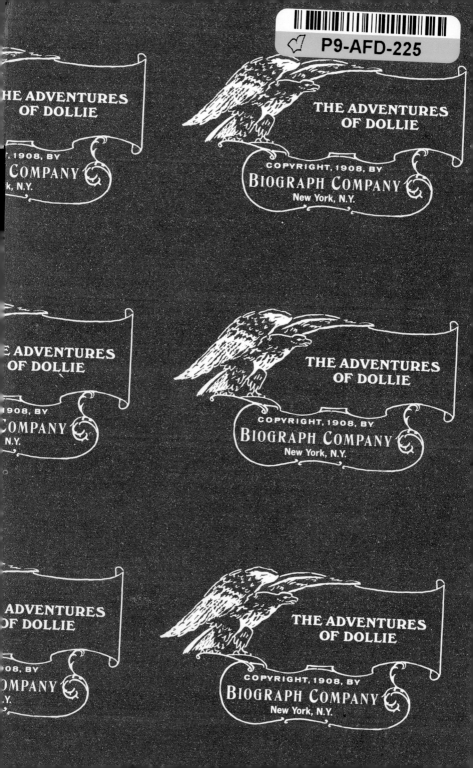

D. W. GRIFFITH:
THE YEARS AT BIOGRAPH

D. W. GRIFFITH

The Years at Biograph

ROBERT M. HENDERSON

FARRAR, STRAUS AND GIROUX
New York

Contents

Illustrations

A classic, Tolstoy's *Resurrection;* a Civil War film, *In Old Kentucky;* and a Western, *The Stage Rustler,* three genres of Biograph films.

Caudebec Inn, and a postcard message from Bitzer to G. V. Predmore, the owner.

A page of the Caudebec Inn's register for July 20, 1910.

The depot at Cuddebackville, New York, and a comedy scene filmed on the spot.

The Mended Lute, filmed at Cuddebackville; and Mary Pickford's note to Mr. Predmore.

Scenes from *The Musketeers of Pig Alley,* with Lillian and Dorothy Gish; *The New York Hat,* with Mary Pickford and Lionel Barrymore; *Man's Genesis,* one of Griffith's last films; and two shots of Griffith directing in 1913.

Scenes from *Judith of Bethulia,* with Blanche Sweet and Henry B. Walthall; and the new Biograph studio in the Bronx, where Griffith completed *Judith.*

D. W. Griffith's announcement of his departure from Biograph, December 1913.

Introduction

Although the motion picture has existed for only eighty years in a practical form, and its life span is relatively short in a historical sense, the early trials, triumphs, and practitioners are known only in the most general ways. Of the thousands of words written about early motion-picture history, most have been based on the memories of pioneer film actors, directors, and technicians. These pioneers have usually recalled the events of the past with anecdotal imprecision and a very human willingness to believe and repeat the fabrications of a later generation of press agents. The historian's problem, as always, is to separate fact from fantasy. The task, in this instance, is doubly difficult since the infant film industry kept few records, and even fewer have survived.

This writer has been fortunate in having available for study the records of The Biograph Company as preserved by R. H. Hammer, the secretary of the corporation, and donated to the collection of the Film Department of the Museum of Modern Art in New York City. In addition, the notes, records, and descriptions of events by Billy Bitzer, the principal Biograph cameraman, were available in the MOMA collection, which also contains the manuscript of the unfinished (and, of course, unpublished) autobiography of D. W. Griffith and other Griffith papers. The valuable assistance of Mrs. Eileen Bowser of the MOMA Film Department staff in assembling pertinent information concerning

Griffith and The Biograph Company cannot be praised too highly.

Invaluable help was also given by Lester Predmore, the son of George Predmore, sometime owner of the Caudebec Inn in Cuddebackville, New York, who had preserved the hotel register and other documents related to The Biograph Company's summer expeditions in the Orange Mountains. It is from these original records, as well as previously published memoirs and accounts, that this history of David Wark Griffith and his film apprenticeship with The Biograph Company was reconstructed.

R.M.H.

New York
January 1970

D. W. GRIFFITH:
THE YEARS AT BIOGRAPH

I

The Background

This book is concerned with the career of David Wark Griffith during the years 1908 to 1913. This was the period of his employment as a director by The American Mutoscope and Biograph Company, later known as Biograph, and these were the years of his apprenticeship.

Over the opposition of Biograph's front office, Griffith advanced during this period from his first one-reel picture, *The Adventures of Dollie* (1908), to the four-reel picture, *Judith of Bethulia* (1913). All his subsequent films were made under the auspices of other production companies. However, the golden age of *The Birth of a Nation* (1915), *Intolerance* (1916), *Broken Blossoms* (1919), *Way Down East* (1920), and *Orphans of the Storm* (1921) was possible only as a result of the mastery of the medium Griffith achieved at Biograph.

It is the theme of this book that D. W. Griffith, during the Biograph period, made unique and original contributions to the development of the motion picture. As another directing genius, Sergei Eisenstein, has declared, "Nothing can take from Griffith the wreath of one of the genuine masters of the American cinema."

The Movies from 1890 to 1908

The motion picture was, for all practical purposes, born in 1889 with the final laboratory development of the Edison Kinetoscope, a peep-show machine projecting fifty-foot movies through a viewing slot directly to the individual viewer. Experiments in projecting pictures on a five-by-five-foot screen had, of course, been made simultaneously with the development of the Kineto-scope. Though Thomas Edison preferred to develop the peep-show machine, others—like William Laurie Dickson—saw greater possibilities in projection. Only nineteen years after the invention of movies, projection on the screen predominated in the industry, and the Kinetoscope had been relegated to the position of a novelty device in penny arcades.

In 1908, motion pictures were being shown in exhibition halls, remodeled store-fronts, former legitimate theatres, and even out-door theatres. They were called nickelodeons, after the admission price of five cents, and they had been opened in almost every city and town in the United States. Millions of dollars were al-ready being invested in the production of films, and some two or three million people were estimated to be going to the movies each week. Despite the impressive growth of this new form of entertainment, the established artists of the legitimate theatre officially ignored the entire undertaking in those early days. Em-ployment in the motion pictures was regarded, at best, as a refuge for those actors who were "at liberty," and needed the five dollars a day paid for film work.

The motion picture theatre in 1908 certainly could not com-pare with the solid, even sumptuous emporium of the legitimate theatre. It was frequently a long, dark, windowless store, stuffy and poorly ventilated. The front of the store, where display windows would normally permit some illumination to enter, was covered by posters over a gaudy "tin" front. A small ticket booth was placed in the center of the store front so that patrons could pass to either right or left when entering the theatre, and the tickets for each performance were sold from a roll in the manner of circus performances. The nickelodeons were generally crowded together, almost side by side, in the immigrant sections of the large cities, where a vacant store could be rented cheaply, and health and sanitary regulations were less rigidly enforced. Occupying as they did former butcher stores and tailor shops, the nickelodeons were also located near their principal customers, the poor. The five-cent admission was well-suited to the purses of a mass audience and the absence of dialogue made the films easily accessible to immigrants unfamiliar with English, not to mention native illiterates as well. The audience at the nickelodeons was described in a contemporary account, *The American Dramatist* (Boston, 1911), by Montrose J. Moses:

The audience that flocks to the Herr Professor's theatre is an interesting mixture of foreigners of all classes. Girls drop in alone, a fact that speaks well for the moral condition of that quarter of town. Boys come in squads. A mother and father and their children count upon such an evening's entertainment. But perhaps the most interesting part of this human spectacle is the people who stand outside, not being able to afford a luxury costing five cents.

At the end of the performance, the audience frequently tried to stay in their seats for the second showing. The managers were forced to employ a burly assistant to usher the patrons out after each show; this fearsome figure came to be known as the "chaser."

At this time films had no stars or featured players, at least none known to their audiences by name. The names of acting personnel and production workers, including that of the director, were omitted from the films. However, the faces of the performers soon became familiar to audiences, and eventually they began requesting more films with particular players, usually identified by some feature of their appearance, such as long curls, or the name of the character they played.

The principal movie companies in 1908 were Edison, Kalem, Vitagraph, Lubin, Selig, Essanay, Méliés, and Pathé. A bitter patent war had been fought by the Edison Company against the others for several years prior to 1907, but in the fall of 1907 an agreement had been reached. These eight companies were licensed to use the Edison equipment, especially the Edison camera, and the group became known as the Edison Licensees. Remaining outside this group was The American Mutoscope and Biograph Company.

This company, formed in 1895, had been an outgrowth of the friendship between Edison's assistant, William Laurie Dickson, and Henry Norton Marvin, a partner in the machinery firm of Marvin and Casler, located in Canastota, New York. Dickson, one of the principal developers of the motion picture, having become disaffected with Edison, suggested to Marvin a new device for competing with the Kinetoscope that would depend upon a series of flipped still photographs viewed by reflected light and producing the effect of motion, rather than upon the continuous strip of film used in the Edison patented machine. After successful demonstrations of the new device, Marvin proceeded to form a company for the manufacture of this new peep-show machine, called a Mutoscope. Backing for the new company came from various sources, including Abner McKinley (brother of the 1896 Presidential candidate, William McKinley) and a bank, the New York Security and Trust Company.[1]

Marvin had gone to Edison to secure the use of the Edison camera for making the still photographs to be used in the Mutoscope, but Edison had refused. The new company therefore undertook to invent a camera for their own use which would not infringe on the Edison patents. This they were able to do, using the advice and knowledge of Dickson concerning the patented features of the Edison camera that had to be avoided. The actual design of the new camera was credited to Marvin's original partner, Herman Casler, since it was not desirable to have Dickson too closely associated with the project because of his former connection with Edison. The new camera was patented by the new film company, christened the American Mutoscope Company. The name "Biograph" was added when the company began

1 Gordon Henricks: *Beginnings of the Biograph* (New York, 1964) , p. 30.

making films for projection on screens. To distinguish these films from those made for the Mutoscopes, they were named "Biographs." Before the end of the period covered in this book, the company changed its name to The Biograph Company, having dropped the production of pictures for the Mutoscopes in the spring of 1908.

At the very start of the new firm's history, one specific event in New York successfully launched Biograph on its future course of presenting motion pictures projected on large screens. On October 12, 1896, they presented at Hammerstein's Olympia Music Hall short films of William McKinley in the midst of his campaign for the Presidency. As the New York *Tribune* reported the next day:

> The biggest part of the enthusiasm began when a view of a McKinley and Hobart parade in Canton was shown. The cheering was incessant as long as the line was passing across the screen, and it grew much greater when the title of the next picture appeared: "Major McKinley at Home."
> . . . Seven boxes were occupied by members of the National Republican Committee and their friends, who came to see Major McKinley walk across his lawn.

Biograph had been invited to join the Edison Licensees but refused, claiming that the patents it held on its own camera were equal to those of the Edison Company. This refusal to join prevented the Edison interests from exercising a monopoly.

Now, in 1908, Biograph's financial fortunes were declining. The Empire Trust Company, another of their backers, became worried about an outstanding Biograph loan of $200,000 and sent Jeremiah J. Kennedy to look into their affairs. His instructions were to liquidate the company, if necessary, to protect the bank's investment. Kennedy, instead, decided to attempt a revival of the fading company, becoming the president and retaining Henry Marvin as vice-president and general manager. Kennedy remained the company president throughout Griffith's association with Biograph.[2]

Throughout 1908 Kennedy and Marvin were involved in negotiations designed to maneuver the Edison group into recognition of the Biograph patents and to accord Biograph a favored position among the licensees. During the period of the negotiations, the Biograph camera was kept from use. The battle was not resolved until December 18, 1908, when the Edison Company capitulated after Kennedy threatened to place the Biograph camera on the open market, licensing its use to all comers. Terry Ramsaye[3] has recorded J. J. Kennedy's final threat, which turned the tide of the negotiations:

"Say!" Kennedy exploded, "if that agreement does not go through, just the way it is, without the change of one word in it, Biograph is going to bust this business wide open. We will put our cameras on the market and license everybody! If we can't get together and control this business, we will make a first-class wreck of it—and we'll have it now."

The new combine, including The American Mutoscope and Biograph Company, was renamed the Motion Picture Patents Company, although popular parlance dubbed it the Film Trust, and its new chief executive officer was Jeremiah J. Kennedy.

By 1908 Biograph was located in studios and offices at 11 East Fourteenth Street in New York City. The building was a typical New York brownstone with four stories, and a commercial basement opening on the street. Entrance to the stores was gained by descending a half flight from the street level. Entrance to the Biograph offices was made by ascending through a set of double doors and then up another short flight to the main floor. The building had originally been a private home, and in terms of

[2] G. W. Bitzer: Unpublished notes about Biograph, in the possession of the Museum of Modern Art Film Library, New York City.

[3] Terry Ramsaye: *A Million and One Nights* (New York, 1927), p. 472.

physical layout very little above the basement level had changed from its former private status. The tenant before Biograph had been the Steck Piano Company.[4] Biograph leased the property for $5,000 a year, rerenting the basement stores. A center hallway ran almost the length of the building, terminating in a large room at the rear that had once been the ballroom. It was this room that Biograph had converted into an indoor studio. On either side of the hallway were the business offices, quite literally the "front offices." The projection facilities where film was viewed, edited, and prepared for shipment were located on the floors above.[5] A building in Hoboken, New Jersey—renamed by J. J. Kennedy a "film laboratory"—was used to process film. The exterior of the building was similar to hundreds of others in New York. A large sign advertising a Singer Sewing Center next door was reflected in the first-floor windows. There were no large signs proclaiming the nature of the business within. The building has long since vanished and the site is presently (1970) occupied by a modern apartment building.

The production phase of The Biograph Company was presided over by George "Old Man" McCutcheon as director. He was assisted from time to time by his eldest son, Wallace. Wallace much preferred a career in musical comedy, but his father insisted on using him at the studio, and frequently used his other seven children in the films. Wallace McCutcheon later became the husband of Pearl White, the heroine of the serial, *The Perils of Pauline.*

The chief bookkeeper at Biograph at the beginning of 1908 was a Mr. Wake, assisted by Herman Breunner. Wake was also the firm's paymaster and comptroller of petty cash. Linda Arvidson Griffith reported that he had an eye for the pretty young

[4] Linda Arvidson Griffith: *When the Movies Were Young* (New York, 1925) . Mrs. Griffith noted that the successor to the Biograph Company on Fourteenth Street was a sculptor named Calder, the father of the creator of the mobile, Alexander Calder.

[5] Blanche Sweet, in a taped interview with the author, June 17, 1965, New York City.

actresses and was dismissed in 1908 for using the petty-cash fund to supply the girls with stockings. Wake's indiscretion was probably not the first of its kind in the film industry, and it was certainly not the last. After Wake's dismissal, Breunner became the chief paymaster. The position won considerable popularity for him among the actors, who would sign pink vouchers for their daily pay and turn them in to Breunner for payment at the end of the day. The customary rate for daily employment in 1908 was five dollars, but only for those days the actor actually worked. It was possible for an actor regularly employed to make from fifteen to forty dollars a week. Many of the actors were tempted to earn additional money by selling story ideas to the film companies, since a story synopsis brought from five to thirty dollars.[6]

The story department at Biograph was a one-man operation, run by an ex-newspaperman and early film exhibitor, Lee Dougherty, whose office was located in the front of the building, directly across from the bookkeeping department. Dougherty was in charge of purchasing story ideas, but it was the practice for the director to authorize story purchases as well. Much of the material that passed over Dougherty's desk consisted of plagiarized material synopsized from novels, plays, short stories, and poems, with the details slightly altered. There was seldom any attempt to secure permission for the use of a copyrighted work. Usually the story was stolen, filmed quickly, sold and exhibited with equal rapidity, and then forgotten before anyone could trace its origin and institute suit.

The average film shown in 1908 lasted five to ten minutes, and a series of films were usually shown on the same program, lasting up to an hour, without interruption. Considerable criticism was levied at the nickelodeons on the grounds that excessive viewing of films constituted a menace to eyesight. This criticism had re-

[6] Payments for story ideas and synopses are noted in a record book of The Biograph Company in the possession of The Museum of Modern Art Film Library, New York City.

sulted in the passage of a law in Massachusetts requiring that five minutes of white light flood the screen every twenty minutes to prevent eyestrain.

The average playing time for a Biograph film was the same as for the others—ten minutes, with a finished length of 800 to 1,000 feet. Slapstick comedies were about half this length, and the few Mutoscopes still being made ranged from 50 to 100 feet. Typical of the Biograph films being made in early 1908 was *Professional Jealousy,* released January 4, 1908, a backstage drama about a feud between the two leading ladies:

> Enough it is to say the two women struggle and fight furiously until the stage manager, whom the maid has called, separates them with the time-worn injunction, "Be a l-a-d-y!"[7]

This film was 609 feet long and the role of the stage manager was played by Tony O'Sullivan. *Energizer,* released January 11, 1908, was a 789-foot farce comedy showing how a "super" breakfast cereal might bring unexpected strength.[8] *Falsely Accused,* released January 18, 1908—990 feet—was "A thrilling drama in which the art of animated photography plays an important part."[9] *Lonesome Junction,* released January 22, 1908—574 feet —showed a group of stereotyped travelers in a railroad station ostensibly located in the Rocky Mountains, including an Englishman; Heine, a "Dutchman," who got a printed title line as he arrived: "Vas ist das, sex stunden zu warten? Oh, vell, I haf a smoke"; a broken-down prizefighter, Mr. Pug; and the villain, who was described as "a black hand dago." The end of the picture came in a rush:

> The arrival of the train is announced, and the party scramble out of the station, in a mad rush to get aboard. A thrilling finish to a screaming farce.[10]

7 Biograph Bulletin No. 118, in possession of The Museum of Modern Art Film Library, New York City.   8 Biograph Bulletin No. 119.
9 Biograph Bulletin No. 120.   10 Biograph Bulletin No. 121.

Others in this period were *Classmates,* 800 feet, "a stirring romance of college days"; *Bobby's Kodak,* 518 feet, "Papa's Present Proves a Prejudicial Portent"; and *The Snowman,* 717 feet, a farce about a snowman who comes to life, gets drunk, and frightens a schoolroom full of pupils before disappearing under the onslaught of the children.[11]

About twenty copies of each Biograph one-reel film were being sold.[12] The price was usually twelve to fourteen cents a running foot, bringing the price of a thousand-foot film to between $120 and $140.[13] Each Biograph film at the beginning of 1908 was bringing a total gross revenue of up to $2,800. Biograph's output ranged from two to three films a week, thus producing a weekly gross revenue on the order of $5,600 to $8,400. Despite a relatively low overhead, this income was not high enough for Biograph's officers.

The content of the 1908 films fell into two general groups. The first group consisted of topical news film concerning the events of the day, although a strict definition of the term "news" would hardly apply since some of the films were concerned only with showing people, animals, and machines in motion. The second group included the dramatic films, generally either comedies or melodramas. The comedies usually dealt with a single comic incident, treated in a slapstick farcical manner. The melodramas followed the standard stage pattern of the time: innocent heroine in the clutches of a foul villain, but rescued at the last moment by a stalwart hero. The plot was the same, but the settings were varied to include natural sights, machinery, or occupations that would intrigue the audience. The use of railroad trains as a device was extremely popular, beginning almost with the first foot-

---

[11] Biograph Bulletins Nos. 122–124. *Bobby's Kodak* had Bobby Harron and Eddie Dillon in the cast.

[12] Bitzer: Unpublished notes.

[13] Bulletins cited above. These bulletins were used to acquaint the exhibitors with the Biograph films as they were released. A price was included on a per foot basis. All films at this time were sold outright. The organization of film-rental arrangements came later.

age of a train in operation; for example, on the same program in 1896 with the films of McKinley was a short film called *Empire State Express* which showed the crack train "rounding a curve." Trains were eventually supplanted by automobiles, first in combination with the trains. Airplanes appeared later.

Subject material, as noted, was frequently pirated from classic or contemporary plays, but always reduced in scale to the standard melodrama formula. There were some who felt that the melodrama was disappearing from the legitimate theatre, and with it the stock characters of the melodrama. Ada Patterson examined this question in a popular article, "Has the Ingenue Disappeared From Our Stage?"[14] She quoted Elizabeth Marbury, a dramatic author's agent:

The drama of the sweet young girl who is separated from her lover by the machinations of a wicked villain has gone out of date with slavery and crinolines and other moments of foolishness. The drama is being born. That is the writing on the theatrical wall.

If the sweet young ingénue was disappearing from the stage, as Elizabeth Marbury suggested, then she had only changed her address. The menaced young girl had become a staple character in the motion pictures.

Even the classics were reduced to the formula of melodrama. *Romeo and Juliet* became a ten-minute pantomime filmed against the background of the Bethesda Fountain in Central Park, New York.[15]

The early film directors, Edwin S. Porter, Stuart Blackton, Sidney Olcott, and others, had discovered that the motion picture had a distinct advantage over the stage in presenting melodrama. The devices available for melodrama in film could have a reality that was impossible to attain on the stage. For example, the

14 Ada Patterson: "Has the Ingenue Disappeared from Our Stage?," *The Theatre Magazine,* June 1908, p. 162.
15 Montrose J. Moses: "Where They Perform Shakespeare for Five Cents," *The Theatre Magazine,* October 1908, p. 264.

Count of Monte Cristo need not escape from his prison through
a canvas sea; the film showed a real ocean. The close connection
between film and stage in 1908 was obvious in another way. The
motion picture was, in large part, merely a photographic record
of a stage play. The length of a shot was synonymous with the
scene in a play. If a play had twelve scenes, the motion picture
corresponding to the play contained twelve shots. Each shot was
made with the camera in a fixed position, approximately center-
orchestra, and both the actors and the setting were photographed
in their entirety.

The ability of film to succeed with melodrama had received
its first noteworthy impetus from a short film produced by the
Edison Company in the fall of 1903—*The Great Train Robbery,*
directed by Edwin S. Porter. This film had enjoyed an unprecedented success, and it had become the model for other films
up to 1908. *The Great Train Robbery* told a simple story about
a train holdup, the pursuit of the bandits, and their final capture in the woods. The structure of the film story was what im-
parted something special to the film. Although the camera was
in its usual fixed position, and each of the shots in the film
represented a complete stage scene, they had been assembled in
an order that began to suggest a special film technique. In the
outdoor scenes, Porter used a moving camera, once in a pan shot
that followed the escaping desperadoes, and once with the camera
mounted on the moving train. The most memorable moment in
the picture, however, is a completely non-sequitur closeup of
George Barnes, playing a bandit, firing his pistol at the audience.
Although this shot is usually placed at the end of the film, Porter
suggested—in the Edison Film Catalogue (1904)—that it might
be used either at the beginning or at the end.

Just as the films had borrowed the plots of the stage melodrama, so the actors brought theatre-acting styles to the films.
The style in the theatre of 1908 was flamboyant, relying on the
grand gesture, the carefully planned pose. Comparing still photographs of the stage plays of 1908 with still photographs from the

motion pictures, one sees that they are almost indistinguishable. The earliest film actors, with rare exceptions, were not of the first rank. They were usually the products of provincial stock companies, who had been unable to find regular employment in New York. Their acting styles were consequently a reflection of the best style in the theatre, but at a generally inferior level. The great Sarah Bernhardt, in her film *Queen Elizabeth* (1912), reveals how ill-suited the manners of even the best actors of the stage were for the motion pictures. To make matters worse, the neophyte film actors were inclined to increase the exaggeration in pantomime because they lacked the restraint ordinarily supplied by dialogue. They elongated their gestures and magnified their movements.

In addition, it was customary for the actors to apply their own makeup, as they did for stage roles and as is still done today in the legitimate theatre. Their lack of understanding of the special problems introduced by black-and-white photography, particularly the problems created by the orthochromatic film used at the time, resulted in a highly artificial look. The normal stage makeup for 1908 depended heavily on pinkish tones, used to overcome the high concentrations of yellow light used onstage. The pink makeup was rendered in gray-to-black tones by the orthochromatic film. Apparently, no one worried overmuch about the sometimes horrendous effects. Makeup, costumes, scenery seemingly were of little consequence. The audiences had no standards for the films, and everything was an exciting novelty. The moment a film did appear that set some sort of standard, the subsequent films had to meet that standard.

Although the established artists of the theatre world attempted to ignore motion pictures, the theatre producers were concerned. Between 1908 and 1910, the chorus of complaints from the legitimate producers increased. In 1910 William A. Brady, an established theatre producer, charged, before a meeting of the American Dramatists Club, that a road company of *Way Down East* had been forced off the road by the competition of pirated

versions of the same play on film. Charles Klein, another producer, also complained that attendance at his production in New
York of *The Music Master* was hurt by the competition of a
motion picture with the same title being presented just up the
street from his Academy of Music Theatre. Montrose Moses
summed up the attitude of the legitimate theatre:

> The motion picture has undoubtedly hurt the theatrical business.
> It steals drama and reduces it to motion. Every road company has its
> tale to tell of business ruined by the kinetoscope; every vaudeville house
> is forced to open its doors to celluloid drama. And when summer ar-
> rives, the legitimate playhouses turn themselves into nickelodeons. In
> a way all this is a menace to the American dramatist.[16]

The financial difficulties at Biograph that had brought in Jeremiah J. Kennedy as president, and involved Kennedy in the complicated maneuverings with the Edison Licensees, caused Henry
Norton Marvin, now the second in command, to attempt to im-
prove the studio's position. Marvin realized that the quality of
the stories being filmed could be better.

Marvin's first move in the search for improvement in the Biograph stories was to hire Stanner E. V. Taylor, an itinerant news-
paperman, to write stories for Biograph. Without much difficulty
Taylor wrote two synopses of approximately three hundred
words each. He submitted them to Lee Dougherty and received
payment of thirty dollars. This was an improvement over the
freelance rates for newspaper stories, and Taylor set out to write
more stories for the films.

With the search for better stories underway, Marvin took a look
at the directing situation at Biograph. The elder McCutcheon,
who was not in the best of health, had retired from the stren-
uous job of directing. His son Wallace tried his hand at directing
a few pictures, including *When Knighthood Was in Flower,* in
which D. W. Griffith and his wife, Linda, acted. But young
Wallace was reluctant to continue with the films, preferring to

[16] Moses: *op. cit.,* p. 214.

return to musical comedy. Stanner Taylor was pressed into service for one film, but the results, according to Linda Griffith, who acted in the melodrama, were rather static. Wallace Mc-Cutcheon agreed to continue for a time making one film a week, but a second director would have to be engaged for the other weekly picture. Marvin began making inquiries to find another director.

The regular employees at Biograph were not interested in the position. The cameramen, particularly, already considered themselves the prime creative minds in the films. To them a director was merely someone to keep the actors in line while *they* made the picture, according to Bitzer's unpublished notes.

There was no established hierarchy in the creative end of the film industry at this time. Biograph's two cameramen in 1908 were Arthur Marvin, a genial, happy-go-lucky man, the brother of Henry Marvin, and G. W. "Billy" Bitzer, who had been a cameraman since the days of the McKinley photographs, and before that an electrician. The task of the director, as the cameramen saw it, was to rehearse the actors for a scene until it was ready to be played; then the cameramen would take over and determine the camera position, the lighting, the length of the shot, and all other matters relevant to the finished film. Although no one at Biograph particularly wanted the job, it seemed to be the prevailing opinion that anyone with enough energy to keep the actors in line could direct a motion picture. The cameraman would take care of all the technical details and cover up the director's mistakes in staging.

Directing for films, then, was generally thought to require little in the way of preparation. Marvin's search was for an energetic person with some knowledge of actors, but no other qualifications were of much significance.

Colonel Griffith's Son

One of the actors hanging around the Biograph studio in June 1908 hoping to pick up a day's work at the five-dollar rate was a lean, hawk-nosed, physical-culture enthusiast from Kentucky, David Wark Griffith. Griffith was using his stage name, Lawrence Griffith, which he had given himself while playing in a variety of provincial stock companies in the preceding twelve years. He was thirty-three years old, and he had ambitions as a playwright. His arrival at Biograph was fortuitously timed. With Henry Marvin looking for story possibilities, Griffith managed to sell him several film synopses, including the plots for *Old Isaacs the Pawnbroker, The Music Master, At the Crossroads of Life, The Stage Rustler,* and *Ostler Joe.* In addition, Griffith was hired as an actor to appear in all but *The Stage Rustler.* He had also appeared in *When Knights Were Bold,* at Biograph.

Since the film synopses that Griffith devised were only short stories outlining a particular plot, and the end product, the film, was completely devised by the director and cameraman, it was not necessary for Griffith to have any technical knowledge of motion pictures. This was fortunate for Griffith, because he had none.

Griffith had had some experience as a playwright. In 1907, the year before, he had sold a play to the actor-producer James K. Hackett. Hackett had produced Griffith's play *The Fool and the Girl* in Washington, D.C., on September 30, 1907, with an experienced cast headed by Fannie Ward and Allison Skipworth. The play was a serious melodramatic tale of the California hop fields and migratory hop pickers, based on Griffith's personal experiences after he had been stranded in San Francisco by the failure of a stock company. The play is a sprawling, not very good colloquial imitation of the typical melodrama in which Griffith had frequently appeared as an actor. Its Washington production was a failure, but Griffith was encouraged to think that his future lay in writing. He took his playwriting very seriously and was incensed at one review by a Washington critic, about which he wrote a letter of protest to the editor of the *Washington Herald.* Griffith was particularly offended by the critic's suggestion that the play contained a somewhat immoral tone.

> In the name of justice, I ask you the courtesy of printing this letter. I am the author of *The Fool and the Girl* now being presented in your city. In the criticisms of no other Washington paper was there the faintest suggestion that anyone was hurt by the immorality of the play. But in Wednesday's issue of the *Washington Herald,* the most vicious, false, and hypocritical criticism is made by an alleged critic who signs himself, Hector Fuller. In our scenes in this prologue, we have not one essential piece of business, not so much as an embrace between man and woman, nor is one profane or foul word used, not even the much hackneyed *damn,* and the most terrible crime committed is the sipping of a little colored water which is supposed to represent champagne, which up until this time we thought might be done upon the stage without causing any great outcry.[17]

The specific criticism to which Griffith reacted with such verbosity was contained in this sentence of the review:

> It may be said that the dramatist wanted to show where his hero's feet strayed, and where he found the girl he was after to make his wife; but if one wants to tell the old, old and beautiful story of redemption of either man or woman through love, it is not necessary to portray the gutters from which they are redeemed . . .

The stage directions in the play constitute the principal point of interest for anyone concerned with Griffith's later film career. They indicate some of his directorial and compositional ideas on the eve of his entry into motion pictures. His suggested staging for the play seems to be of a kind that would be easier to obtain on film than in the theatre of 1907. Griffith described a señorita in

> . . . semi-Mexican costume who executes a wild solo dance upon the platform, during which some of the figures on the stage move in and out between her and the front of the stage chatting and drinking while watching the dancing, and then closing up so that she is lost in the

17 David Wark Griffith, in a letter to the editor of the *Washington Herald,* October 3, 1907, in the possession of The Museum of Modern Art Film Library.

picture in order to keep away from the idea of the dance being a specialty.[18]

In the description of the play's climactic fifth act, Griffith wrote:

It is sunset and red lights fall through the window. The room is dim with evening light. Effie is seen distinctly in the white light from the street which falls in latticed splashes of white upon the floor.

Griffith's fee of a thousand dollars for the production was soon gone for living expenses, but Griffith's faith in his writing ability was confirmed. He felt that anything else he might work at was only interim employment. Back in New York with his wife, he began work on another play, *War,* concerning the American Revolutionary War. The play involved considerable research in letters and diaries at The New York Public Library. Linda Griffith reported that he received a nibble from Henry Miller, but the play was finally turned down because it had a cast of fifty-six principals and many extras; it was just too large and expensive to produce.

Griffith described the opening of the third act of *War:*

Night-time, December 24th, 1776—The "King George" Chamber of the "Red Fix" [sic] Inn at Trenton—built according to the old houses in Trenton at that date. . . . Room is lighted with great candelabra set in walls R. & L. holding lighted candles, giving the soft, flickering lights that make shadows in the room, as the bright glare of the ordinary foot-lights would destroy entirely the atmosphere of the act.

Opening of act, all possible brightness, and wild half-drunken hilarity. In the center of stage, six men and six women dancing the Morris Dance to the air of the "Beggar Daughter of Bednal Green"—around the figure of a Hobby Horse which is fantastically made up over a man, musicians . . . are playing wildly . . . on wall seat, extreme right is a civilian, fairly well dressed, rather dishevelled, without coat. A girl gaudily dressed, highly rouged, patched and powdered has her head

[18] Griffith: *The Fool and the Girl,* an unpublished manuscript play in the possession of the Library of Congress, Rare Book Collection, Washington, D.C., copyright 1907.

resting on a pillow which he holds in his arms. . . . A very small dissipated looking old man of about 60 is being driven around the room by a young girl of about 18; she has bridle reins about his neck, and she strikes him with a driving whip, calling "Get up, get up, get up horsie, kick nice horsie, kick," at which the old man squeals kicking up one leg and then the other in imitation of a horse. Two men carrying an immense metal punch bowl half full of punch pass in and out among the crowd, all of them have pewter mugs which they dip into the bowl and drink at pleasure. Two re-faced [sic], fleshy, middle aged men, decidedly the worse for liquor, follow the punch bowl, singing in time to the music:

> *Oh my beak, oh my beak*
> *The Punch is wet,*
> *And the Punch is weak.*[19]

Griffith had certainly paid little attention to Hector Fuller's criticism. Although *War* was never produced, the fruits of the research for the play, and some of the material from the play itself, were used again and again during his later career.

When Griffith first approached a film company looking for employment, he styled himself a writer who would accept an acting job rather reluctantly. Actually, his success as a writer, other than with *The Fool and the Girl,* was limited. He had had some short verse accepted for publication, but little else. Judging by one of his published poems, "The Wild Duck," which appeared in *Leslie's Weekly* for January 10, 1907, his powers as a poet were limited:

> *Look—how beautiful he is,*
> *Swift his flight*
> *As a bullet he comes in*
> *From the sea in the morning,*
> *For the wind is*
> *From the sea in the morning.*
> *See! He's bound for the hill tops,*
> *The gold hill tops,*
> *The gold hill tops . . .*

---

[19] Griffith: *War*, an unpublished manuscript play in the possession of The Museum of Modern Art Film Library, uncopyrighted.

Griffith's other efforts failed to impress the editors, and there was no demand for his work.

Griffith's principal experience as an adult was in the provincial theatre and touring stock companies, beginning in 1896 as a "super" with a touring company, headed by Julia Marlowe, which was presenting *Romeo and Juliet* and *Romola*. That same year he also did a brief stint as a spear carrier with Sarah Bernhardt's company in *Gismonda* and *La Dame aux Camélias*.

Griffith had become involved with the theatre by accident. Nothing in his youth particularly prepared him for a theatre career, although it has been said that his father liked to read Shakespeare to the family. Griffith was the fourth son of a former Confederate officer, Jacob Wark Griffith, and Mary Perkins Oglesby. The middle name, Wark, which he shared with his father, had descended through his paternal grandmother, Margaret Wark.

Griffith's father was a hearty, blustering man who had acquired the nickname "Roaring Jake" in Oldham County, Kentucky, as a result of his loud, authoritative tone. His direct influence on his son, David, was perhaps minimal, since he died when David was only ten years old.

Griffith did retain a romantic image of his boyhood, an image which did have some possible influence on his selection of dramatic subjects during his film career. He later wrote about his own birth in 1875:

> In the first place, I was born. I don't think there were any shooting stars, earthquakes, or anything else happened about it [sic].[20]

A major memory of his father involved the story of his first "friend," a nondescript yellow dog. The image that Griffith retained was that of the dog's final moments when, a victim of some canine disease, the dog had to be destroyed by Griffith's father.

20 Griffith: Manuscript of a projected autobiography, in the possession of The Museum of Modern Art Film Library, New York, from which this and subsequent quotes are taken.

I heard the news that the execution was about to come off. Then I saw them lead the dog down to the side orchard with a rope around his neck so they could tie him to a tree. Then I saw my father go into the house to get a gun. I knew it wouldn't be long now for the dog because father had been a colonel in a couple of wars, and a captain of one and fought Indians and most anyone who came around and was a good shot. When I saw him go down into the orchard with the gun, I started running in the opposite direction. I didn't want to see the execution, but I couldn't run fast enough to get away from the report of the gun. Colonel Griffith had a good aim. There was only one shot and I knew the poor old yellow dog was turning over on his back with his feet in the air like dogs generally do when the shot is corrected [sic] at the place. I asked afterwards what they did with the body, but nobody told me. That was the last of my first friend.

Griffith's boyhood home was one of the outbuildings of a farm at La Grange, Kentucky. There were two other buildings, small cabins, in which two Negro families still lived. One was presided over by a large black woman, known as "Aunt" Easter, whom he particularly remembered for her interest in small boys and her special combination of hot biscuits and watermelon.

Griffith's memories of his boyhood were usually pleasant ones, but, although professing love for his father, he wrote:

I often wonder if he cared anything about me particularly. I am forced to doubt it. As far as I can remember, he never seemed to show anybody his feelings toward them . . . What he did, which he did only occasionally, was to put his hand on my head and said [sic] "Son, how are you this day?" This simple action seemed to me an overwhelming miracle of some kind.

Griffith's father died in 1885 from the delayed effects of some bad surgery performed during the Civil War. Mary Oglesby Griffith was forced to move her brood of children to a small farm in Shelby County, Kentucky.

Griffith's education was continued in a small country school. A vivid memory from his school days was that of his first love:

. . . I fell in love with a vista of memories. I see her being a very beautiful girl, just what type I don't know, but she was very thin and could run like hell. This made her greatly desired by the Captain of the prisoner base teams. My God, how I loved her! I really do remember that she was little and slim and that she had beautiful legs and she could use them.

Griffith was twelve at the time of his first love, and his dream girl was ten.

Griffith's mother found the small farm impossible to operate, and she moved the family again, to Louisville, Kentucky. There she took over the operation of a run-down boardinghouse. The new business was also a failure. The Griffith family was barely able to make ends meet.

Griffith completed his formal education in the Louisville public schools. Two of his classmates were Henry and Harvey Waterson, sons of the editor of the *Louisville Courier Journal*. Griffith was particularly impressed by Henry because he always treated Griffith, the poor boy, without condescension.

With the boardinghouse failing, Griffith had to leave school and go to work. His first job was operating a wire-controlled elevator at the J. C. Lewis Dry Goods Store. This job produced more calluses than money, so when a cousin offered to help him get a job in a new bookstore owned by Simon Flexner, Griffith readily accepted. The bookstore was a more congenial situation than the dry-goods store. Griffith was delighted by his introduction to the world of letters, even though that world came through the doors only occasionally as a customer. The store was visited by a local novelist, Mary Johnson, and the "Hoosier poet," James Whitcomb Riley. Another customer who made a great impression on the young Griffith was Adolph Claubers, afterwards a critic for *The New York Times* and the husband of actress Jane Cowl.

During his employ at the Flexner Bookstore, Griffith fell in love again.

She was a blonde. I don't know how it is, but somehow blondes seem to have a fatal effect on me. I did her a lot of good anyhow. I had to walk about forty blocks to get to her house from where I lived . . . we had to meet unbeknownst [sic] as it were. My courtship gave her a splendid physique because in pleasant weather, I walked her miles and miles up and down the canal . . . and told her of my great ambition to be a writer . . . her answer . . . was to the effect that I would do marvelously well in such stories as "Deerfoot" and "The Indian Runner," popular stories running in *The Boy's Home Companion*. The little blonde may have been right at that.

Griffith was now twenty. At the bookstore he met Mr. Ellis,[21] a blacksmith who had founded an amateur theatre group that rehearsed in the back of his forge. He was then attempting to raise enough money for a short tour with his group. Griffith was invited to join. Somehow Ellis raised the money for the tour, and the new troupe gave its first performance across the river from Louisville, in Jeffersonville, Indiana. Ellis had dubbed his company the Twilight Revelers. Griffith commented on this first performance:

. . . the benignant [sic] citizens of this city must have had some curiosity of what the hell was a Twilight Reveler for we did fair business.

Despite the "fair" opening, the remainder of the tour was a failure and the actors were stranded in a hotel, without the funds to pay laundry bills or room rent. The problem was solved in the manner frequently associated with stranded theatrical troupes. Griffith and the company decamped through the hotel's second-story window during the early morning hours.

One of Griffith's associates in the Twilight Revelers was Max Davidson, who became a close friend. Griffith describes a stage mishap in which they were both involved:

We had, during rehearsals, become fast friends, talking about acting and such things. There was a big safe-opening scene in the climax of the play. Max's business was to open the safe. My cue as the great hero of the occasion was "Oh, this is easy!" He started work on the safe. I

[21] Griffith refers to the blacksmith as "Ellis." However, Iris Barry notes in *D. W. Griffith: American Film Master* (New York: The Museum of Modern Art, 1940) that the blacksmith's name was Jim White.

wasn't worried about the scene, but I was very much troubled about the last act . . . and was busy walking up and down the cellar beneath the stage trying to get the lines in my head. Max gave the cue all right, but I was walking. . . . The safe flew open. That was my cue for entrance and to proclaim dramatically, "You devil, get away from that safe, or I'll blow you to kingdom come!" It happened that there was only one entrance to the stage from the cellar and that was on the right side. It also happened that all the actors were on the other side of the stage . . . [and the passage across the stage was blocked by] the backdrop against the wall so there was no way of getting to me except to cross the stage which would certainly have spoiled the act. Again and again Max repeated the cue which must have become slightly monotonous to the audience. Finally I woke up from my reverie and hurried up the steps, but Max had given up in despair as the audience was laughing its head off and made his exit on the left side. I rushed on shouting, "Stand back, you villain, or I'll blow you to kingdom come!", but there was no villain to stand back, the stage being empty. This was a dramatic play, and it had received lots of good laughs already, but this was the climax. The audience nearly fell out of their chairs.

It was Davidson who suggested later in 1908 that Griffith ought to try for a job in motion pictures.

After the breakup of the Twilight Revelers, Griffith had his two experiences as a "super" with the touring companies. Late in 1896, Griffith was employed as an actor by the Meffert Stock Company, playing in the Temple Theatre in Louisville. Griffith played the smallest roles, such as Marks in *Lights of London,* a servant in *The Wages of Sin,* and a walk-on part in *All the Comforts of Home.* He was rehired for a second season at the Temple Theatre in 1897 and appeared in another series of small supporting roles: Parker Serrant in *Lady Windermere's Fan,* Mr. Randolph in *The Wife,* and as Captain Woodford in *Held by the Enemy,* a Civil War melodrama. Griffith continued with the Meffert Company for a third season in 1898, playing Thomas in *Little Lord Fauntleroy,* "a villain" in *The Count of Monte Cristo,* Lord Drelincourt in *Jim the Penman,* and Frank Bedloe in *Shenandoah,* another Civil War melodrama. In his fourth season at the Temple Theatre, Griffith had a somewhat larger role as Athos in *The Three Musketeers*.[22]

By 1904 Griffith had become a member of Ada Gray's company, playing small roles in *Trilby* and *East Lynne* on tour. Toward the end of that year, he joined the Neil Alhambra Stock Company in Chicago. His lean, bony physique made him a natural for the role of Lincoln in that company's production of *The Ensign*.[23] It is possible that his casting in the role of Lincoln gave him a sympathy for the Civil War President that went beyond his Southern sympathies, for he handled the character of Lincoln most sympathetically in later years in both *The Birth of a Nation* and the biographical picture *Abraham Lincoln* which he directed in 1930.

In 1905 Griffith joined the Melbourne MacDowell company on the West Coast. He appeared in small roles in *Fedora*, *The Financier*, and as Alessandro in a stage version of Helen Hunt Jackson's *Ramona*. Griffith apparently developed a fondness for *Ramona* because it appeared later as one of his major efforts with The Biograph Company. It was during the engagement in *Fedora* that Griffith met Linda Arvidson. She was highly intrigued by his deep, stern voice, but detested his stage name Lawrence and was relieved to discover that his real name was David.

Earlier in the season, Griffith had arrived on the Coast with Catherine Osterman in a production of *Miss Petticoats*, which folded in San Francisco. The engagement with the Melbourne MacDowell Company followed, but this in turn went under.[24]

This time there was no other theatrical employment in sight. The hop harvest near Ukiah, California, was underway, and Griffith was able to survive by joining the pickers. It was this

[22] Theatre programs of the Meffert Stock Company, Temple Theatre, Louisville, Kentucky, for 1896, 1897, 1898, and 1899, in the possession of The Museum of Modern Art Film Library.

[23] Theatre programs of the Ada Gray Company and the Neil Alhambra Company, in possession of The Museum of Modern Art Film Library.

[24] Programs and other records of the MacDowell Stock Company, in the possession of the Museum of Modern Art Film Library.

experience that provided the background for his play *The Fool and the Girl*. Griffith was finally rescued from a future as a hop picker by a call from Los Angeles to play the Alessandro role in *Ramona* again. Linda Arvidson was also working in Los Angeles at the time. They spent a great deal of time together, visiting many of the historic places about Los Angeles, including the San Gabriel Mission.

Returning to San Francisco after the closing of *Ramona*, Griffith was hired by Nance O'Neill, who had just come back from a tour of Australia. Griffith played the role of Francis Drake in *Elizabeth the Queen of England*. In March he appeared with Walker Whiteside and played roles in *Rosmersholm* and Sudermann's *Magda*. In the latter play he replaced the leading man, McKee Rankin, in the role of Hefterdinct, the pastor of St. Mary's. His notices were good, and Nance O'Neill promised him additional leading roles.

The O'Neill Company began gradually moving eastward, touring Iowa, playing in Des Moines, and finally arriving in Boston, Massachusetts. The O'Neill Company had a six-week booking in Boston, so Griffith sent for Linda Arvidson, who had been caught in the San Francisco earthquake but was uninjured. She arrived in Boston the second week in May, and they were promptly married in the Old North Church. The newlyweds agreed not to publicize their marriage so that it would not jeopardize their respective theatre careers.

In the fall of 1906, Griffith was engaged to appear in a road tryout of Thomas Dixon's *The One Woman,* a new play following on the heels of Dixon's success with a dramatization of his novel *The Clansman*.[25] Griffith was given notice, however, two weeks before the New York opening. Between engagements, Griffith had been hard at work on his play, *The Fool and the Girl*. On returning to New York, he was hired for a small role

25 *The Clansman* became the basis for Griffith's film *The Birth of a Nation*. The film opened in Los Angeles under the title *The Clansman,* which was not changed until it played in New York.

in *Salome* at the Astor Theatre. In May 1907, Mr. and Mrs. Griffith were both hired to appear in a pageant honoring the Centennial of the first Virginia Colony at Norfolk, Virginia. Griffith played "John Smith," and Linda Arvidson appeared as "Pocahontas."

The dearth of acting jobs after *Salome* was broken by the Washington production of *The Fool and the Girl*. The thousand-dollar fee for the production rights was the largest single sum that either Griffith or Linda Arvidson had received during their respective theatrical careers. The money lasted only a brief time, but it helped to restore their fading confidence.

When the income from the play was used up, Linda Griffith withdrew three hundred dollars from her savings bank in San Francisco. That was fortunate, because no jobs were forthcoming that winter.

In New York in the spring of 1908, Griffith met his old friend, Max Davidson, who suggested that Griffith might try selling some of his stories to the film companies or perhaps, although this would be a last resort, acting in some films. Griffith was initially cool to Davidson's suggestion, but dwindling finances finally sent him to the Edison Company in the Bronx. Griffith attempted to sell them a synopsis of the opera *La Tosca*. The Edison director, Edwin S. Porter, turned the script down not because of the literary piracy, but because Griffith had written too many scenes for a film production. Griffith then suggested that he could act as well as write, and Porter hired him to play the role of the woodsman hero in *Rescued from an Eagle's Nest*.

The plot of *Rescued from an Eagle's Nest* was a simple one. A baby is carried off by an eagle, and after great consternation—actors run wildly about in front of the camera—the brave mountaineer (Griffith) climbs the mountain, fights off the eagle, and saves the baby. The exteriors for the film were shot along the palisades of the Hudson River near Fort Lee, New Jersey, but the details of the filmed rescue were made on a canvas mountain in the Edison Studio. In viewing the film today, one can see that

Griffith's battle is against an eagle that bears a remarkable resemblance to a stuffed turkey and is quite obviously manipulated on wires. This picture marked the beginning of Griffith's film career.

Max Davidson had also suggested that Griffith try the Biograph studio at 11 East Fourteenth Street. When Porter had no further work for him, Griffith began going to the Biograph studios.

The next step in Griffith's progress came as a result, not of his story writing, but of the observations of Henry Marvin, the Biograph cameraman and brother of the boss. Marvin was struck by the energetic activities of the young actor. When the search for a new director seemed to have reached a dead end, it was Arthur Marvin who suggested to his brother that calling in young Griffith and giving him a chance might not be a bad idea.

At first, Griffith was hesitant to accept Arthur Marvin's offer of a chance to direct, although he and his wife had discussed this possibility with anticipation at home. Marvin made it plain that this was a trial proposition. Griffith would direct one picture on probation, and if that one went well, he would be given another to direct. There was no discussion of any long-term arrangements, and Griffith was fearful that if he failed as a director he might lose the chance of acting as well. Griffith explained to Marvin that he was a married man and needed some job security. The Griffith family budget had come to depend upon the sale of synopses and the acting jobs. Between both Griffiths, sixty or seventy dollars a week were being earned. Marvin finally assured Griffith that he would not lose his other work if he failed as a director, and Griffith agreed to try his hand at the new endeavor. This was to be his first attempt in any medium, for Griffith had not directed in the theatre.

Griffith was given the synopsis of a story written by Stanner E. V. Taylor, the ex-newspaperman recruited by Henry Marvin as a writer. The story was called *The Adventures of Dollie,* and according to Linda Griffith it had been considered something of a "lemon" at the studio. This is the description that Lee Dougherty wrote for the Biograph Bulletin No. 3454, announcing the production's release, on July 14, 1908:

On the lawn of a country residence we find the little family comprising father, mother, and little Dollie, their daughter. In front of the grounds there flows a picturesque stream to which the mother and little one go to watch the boys fishing . . . While the mother and child are seated on the wall beside the stream, one of these Gypsies approaches and offers for sale several baskets. A refusal raises his ire and he seizes the woman's purse and is about to make off with it when the husband, hearing her cries of alarm, rushes down to her aid, and with a heavy snakewhip lashes the Gypsy unmercifully, leaving great welts upon his swarthy body, at the same time arousing the venom of his black heart.

. . . [The gypsy] seizes the child and carries her to his camp where he gags and conceals her in a watercask.

. . . [Later] as they ford a stream the cask falls off the wagon into the water and is carried away by the current. Next we see the cask floating downstream toward a waterfall, over which it goes; then through the seething spray of the rapids, and on, on until it finally enters the quiet cove of the first scene, where it is brought ashore by the fisherboys. Hearing strange sounds emitted from the barrel, the boys call for the bereft father, who is still searching for the lost one. Breaking the head from the barrel the amazed and happy parents now fold in their arms their loved one, who is not much worse off for her marvelous experience.

Griffith had his story and his first directorial assignment. The boss's brother, Arthur Marvin, was to be his cameraman, since the other cameraman, Billy Bitzer, was working exclusively for Wallace McCutcheon. Now Griffith's problem was where to begin as a film director.

I I

1908: The Beginning

How should a motion-picture director begin? Griffith had observed Edwin Porter and both McCutcheons, but he still felt
insecure on his first assignment. He turned to the experienced
cameraman Billy Bitzer for advice. Bitzer gladly offered to help,
inviting Griffith to his rooms for an evening conference about
the problems of directing in general and *The Adventures of
Dollie* in particular. In his room, Bitzer scribbled some notes on
the back of a shirtboard. In four different columns, he outlined
the values that should be realized in the picture. Each of the
columns was headed with a value title: comedy, drama, pathos,
pretty shots. Under each column, Bitzer wrote an outline of the
scene that should be filmed to carry out the theme. After showing
this to Griffith and explaining its meaning, Bitzer offered to write
any other action scenes that Griffith might require. Griffith gave
no sign that he would either accept or reject Bitzer's suggestions.
He listened politely, thanked Bitzer, and went home.[1]

"The Adventures of Dollie"

Griffith's first two tasks on the picture were to cast it and to
find a suitable outdoor location for the story. The location that
best suited Griffith was discovered at Sound Beach, Connecticut,

[1] Bitzer: Unpublished notes.

a spot that had been used by other directors. Marvin approved the location. Although Marvin had been assigned by his brother to keep an eye on the neophyte director, he was not the type of person to offer much opposition to any ideas Griffith might have. He was a rather happy-go-lucky, unambitious man who often referred to himself as "the captain of the good ship Take-It-Easy with nine decks and no bottom, which sails on forever and forever sails on."[2] Billy Bitzer also described Marvin as "seldom affected with the exuberance of ambition." Linda Griffith called him "genial Arthur." Marvin was the perfect man to calm the nerves of the novice director; in addition, he was a first-class photographer.

Although Billy Bitzer eventually became Griffith's principal cameraman, Arthur Marvin continued to photograph many of Griffith's films until his untimely death early in 1911. Both Bitzer and Marvin frequently worked on sections of the same film, with Bitzer doing the location shots and Marvin photographing the studio shots.[3]

Bitzer later admitted that Griffith gained the upper hand over his cameramen by playing Marvin off against him. Marvin jokingly attributed one Griffith assignment that went to him instead of Bitzer to the few inches' difference in their heights. A scene required that the cameraman make the shot while standing in a river up to his neck. Marvin claimed that Bitzer would not have been able to handle the assignment; the water would have been over his head.

The first item in the casting of *The Adventures of Dollie* was easily taken care of. Griffith cast his wife, Linda Arvidson, as the mother. An actor friend who specialized in villains, Charles Inslee, was cast as the evil gypsy. The husband was more of a problem. According to Terry Ramsaye, Griffith made the rounds of the actors' agencies looking for the right young man to play

2 Bitzer: *op. cit.*
3 Cameraman's record book, Biograph records, in the possession of The Museum of Modern Art Film Library.

the husband. As he went up the steps of one agency, he passed a good-looking young man who was on his way down. Griffith asked the front-office clerk at the agency if the man he had just passed was an actor; the clerk thought he might be. Griffith turned and pursued the young man down the street, catching him at the corner. The young actor's name was Arthur Johnson. He was interested in Griffith's proposition, particularly since he was "at liberty," and suggested it would be easier to discuss matters over a few drinks. Linda Arvidson's version of this meeting is somewhat shorter. She claimed that Griffith passed a handsome young man on the street, decided that he must be an actor, and approached him with an offer of a role in a motion picture. According to her, Johnson replied that he knew nothing of motion-picture acting. Griffith answered: "You don't need to know—just meet me at the Grand Central depot at nine o'clock to-morrow morning." In view of Arthur Johnson's later problems with alcohol, the story that the hiring was completed over a few drinks seems quite probable.

The other major part in *The Adventures of Dollie* went to Mrs. Frank Gebhardt, the wife of a Biograph actor, who played the gypsy's wife.

The pattern of this first Griffith picture followed that of the other films of the day. Each scene was photographed with the camera in a fixed location. The scene was played before the camera as though it were being performed on a stage in a medium shot, with the actors always photographed full-length. There were about twelve scenes in the film, and as was the case for films in 1908, each scene was a single shot. The film was photographed in two days, on June 18 and 19, and the laboratory completed the development and processing on June 22.[4]

Griffith and his wife waited impatiently for the results. Griffith was whistling in the dark: "If the photography is there, the picture will be all right; if it looks as good on the negative as it

[4] Biograph laboratory records, The Museum of Modern Art Film Library.

looked while we were taking it, it ought to get by," he told her.

Arthur Marvin brought the first strip of film out of the dark-room and Griffith asked how it had turned out. Marvin replied: "Looks pretty good, nice and sharp."

"Think it's all right?"

"Yeh, think it is."

The laboratory records are somewhat less enthusiastic about the quality of the film—only "fair," they say. Linda Griffith reported the anxious moments when the film was first shown in the little projection room above the studio:

No sound but the buzz and whir of the projection machine. The seven hundred and thirteen feet of the "Adventures" was reeled off. Silence. Then Mr. Marvin (Henry) spoke:

"That's it—that's something like it—at last!"

Afterwards, upstairs in the executive offices, Mr. Marvin and Mr. Dougherty talked it over, and they concluded that if the next picture were half as good, Lawrence Griffith was the man they wanted.

The official first showing of *The Adventures of Dollie* took place at Keith and Proctor's Theatre, Union Square, New York, on July 14, 1908. Linda Griffith somehow felt that this opening night ought to be a glamorous affair, but:

The house filled up from passers-by—frequenters of Union Square—lured by a ten-cent entertainment. These were the people to be pleased—they who had paid out their little nickels and dimes. So when they sat through Dolly's seven hundred feet, interested, and not a snore was to be heard, we concluded we'd had a successful opening night.

Although this first picture gave little sign of Griffith's ability, the process of filming it had gone smoothly. Griffith had demonstrated that he could handle actors and could put together a film with plausible continuity. Henry Marvin was apparently satisfied with his new director, because he quickly assigned him another picture, *The Redman and the Child*. He did not even wait for the public's reaction to Griffith's work. By the time *The Adven-*

tures of Dollie was shown to the public on July 14, Griffith had completed five films of his own and completed one other film started under Wallace McCutcheon's direction.[5]

The Redman and the Child was an Indian picture. Griffith had some free time between the conclusion of his work on *The Adventures of Dollie* and the beginning of this next film. *Dollie* was completed on June 19, and work did not start on *The Redman and the Child* until June 30. Griffith again set out to hunt for a location suitable for the new film, and found just the spot near Little Falls, New Jersey.

Griffith and the company, including Charles Inslee and Harry Salter, with Arthur Marvin again as the cameraman, took the ferry across the Hudson River to the Weehawken ferry terminal for the train trip to Little Falls. Exterior scenes were filmed on the river on June 30. Footage was processed in the laboratory on July 1, and examined. Griffith and the company returned to Little Falls on July 3 and completed filming the picture. On the day before, July 2, Griffith started another picture, *The Tavern Keeper's Daughter,* with Frank Gebhardt and Marion Sunshine, in the studio. After the Independence Day holiday on July 6, Griffith began his fourth picture, *The Bandit's Waterloo,* in the studio. This was completed on July 8. Picture number five, *A Calamitous Elopement,* followed on July 9 and 11. Griffith then returned to *The Tavern Keeper's Daughter* and completed it on July 13, one day ahead of the first public showing of *The Adventures of Dollie.*

The Tavern Keeper's Daughter was released at 410 feet, approximately four and a half minutes' running time, on July 24, 1908. *The Redman and the Child,* 857 feet long, or nine and a half minutes of running time, was released on July 28, 1908. *The Bandit's Waterloo,* 839 feet, was released on August 4, 1908;

---

[5] Lab records, *op. cit.* The lists of Griffith's films in this book are based on research done for The Museum of Modern Art Film Library by Katherine Stone, and work done by Seymour Stern, "An Index to the Creative Work of D. W. Griffith," *Index Series,* British Film Institute, No. 2, April 1944.

and *A Calamitous Elopement*, 738 feet, was released on August 7, 1908.[6]

Griffith's sixth picture, made in the studio on July 14 and at Shadyside, New Jersey, on July 15, *The Greaser's Gauntlet*, was 1,027 feet long, with a running time of eleven and a quarter minutes. The thousand-foot length, one reel, became the standard length for a feature picture, and most of Griffith's films during the Biograph period were approximately this long. It was generally the policy to make farce comedies just half as long, and two comedies would be issued on a single reel. The half-reel comedy, about 500 feet, became known as a "split-reel."

The Redman and the Child was the first of a long series of pictures that Griffith made with an American Indian as the central figure. This first Indian character was treated by Griffith in the tradition of "the noble red man." The character, played in this instance by Charles Inslee, was described as:

a magnificent type of the aboriginal American . . . a noble creature, as kind-hearted as a woman and as brave as a lion. . . . What a magnificent picture he strikes as he stands there, his tawny skin silhouetted against the sky, with muscles turgid and jaws set in grim determination.[7]

The villains of this film are white bandits, and it is the Indian hero who gives chase in his canoe, subdues the villains by drowning one in the river and stabbing the other on the riverbank, and finally rescues a kidnapped child.

The Tavern Keeper's Daughter was a simple morality drama in which the heart of a Mexican bandit was softened by the miner's baby.

His heart is softened by the childish prattle of the miner's baby who sits in its cradle playing with her dollie. He drops on his knees before the crib and prays to God to help him to resist his brutal inclinations.[8]

6 Biograph Bulletins Nos. 156, 158, 159.
7 Biograph Bulletin No. 156.   8 Biograph Bulletin No. 155.

The Bandit's Waterloo was given a Spanish setting in the studio. It was subtitled "The Outwitting of an Andalusian Brigand by a Pretty Señora." *A Calamitous Elopement* was chiefly concerned with some antics and broad farce built around a balcony set in the studio. Frank and Jennie, played by Harry Salter and his wife, Florence Lawrence, are trying to elope against her father's wishes. "Bill, the burglar," intent on carrying on his trade, becomes mixed up in the elopement. At the end of the picture everyone is satisfied: the love birds are united, the burglar has successfully carried out his robbery of the honeymooners' effects, and the tyrannical father has been outwitted.

The Greaser's Gauntlet had a young Mexican as the hero. He sets out from his home in Mexico to seek his fortune in the United States. Falling in with a rough tavern crowd, young Jose is framed for a burglary and almost lynched. His rescuer, a young American girl, played by Linda Arvidson, saves him, and he vows eternal gratitude: ". . . her eyes sink deep into his heart, enkindling a hopeless passion for her." Shortly after, when the girl falls into the clutches of the usual villains, Jose comes to the rescue. "The tables are now turned and Mildred has a chance to thank him for his deliverance."

The Biograph Camera

Griffith enjoyed one important technical advantage over his immediate predecessors and the competition when he first began directing, and that was the Biograph camera. This unique instrument, kept out of sight during the early litigation with the Edison Licensees, was now available for use. In addition, Bitzer had just received a new Zeiss Tessar f/3.5 lens from Germany which had better image-resolving power than previous lenses.[9] This combination of lens and camera was capable of delivering a superior photographic image, giving Biograph a visible superiority over the competition.

9 Bitzer: Unpublished notes.

The Biograph camera was an ungainly creation, looking somewhat like an oversized version of the box camera familiar in every
home in the twenties and thirties. The camera box, in this instance, was made of polished wood, with the lens protruding from
one end and with a hand crank on the side. The lens had a two-
inch focal length, and with a maximum aperture of f/3.5, it was
comparatively slow. This meant that a maximum amount of light
was necessary to record an image on the insensitive film materials
of the day. The camera used plain, unperforated film, unlike the
film used by the Edison Licensees, which had sprocket holes along
the sides. In the Edison camera the film was carried forward for
each exposure by means of sprocketed rollers and a claw mecha-
nism that pulled the film along. In the Biograph camera, the film
was carried forward from an upper wooden magazine over smooth
rollers by friction. The necessary intermittent motion of the
film at the aperture was managed by a beater-movement roller.
This movement placed an unexposed section of film behind the
aperture for the moment of exposure, and then, after the exposure, swung a new, unexposed section into place. In order to
keep this action smooth, a film loop was formed above and below
the aperture. This was called the Latham loop after its inventor,
Woodville Latham.[10] At the moment of exposure, two registra-
tion holes were punched in the film, forming master holes that
could be used for precise matching when release positive prints
were made from the camera negative. The punchings were sucked
out of the camera by means of little blades mounted behind the
camera shutter. The blades created a momentary vacuum and
then blew the celluloid punchings out an opening in the bottom
right of the camera. Billy Bitzer remembered that he could always

---

[10] It was J. J. Kennedy's purchase of the Latham patents that helped enormously in the litigation with the Edison Licensees, whose cameras were also
using a version of the Latham loop but without official sanction. Doubt has
been expressed that the Latham patents would have held up in open court,
but they were never tested. See both Terry Ramsaye's account and Benjamin
B. Hampton: *A History of the Movies,* New York, 1931, for accounts of Kennedy's successful maneuvering.

return the camera to a previous placement by locating where the little pile of punchings fell on the ground. The camera was equipped with a reflex viewer that made it possible to focus the lens with precision. The actual focusing was somewhat time-consuming, however, since the wooden film magazines on top of the camera had to be swung aside, a metal frame containing a ground glass put in the magazine's place, the lens focused on the ground glass, and the magazine returned to its proper position after the ground glass was removed.

Griffith had an additional advantage which was not unique but which he was able to capitalize on by careful use. The slow, orthochromatic film stock, with its sharply contrasted images, gave the resulting photographs the quality of steel engravings. Griffith recognized this effect and its pictorial relationship to still photographs such as those taken by Mathew Brady during the Civil War. He studied and consciously copied Brady's pictures in many sections of his Civil War films, particularly in *The Birth of a Nation*.[11]

In a great many individual shots, Griffith was quite successful in matching the Brady photographs. A heightened realism is one of the remarkable qualities in all of Griffith's battle sequences. The effect is lost, however, by the staginess of the studio interiors and the occasional intrusion of the standard movie cabin, like the one used in *Rescued from an Eagle's Nest*.

The film passed through the camera at a rate of approximately sixteen frames, or exposures, a second, a rate comparable to the present standard for amateur 8 mm. cameras. The speed was variable, however, despite a governor device, because the camera was operated with a manual crank. The speed, then, depended heavily on the cameraman's skill in turning the crank at a steady rate. Two turns of the crank were required per second. This accounts for the slight variations in movement in the figures in early silent films. The skill of Bitzer and Marvin as cameramen

11 Bitzer: *op. cit.*

is no more evident than in the observable fact that there is little speed variation in the Biograph films.

The original Biograph camera was built by the Marvin and Casler machinery firm, sometimes also known as the Marvin Electric Rock Drill Company, in Canastota, New York. As a result of Marvin and Casler's interest in drilling equipment, the camera came equipped with a standard rock-drilling tripod. Only the heavy iron blocks that anchored the legs for rock drilling were removed.

Bitzer was pleased with the camera-and-lens combination on medium and long shots, but he was not happy about the camera in closeups. The shallow depth-of-field made it necessary for the cameraman to decide which small area of the scene should be in sharp focus. The blurred, misty, out-of-focus shot was not for Billy Bitzer.

During the relatively brief periods when he was not involved in directing his first films, Griffith invaded the territories of the other Biograph workers. He spent hours talking with Lee Dougherty. He viewed films made by the other companies: Edison, Vitagraph, Lubin, Selig, Essanay, Méliés, and Pathé. Griffith was particularly impressed by the Vitagraph films directed by a Mr. Rainous and his leading lady, Florence Lawrence, and he remarked that he would like to work with Rainous and learn the movie business. But in fact he was more interested in Miss Lawrence. With Harry Salter's help, Griffith called on her and offered her twenty-five dollars a week, a ten-dollar increase over her Vitagraph salary, to work for Biograph. At Vitagraph, for the lower salary, she had sewed costumes and canvas scenery as well as playing leading roles. She promptly accepted Griffith's offer and became Biograph's first leading lady.

Griffith's curiosity about the motion-picture business was insatiable. His personal work day often stretched to sixteen hours, and a seven-day week was customary. Griffith looked into every facet of the business. The technique of using a question to elicit the answer he wanted became a personal Griffith technique. He

employed this technique frequently as a director, sometimes leading an untutored observer to believe that the person answering
the question was really doing the creating. Griffith would say,
"Billy, don't you think Mary ought to come through from the
door?" The affirmative answer would only confirm Griffith's plan
of action.[12]

Because Biograph had only a single indoor studio, the former
mansion ballroom, it was frequently unavailable for filming while
scenery was being constructed. During these periods Griffith
would schedule exterior filming in whatever locations seemed
appropriate. The actors were always eager to leave the confines
of the Biograph building and studio. Linda Arvidson described
the cramped, cluttered conditions there:

A "scene" was set back center, just allowing passage room. What
little light came through the few windows was soon blocked by dusty
old scenery. On the side spaces of the room and on the small gallery
above, the carpenters made scenery and the scene painters painted it—
scenery, paint pots, and actors were all huddled together in one friendly
chaos. We always had to be mindful of our costumes. To the smell of
fresh paint and the noise of the carpenters' hammers, we rehearsed our
first crude little movies . . .
    . . . Rolls of old carpet and bundles of canvas had to be climbed
over in wending one's way about. To the right of the camera a stair-
way led to the basement where there were three dressing-rooms; and no
matter how many actors were working in a picture those three dark
little closets had to take care of them all. The developing or "dark"
room adjoined the last dressing-room, and all opened into a cavernous
cellar where the stage properties were kept. Here at the foot of the
stairs and always in everyone's way, the large wardrobe baskets would
be deposited.[13]

Along with the other film companies based in New York,
Griffith made extensive use of the Hudson River palisades and
the dusty, unpaved streets of Fort Lee, New Jersey. Other loca-

12 Lester C. Predmore, in a taped interview, May 1, 1965, Middletown, New
York.
13 Linda Griffith: *op. cit.*, p. 56.

tions in New Jersey, Long Island, and Connecticut were used somewhat less regularly. Fort Lee was easily and cheaply reached by a ten-cent ferry ride from 125th Street in Manhattan. Palisades State Park, next to Fort Lee, offered a wide range of scenic contrasts for filming outdoor dramas—ranging from deep woods and high rocky cliffs to the "thousand foot bathing beach at a point opposite 158th Street . . ." in New York City and the rural town atmosphere of Fort Lee. The railroad connections from the Weehawken terminal made it easy for the company to journey to any number of interior locations in New Jersey with an even wider choice of backgrounds. Griffith continuously broadened his selection of locations, searching always for variety and for backgrounds that were better related to the films he was directing. By the end of his first half year as a director, Griffith had taken his acting company to Little Falls, Fort Lee, Cliffside, Sea Bright, Atlantic Highlands, Coytesville, Shadyside, and Hoboken, all in New Jersey, as well as to Sound Beach, Connecticut.[14]

At the beginning of July 1908, both McCutcheons had left Biograph, and Griffith became the sole director. Whereas Wallace McCutcheon had been unwilling to direct more than one production a week, Griffith was eager to carry the full load by himself. The tempo of production gradually increased. Griffith completed ten films in July 1908, including *The Man and the Woman, For Love of Gold, The Fatal Hour, For a Wife's Honor,* and *Balked at the Altar,* in addition to the pictures already mentioned. (This pace continued for the next three years and then gradually dropped from almost three films a week to two. In his last half year at Biograph, during 1913, Griffith made only one picture a week, but a number of the pictures during this phase were two-reelers, and one film, *Judith of Bethulia,* was four reels.) The output of finished film, about three thousand feet of film a week, or an hour and a half of drama, remained the same during the entire Biograph period. This rate of production exceeds that

14 Lab records.

of today's major television series, which amounts to about fifty minutes of film a week and approximately thirty-nine programs a year. Griffith's output in 1909, his first full year, was the equivalent of seventy-one hours, almost double the rate of a successful television series.

Despite the fast pace of production set for him, Griffith began to call for more rehearsals before filming. He had been unhappy with the length of rehearsals before filming, and the generally slapdash attitude of the actors as they performed. This had not been the regimen that Griffith had admired in the Nance O'Neill Company, nor was it a practice that would appeal to an energetic young man eager to demonstrate his competence. Henry Marvin was not happy with the increased costs of additional rehearsals, but Griffith's production pace, and reports of increased interest in the new Biograph films, kept him for the moment from interfering with Griffith.

Griffith experimented little in his first films. He was satisfied to let Marvin and Bitzer film the stories in their accustomed manner, the camera in a fixed position and in medium shot for the entire scene. In the studio, the camera was mounted on a rolling platform just in back of the double entrance doors to the ballroom. It was capable of moving forward or back but was never moved during a shot, only moved closer for a small setting or back to cover a large set. In his eighth picture, *For Love of Gold,* Griffith for the first time became dissatisfied with the standard method of filming.

The scene was a card game on a studio set. Griffith was anxious to show the reactions of the card players to the game. The traditional medium shot did not show the actors' faces in enough detail. Griffith asked that the camera be moved closer on the rolling platform until the faces could be seen. This meant that the scene would consist of two shots, a medium shot and a three-quarter shot. Now the actors could make their expressions count in the scene, reflecting their thoughts clearly. Griffith had accomplished two things. In previous films, the only way a film director could show what a character was thinking was through the addition of cartoon balloons with titles, drawn in after the film was made. Now Griffith was able to express thought visually. He had also destroyed for all time the idea that a shot and a scene were synonymous. The shot was now the basic film unit, and a scene, or sequence as it came to be known, might consist of an unlimited number of shots.

Despite Griffith's concern over the inadequacy of rehearsals and his attempts to remedy this situation, motion pictures in 1908 were still produced in a highly improvised manner. No shooting scripts or detailed action outlines were prepared. The synopsis was carried in the director's head, and he could vary it as the filming situation changed. If one scenic background called for by the story was not available, the director could change backgrounds and alter the story to suit. Billy Bitzer noted this improvisation atmosphere during the early days, relating an incident that happened in Fort Lee. Griffith had used a variety of home fronts in Fort Lee for his films, and in most cases the home owners had not objected. If a question arose, it was Griffith's custom to take five dollars from his pocket and hand it to Bitzer with instructions to give it to the home owner for permission to film in front of the house. After most of the homes that met his requirements had been used, Griffith decided to try one he had not filmed before. The front yard was guarded by a large, ferocious-looking dog. Griffith handed Bitzer five dollars and told him to secure permission to film in front of the house. But the presence of the dog suggested that the owner of the house might not be too receptive to movie people, even for five dollars. So when Bitzer noticed the name Fitzpatrick on a metal name plate next to the front door, he decided to send an actor from the company, an actor with that name, to do the necessary negotiating. Fitzpatrick was then dispatched. He knocked on the door with a flourish and after giving his name explained the purpose of his call. The woman slammed the door in his face, shouting that she would have nothing to do with anyone named Fitzpatrick; the previous person with that name she'd seen had cheated her out of a month's rent. Griffith thought the incident amusing. He easily selected another location for the film, making the necessary adjustment in the action.[15]

Although Griffith apparently pleased the Biograph front office sufficiently to continue as a director, even before any public reaction to his pictures could be measured, some of his co-workers viewed him with misgivings. Bitzer recalled that Griffith the actor had indulged in an acting style that bordered on the violent, waving his arms about and moving with such rapidity that the camera recorded only a blurred image. His appearance in one film had been cut for that very reason. When he asked Bitzer why his scene was cut, Bitzer explained that it would take a shutter speed of a hundredth of a second to stop this frantic motion, and the Biograph camera operated at only a twenty-fifth of a second under the dim Cooper-Hewitt lamps used for indoor filming. Griffith expressed surprise that he had not been told about this before. Bitzer's concern that Griffith might encourage the same frantic style as a director was unfounded. Griffith had learned his lesson; from this point on, he worked for increasing realism in the acting of the company.[16]

Another practice that Griffith found unsatisfactory was the actors' makeup. The weird pink makeup failed to photograph naturally, and in addition the actors were easily spotted by local inhabitants when the company was on location. Griffith encouraged experimentation that would promote a more natural look, even though he was rather rigidly tied to the stage concepts of the period that depended upon certain stereotyped makeup for specific characters—heavy black beard stubbles for tramps, heavy eyeshadow for heroines, chin whiskers fashioned in the Uncle Sam manner for fathers, bankers, and assorted blue-nosed busi-

[15] Bitzer: *op. cit.*   [16] Bitzer: *op cit.*

nessmen.[17] Any technique was tried at least once, sometimes with
disastrous results. Bitzer endeavored, in his usual helpful manner,
to age an actor by powdering his hair, a traditional stage technique. When the actor raised his hat during the filming, a cloud
of talcum powder rose with the hat, photographing as a cloud of
smoke. Bitzer felt that another director might have fired him for
his meddling, but Griffith was unperturbed. He merely remarked
that the scene was unnecessary and should be cut; he did not
reprimand Bitzer for his efforts.

The change toward a makeup which would photograph realis-
tically is quite noticeable between early films such as *Monday
Morning in a Coney Island Police Court, The Curtain Pole,* or
Edgar Allen [sic] *Poe,* and such later films as *The Lonedale
Operator, The Crooked Road,* or *The New York Hat.*

Griffith's First Contract

By the middle of August 1908, Griffith had completed five more
films, for a total of seventeen in his first two months as a director.
He was offered his first written contract as director by Henry
Marvin. The contract was to run for one year and it specified in
some detail Griffith's obligations as director. None of his later
contracts specified the directorial duties quite so precisely, perhaps because these duties had become tradition. Under the terms
of the contract, Griffith was to receive a base salary of fifty dollars
a week, plus a commission of "$\frac{1}{20}$ of one cent for each linear foot
of positive motion picture film that the Party of the Second Part
sells from negatives of stories, plays and performances executed
under the direction of the Party of the First Part [Griffith]." A
further provision stated that the combined salary and commission
were not to fall below a hundred dollars a week. The commission
was to be paid monthly. Griffith signed the contract with his
stage name, Lawrence Griffith, on Monday, August 17, 1908. It

17 Note the makeup worn by Charles Mailes, as the tyrannical father, in
The New York Hat (released December 5, 1912), directed by D. W. Griffith.
The Museum of Modern Art Film Library, New York.

was signed on behalf of the Biograph Company by J. J. Kennedy, president, and James A. Gausman, secretary.[18]

During the remainder of August following the signing of the contract, and in the month of September, Griffith completed fourteen more films, at a rate of approximately two a week. The shooting schedule was put on a six-day basis, with only Sunday off. Griffith used the Sunday to view other companies' films, supervise the editing of his own productions, and plan the following week's efforts. Bitzer noted that the only vacations taken by Griffith during the entire Biograph period were the train trips he eventually took to California.

During his first few months as director, Griffith had brought some new faces into the company—Arthur Johnson, Charles Inslee, Mr. and Mrs. Frank Gebhardt, Florence Lawrence, Jeannie MacPherson, and John Compson. He made occasional use of Marion Sunshine from the vaudeville stage, and kept on a number of the Biograph players from the previous regime, including the prop boy, Bobby Harron, and Tony O'Sullivan. His wife, Linda Arvidson, shared the leading roles with Marion Leonard and Florence Lawrence.

In July 1908, Griffith used a young, stocky Irish-Canadian named Michael Sinnott, who had taken the stage name Mack Sennett. Sennett was twenty-four and had had a limited experience in stock companies after leaving his home town of Richmond, Quebec.[19] Sennett's first appearance under Griffith's direction was a small part in a comedy, *Balked at the Altar,* filmed on July 19 and 30. He was used primarily as an extra, but Griffith found his ebullient spirits well suited to additional duties as an assistant, a "gopher" in theatrical parlance. Sennett would "go for" coffee, props, actors, or whatever might be required. Sennett

18 Contract between Lawrence W. Griffith (pseudonym for David Wark Griffith) and The American Mutoscope and Biograph Company, August 17, 1908. In the possession of The Museum of Modern Art Film Library.

19 Mack Sennett: *King of Comedy,* with Cameron Shipp (New York, 1954), p. 14.

appeared again on the screen in a larger role in *Father Gets in the Game,* filmed September 3 and 4.

Sennett was not the only employee who doubled from a production job to acting chores. Harry Salter doubled as assistant director, and the boy in charge of props, Robert "Bobby" Harron, then only twelve years old, also appeared in films. Harron had started to work for Biograph in 1907, on an after-school basis, hired by Wallace McCutcheon to work in the cutting room for five dollars a week. He played in several pictures before Griffith arrived, including the role of office boy in *Dr. Skinum* (1907) and with Eddie Dillon in *Bobby's Kodak* (1908). For a time he adopted the stage name of Willie McBain, but by the time Biograph began publicizing its players in 1913, he had reverted to his own name. In 1908, despite his youth, Harron was the sole support of a large family of brothers and sisters.[20]

Florence Lawrence was the first popular favorite in the Biograph acting company. She had been acting in the theatre since childhood, when, managed by her mother, she was billed as "Baby Flo, the child wonder-whistler." Linda Arvidson recalled:

. . . she never minded work. The movies were the breath of life to her. When she wasn't working in a picture, she was in some movie theatre seeing a picture. After the hardest day, she was never too tired to see the new release and if work ran into the night hours, between scenes she'd wipe off the make-up and slip out to a movie show.

Despite the fact that members of the acting company received no screen credit for their efforts—neither did Griffith as director— Florence Lawrence became known to the public as "The Biograph Girl." This title, as well as a banner announcing "Biograph Day," became a common sight on the fronts of the nickelodeons. Florence Lawrence and her husband, Harry Salter, worked for Griffith and Biograph until June 1909. Salter played villains and,

[20] Harold Dunham: "The Tragedy of Robert Harron," *Films in Review,* Vol. XIV, No. 10, December 1963.

as an assistant director, did the preliminary interviewing of pro-
spective actors.

One of the early Florence Lawrence films was *The Taming of
the Shrew* (November 1908), Griffith's only film based on a play
by Shakespeare. The *Motion Picture World* carried a review of
the film:

> Too much praise cannot be bestowed on this picture. After seeing
> the play and moving picture, my first duty is to speak in unreserved
> praise of the lady who took the part of the Shrew and the gentleman
> who portrayed Petruchio. There is not a false move anywhere. The
> staging is good and the costuming nearly faultless. High praise for
> such a play. A word of acknowledgement is also due to the adaptor who
> has done his work well. The subject as presented will please an audience
> of Shakespearean scholars, and at the same time, delight the humblest
> intelligence.[21]

Harry Salter played Petruchio.

The motion-picture market in 1908 demanded a wide variety
of films. Griffith preferred to direct serious films and melodramas,
but it was also his responsibility to direct comedies. In September
he began his only sustained series of comedy films, the Jones
series. Each of the films was built around a central couple,
played by John Compson and Florence Lawrence, and a humor-
ous situation in which they found themselves. The first film in
the series, *A Smoked Husband,* was filmed August 26 and 27,
1908; the leading characters were called Mr. and Mrs. Bibb. It
was not intended as part of a series, but after its release in September and its favorable reception, Griffith decided to do new
stories with the same characters.

It was often charged by some of Griffith's staff, notably Mack
Sennett and Mary Pickford, that Griffith was a rather humorless
man with little appreciation for comedy.[22] Sennett claimed that

21 *The Motion Picture World,* November 21, 1908, p. 398. This was the first
year of publication for this important trade journal.

22 Sennett: *op. cit.,* p. 52. Mary Pickford: *Sunshine and Shadow,* with Cameron Shipp (New York: Doubleday, 1955), p. 129.

his repeated attempts to interest Griffith in films featuring farcical policemen met with failure because Griffith saw nothing funny about the police. The truth of these allegations is doubtful. Even before Griffith, Biograph produced a considerable number of slapstick comedies, and Griffith later permitted Sennett to direct comedies centering on a broadly comic pair of private detectives, "hawkshaws," played by Sennett and Fred Mace. The basic concepts behind the bumbling private detectives were those that developed into Sennett's own Keystone Cops.

The Jones pictures were constructed around a single incident, the comedy arising from a specific situation in which the Joneses found themselves. In *Mr. Jones at the Ball,* John Compson, in the title role, splits his trousers on the evening of a large party. Mrs. Jones takes him into a side room to repair the trousers.

She takes him into the ladies parlor, bribes the matron to keep the ladies out while she repairs the rent. After lacerating poor Jones with the needle, she finds that he must take his trousers off, which he does behind a screen. Hardly has he done so, when there is a clamoring on the outside by several ladies, who wish to enter. Their number is greatly increased by other indignant dames who finally overcome the matron and rush in just as Mrs. Jones has pushed poor Jones, still *en deshabille,* through a door on the opposite side into what she imagines to be a closet, but, Great Heavens! it proves to be the ballroom . . . Grabbing up a rug from the floor and putting it about him, he dashes back into the room . . . Jones . . . makes a flying leap through the window landing on the head of a policeman in the street below, who carts him away to the station-house on a wheelbarrow. Thus ends one of the funniest Biograph films ever produced.[23]

There is no evidence that Griffith was the first director of a situation-comedy series, but research has failed to record a similar effort in 1908 by any of the other active production companies. The durability of this genre of comedy films is attested to by the fact that contemporary television offers many such series. Other films in the Jones series included *Mrs. Jones Entertains, Mr.*

[23] Biograph Bulletin No. 199.

Jones Has a Card Party, Jones and the Lady Book Agent, The Jones Have Amateur Theatricals, and *Jones and His New Neighbors.* All the Jones pictures were split-reels, approximately five hundred feet, or five minutes in running time.

Griffith's approach to comedy differed considerably from much of the work being done at the other studios. The basis for much of the competing comedy was either a physical joke, frequently depending on some form of cruelty, or trick photography derived from the early films and experiments of Méliés.[24] Griffith, on the other hand, allowed the comedy, and the film techniques used, to grow out of the needs of the story itself. As Biograph became larger and more successful, Griffith moved away from making comedies, turning their direction over to his former assistants, Mack Sennett, Dell Henderson, Frank Powell, and Christy Cabanne, while he concentrated on serious pictures. However, even after his withdrawal from comedies, Griffith included considerable comedy in his serious pictures. To the modern viewer, this later comedy sometimes seems self-conscious, coy, or even saccharine, but even so, it is usually clear that there is an attempt at satire or irony growing out of a carefully plotted character, and it is always an integral part of the serious design.

Griffith's attempt at broad comedy cannot be characterized as funny in the same sense as the later Sennett or Chaplin films, and they do betray Griffith's uneasiness in handling farce. He is, on the other hand, quite successful in realizing the comedy in real situations and characters. Some of his plots and situations may appear ludicrous today, but no more so than did the same plots and situations in the stage melodramas of that day.

Audience reaction was beginning to come to the attention of Biograph. The first letter of public record was written to the editor of *The Motion Picture World,* July 17, 1909, and it commented on two Griffith pictures from earlier that year:

[24] Note particularly Méliés's films *Cinderella* (1900), *Red Riding Hood* (1901), and *A Trip to the Moon* (1902), available in the film collection of The Museum of Modern Art Film Library, New York.

For what appeals to me more than all the other things about the Biograph subjects is the finish, the roundness, and the completeness of the story. It seems that they forget nothing. Every little detail receives just the attention it should have before the public sees it.

The Drunkard's Reformation (April, 1909) is the story of exceptional cleverness. The little girl in the play hesitating between fear and love for her father tells the story of her thoughts through her wonderful eyes and the story is a sermon—a masterful, powerful sermon on the evils of the drink habit.

The Biograph subjects all mean something, and they help those who see them. And their comedies are clean, wholesome. There is no slapstick, knock-about stuff in them to disgust people. *The Sacrifice* (January, 1909) is a quiet, droll little thing, sort of a Mark Twain skit that appeals to people; and when they want to scream, they give us *The Curtain Pole* (February, 1909) or *Jones at the Ball*. The Jones are a great pair of clever actors and irresistibly funny. In our little city, we have a change of program nightly, and the manager knows that he has only to advertise a Biograph subject to fill his house, and we know that when we go, we will not be disappointed.[25]

Edward Wagenknecht notes:

Even we children sensed that Biograph pictures were "different," although we could not, for the life of us, have told you wherein their difference might consist. . . .[26]

With the aid of Billy Bitzer, an inveterate tinkerer and inventor, Griffith continued his experiments in methods of telling film stories more effectively. Griffith got along well with both his cameramen, and Bitzer never repeated his efforts to tell Griffith how to make films. Bitzer was always ready with suggestions, but the final choice of method to achieve a desired result was made by Griffith. Griffith would frequently outline an effect that he wished to use, or a result that should come from a specific sequence, and Bitzer would experiment with the camera in an

[25] Carl Anderson: Letter to the editor, *The Moving Picture World,* July 23, 1909, p. 165.

[26] Edward Charles Wagenknecht: *The Movies in the Age of Innocence* (University of Oklahoma Press, 1962), p. 89.

attempt to realize Griffith's objective. After moving the camera closer to the actors in *For Love of Gold,* Griffith asked that the camera be moved even closer to their faces in *After Many Years.* This was filmed in September and October 1908, at both Sea Bright and Atlantic Highlands, New Jersey, and in the Fourteenth Street studio. Again, Griffith's reason for moving the camera closer was to show more clearly the reactions of the characters. Although the closeup was not a new device, Edwin Porter having employed it in *The Great Train Robbery,* and early Mutoscopes having featured closeups, it was not an accepted technique within the structure of the dramatic story. The Biograph front office was upset when they viewed the shot in the finished film. They were afraid that the audience would never accept a picture of a truncated human being. There is no evidence that the audience reacted unfavorably, however. The closeup became, in many filmmakers' theories, the one shot which best crystallized the motion picture's unique distinction over other theatrical forms. It became a normal part of motion-picture syntax.

Only one element in the closeup bothered Griffith. When the camera was moved in for a shot, a change of scale resulted in the projected picture. This change of scale has no apparent effect on a modern observer, accustomed to the technique of the closeup, but Griffith, still viewing the film through the eyes of the stock actor, was disturbed. He wanted some method of concentrating the audience's attention on the central figure, or on some detail within a large scene, but without moving the camera in and changing the scale. Bitzer tried a number of experiments in an attempt to achieve the desired effect. First, he attempted to shoot a scene with the background out of focus and only the central figure in sharp focus. This was done by shooting through a gauze mask with a hole cut around the outline of the figures desired to remain sharp. Griffith rejected this technique as much too distracting. Too much attention was drawn to the fuzzy background. Griffith then told Bitzer to find some way of giving him a piece of film with only the actor on it.[27]

Bitzer was stumped. He had been conducting a number of experiments in his basement with electric lights. Needing some means of keeping stray light rays from entering his lens from the side and spoiling the exposure through streaking the films, a phenomena now known as "lens flare," Bitzer rummaged through his tools and spare parts and finally came up with an old glue pot. He knocked the bottom out of the pot and fastened it over the camera lens as an improvised lens hood. It seemed to serve its purpose under the studio's artificial light when the camera lens was at full aperture. And when he tried the glue-pot device outdoors, it worked equally well. In the outdoor situation, however, the camera lens was closed or stopped down, to control the increased amounts of light. When the outdoor film was developed, Bitzer noticed that the corners of each frame were dark. The edge of the glue pot had been brought into focus, producing a rounded image instead of the expected rectangular one. Bitzer was ready to toss the film away, but Griffith recognized that accident had given them the means to throw emphasis on a single element in a scene. Further refinement of the glue-pot device led to the vignette mask, which, when placed over the lens on the front of the lens hood, blacked out portions of the screen in any desired shape, usually for Griffith a circle, and left only the desired figure or object on the screen. The normal procedure was to give a full shot of the scene and then follow it with a vignette shot from the same camera position, showing only the detail that was to be highlighted. The scale of the figure in the second shot remained the same as in the first shot. Griffith employed the vignette shot increasingly during the period as an alternate method of concentrating attention to the closeup.[28]

One more practice in the films of 1908 annoyed Griffith. It was customary for a comedy or romantic film to end with a kiss.

27 Bitzer: Unpublished notes.   28 Bitzer: *op. cit.*

Griffith had no objections to the kiss but, perhaps because of his stage background, he felt that if the kiss was held too long, the proper mood for the conclusion of the picture was destroyed. The audience would begin to titter. Something akin to the theatre's slow curtain and slowly dimming lights was needed in the film. Griffith had observed the effect caused by stopping down the lens during an exposure out of doors. Such shots were generally trimmed from the final picture because they got gradually darker, the film becoming increasingly underexposed. Griffith asked Bitzer to try this deliberately on the last shot of the picture. The effect was a sort of semi-fadeout, but one which never went to complete black.

The technique served its purpose and Griffith continued it, even eventually extending its use to a separation between episodes within a film. Research has shown that the fade was used in a small number of films before 1904, so that Griffith and Bitzer can be credited only with a rediscovery. The earlier attempts were apparently unknown to them. It was the Griffith efforts, however, that have been influential in the adoption of the device by his contemporaries, since it had not been used in dramatic films before.[29]

After Many Years was the first of several pictures directed by Griffith based on Tennyson's *Enoch Arden*. The synopsis for this first version had been prepared by Frank Woods, a member of the staff of *The Dramatic Mirror*. Linda Griffith writes:

It was the first movie without a chase. That was something, for those days, a movie without a chase was not a movie. How could a movie be made without a chase? How could there be suspense? How action? *After Many Years* was also the first picture to have a *dramatic* close-up—the first picture to have a cut-back. When Mr. Griffith suggested a scene showing Annie Lee waiting for her husband's return to be followed by

[29] Richard Arlo Sanderson: "A Historical Study of the Development of American Motion Picture Content and Techniques Prior to 1904," unpublished Ph.D. dissertation, Dept. of Communications, University of Southern California, 1961, p. 11.

a scene of Enoch cast away on a desert island, it was altogether too distracting. "How can you tell a story jumping about like that? The people won't know what it's about."

"Well," said Mr. Griffith, "doesn't Dickens write that way?"

. . . The picture was so unusual—how could it succeed? It was the first picture to be recognized by foreign markets.

Billy Bitzer made his one contribution as a scriptwriter to *The Curtain Pole* (October 1908). Bitzer had long tried to sell Griffith on the idea of building a comic film around a man's attempt to install a curtain pole. Griffith turned the idea aside a number of times but finally relented and agreed to film the story on one of the location trips to Fort Lee. The picture provided Mack Sennett with one of his best comic opportunities as Monsieur Du Pont, a natty, wax-mustached, inherently inept *boulevardier*. The characterization was undoubtedly out of place in a story set in a Fort Lee home, but this only added to the farce. Sennett, as Du Pont, smashes the curtain pole during a party. He endeavors without success to replace the pole, finally leaving the party to get a new pole. The climax of the picture was a long, wild taxi ride back to the party, with the long curtain pole projecting from the taxi's windows on both sides, sweeping with it everything in its path. The ending of the picture comes as Du Pont enters with the pole:

He is a wreck as he enters with the pole, and no one pays the slightest attention to him, which makes him furious. "Sacrebleu! Zis is ze ingratitude!" And in a rage he bites the pole in two.[30]

Linda Arvidson remembered some of the details concerning the production of *The Curtain Pole:*

The natives of Fort Lee, where *The Curtain Pole* was taken, were all worked up over it. Carpenters had been sent over a few days in advance, to erect, in a clearing in the wooded part of Fort Lee, stalls for fruits, vegetables and other foodstuffs. The wreckage of these booths . . . was

[30] Biograph Bulletin No. 214.

to be the big climax of the picture. The "set" when finished was of such ambitious proportions—and for a comedy, mind you—that we were all terribly excited.

In the melee caused by the careening taxi and curtain pole, Linda Arvidson was momentarily knocked unconscious in the middle of the set, and though she recognized the worth of Sennett's comic performance in the film, she never quite forgave him. She particularly noted that the origin of the character of Monsieur Du Pont was derived from the European film comedian Max Linder and that Sennett had first borrowed the characterization in *Father Gets in the Game,* earlier in the year.

By the end of December 1908, Griffith had completed fifty-seven pictures. In terms of story content, the pictures fell into certain patterns that Griffith kept repeating throughout his stay at Biograph. He made Indian pictures featuring his concept of the noble red man as a frontier hero, beginning, as mentioned, with *The Redman and the Child,* and including *The Red Girl, The Call of the Wild,* and variants on this same theme in two pictures about the Canadian north woods, *The Ingrate* and *A Woman's Way;* pictures about the sea, or the fishermen who must live by the sea, including *Where the Breakers Roar, After Many Years, The Pirate's Gold;* and pictures about Mexican characters in Western settings, including *The Bandit's Waterloo, The Greaser's Gauntlet,* and *The Vaquaro's Vow.* In addition, Griffith had made his first picture about the Civil War, *The Guerrilla,* in which a faithful Negro servant rides for help, has his horse shot out from under him, but manages to get through with the message.

The range of settings in the 1908 films had been varied from the mountains, woods, and rivers of northern New Jersey to the seaside; the streets of New York City and Central Park to a manicured estate in Cos Cob, Connecticut. Griffith made his only picture based on Shakespeare, and he made his only picture with a Japanese setting, *The Heart of Oyama,* with a hand-tinted release print. Costuming ranged from the standard stage Renaissance in *The Taming of the Shrew* to contemporary.

One major innovation in editing also occurred in Griffith's ninth film, *The Fatal Hour,* described in the Biograph Bulletin:

Certain death seems to be her fate, and would have been had not an accident disclosed her plight. Hendricks after leaving the place is thrown by a street car and this serves to discover his identity, so he is captured and a wild ride is made to the house in which the poor girl is incarcerated. *This incident is shown in alternate scenes* [italics mine]. There is the helpless girl, with the clock ticking its way towards her destruction, and out on the road is the carriage, tearing along at breakneck speed to the rescue, arriving just in time to get her safely out of range of the pistol as it goes off.[31]

This would seem to be the earliest example of crosscutting for suspense, or parallel action.[32]

[31] Biograph Bulletin No. 162.

[32] Edward Wagenknecht reports that this is the earliest example of crosscutting found by George Pratt of the Eastman House Museum, Rochester, New York. Wagenknecht: *op. cit.*

III

1909: Cuddebackville

After the Christmas holidays of 1908, Griffith returned to the heavy pace of filmmaking. He completed nineteen films in January 1909, and started a number of others. It became his method to work on more than one film at a time. A series of films would be started in the studio, and then at various other times the exteriors would be filmed. The production of one film frequently overlapped production of other films.

In mid-January Griffith, Sennett, Frank Powell, and Linda Arvidson, pushed out of the studio by scenery construction, set out to film in Central Park. Arthur Marvin was the cameraman. Linda Arvidson remembered:

New York's Central Park awoke one February [actually January] morning to find her leafless trees and brush all a-glisten with a sleet that made them look like fantastic crystal branches. When the actors reported at the studio that morning, they found Mr. Griffith in consultation with himself. He did not want to waste that fairyland just a few blocks away.

A hurried look through pigeon-holed scripts unearthed no winter story. "Well," announced our director, "make up everybody, straight make-up. Bobby, pack up the one top hat, the one fur coat and cap, I'll call a couple of taxis, and on the way we'll change this summer story into a winter one."

The summer story, altered to fit the winter scene in Central Park, was called *The Politician's Love Story*. For Mack Sennett this represented his first leading role in a film without a slapstick base, although technically *The Politician's Love Story* was a comedy. It provided one of those accidents that lead to innovation. Marvin was forced to photograph some of the scenes against the sun. The sunlight shining through the snow and frost-laden trees produced a startlingly beautiful effect. The company was particularly satisfied with the results and commented in the Bulletin: "The subject is a photographic work of art, comprising the most beautiful winter scenes ever obtained." Bitzer was frequently credited with the outdoor photography for this film. Actually, the Biograph records show that Marvin did the exterior camera work on January 18, and Billy Bitzer finished the film in the studio on January 19.

Just two days after completing *The Politician's Love Story,* with one Jones picture in between, Griffith began work on *Edgar Allen Poe,* a story about Poe's creation of the poem "The Raven." Herbert Yost, a Broadway actor of some considerable reputation at that time, was hired to play Poe. Linda Arvidson played the role of Virginia, Poe's sick wife. Griffith's attitude toward his subject is revealed by Biograph Bulletin No. 212:

> He was undoubtedly the most original poetical genius ever produced by America, and might be regarded as the literary lion of the universe, to which fact the public are becoming alive. . . .

In this instance Griffith did not wish to settle for a happy ending or a last-minute rescue. To save his sick wife, Poe

> hastens to the store and procures food, a heavy comfortable for the cot and medicine, and with a much lighter heart returns home. Spreading the quilt tenderly over Virginia, he takes her hand and gazes fondly into her sightless eyes, but the cold unresponsive hand tells him the awful truth. "My God, she is dead," and he falls prostrate across the cot.

Griffith asked Bitzer to attempt a lighting effect in this film that paralleled the effect he had called for in his play *The Fool and the Girl*. The main source of light in the Poe tenement room was to come from the window rather than, as had been customary before, from utilitarian front lighting. Bitzer thought that Griffith was headed for trouble in securing adequate exposures. The results, however, were exciting. The set was shadowy, but the effect was one of naturalness and a mood suited to the subject matter. Lee Dougherty was quite ready to close the Bulletin with: "The subject is one of the most artistic films ever produced."

In his autobiography, Cecil B. DeMille was to take credit for the invention of the term "Rembrandt lighting" as a description of a moody interplay of light countered with deep shadow. Perhaps DeMille did invent the term, but the credit for the effect itself must go to Griffith and Bitzer.

Griffith directed fifteen films in February 1909. Among them was an anti-Communist film, *The Voice of the Violin.* A young German violin teacher is spurned by his pupil, the daughter of a wealthy capitalist. He turns for comfort to a group of plotters,

imbued with the doctrines of Karl Marx, the promoter of the communist principles of socialism, the alleged utopian scheme of universal cooperation, which in time and under the control of intemperate minds becomes absolute anarchy.

The violinist agrees to participate in a bomb plot against the capitalist. His confederates plant a bomb in the cellar beneath the capitalist's mansion while a violin concert is being given upstairs. As the young musician stands outside the window as the lookout, he hears his former love playing his concerto. His new Communist principles are shaken and he leaps into the cellar to stop the bomb going off. He is seized and bound by his confederates. As the concert continues, he manages to inch his way to the bomb and bite the fuse in two with his teeth.

Calling for help he arouses the household who release him from his position. Well, you may guess what the finish will be. Well it did, and they lived happily ever after.[1]

1 Biograph Bulletin No. 223.

The role of the violinist was played by Arthur Johnson, and the rich girl was portrayed by Marion Leonard.

The production record for March 1909 was fourteen films, with Griffith continuing his experiments with natural lighting in *Resurrection*. Bitzer and Marvin shared the camera work on this adaptation of Tolstoy's novel. The editing and camera work on *Resurrection* were not particularly unusual, but Griffith did use one closeup for expository purposes, a finger moving across the pages of a Bible. The actors were photographed in medium shots, showing them full-length, but Griffith did bring the camera in for the closing shot framing the actors across the knees, thus giving a greater emphasis to the final moment. And he continued his experiments with changing the camera setup in mid-scene.

At the beginning of March, Griffith had tried a variation of the lighting effect previously used in *Edgar Allen Poe* with a light from the fireplace as the main source for the closing scene of the picture *A Drunkard's Reformation*. This film followed the usual melodramatic formula for showing the evils of drink. The father is enticed into a neighborhood saloon by evil companions. The first convivial drink leads to a second, and the "good" father is quickly turned into an irresponsible drunkard. In the film, Griffith employs several "switchbacks" to contrast the saloon scenes with scenes of the wife and daughter at home. Then Griffith, in a dinner scene, shows the effect of the drunkard's return on his family. The wife attempts to serve her husband dinner, but he rejects it. A jump cut[2] bridges the time between the beginning of dinner and the end. Griffith then cuts to a theatre scene.

The father and daughter are watching a temperance drama on

[2] A jump cut is a cut between two shots made of the same subject in the same physical location and from the same camera angle. It can be the result of accident caused by the camera stopping in mid-shot and then resuming a moment later, or it can be deliberate technique, as is the case in *The Drunkard's Reformation*, to bridge an interval of time. Most contemporary editing would employ a dissolve rather than a jump cut because a dissolve has less of a shock than the cut.

the stage. The stage play parallels the father's own experiences. Griffith cuts back and forth between shots of the stage play and the audience to show the father's reactions to the play. The father is visibly affected and vows never to drink again. The process of reformation is a direct result of the play. The shots of the stage were made from the audience point of view, and those of the audience were made from the upper level of the stage. The last shot in the film shows the father, mother, and daughter in a close, triangular grouping before the home fireplace. The lighting is effective, although the realism is weakened both by the absence of flicker in the firelight and by the static composition. The cast included Linda Arvidson as the mother and Arthur Johnson as the father, and Mack Sennett played an evil companion in the play-within-a-play. Bitzer was the cameraman.

Griffith directed only eleven films in April 1909, but the month marked a turning point for Biograph. The American Mutoscope and Biograph Company changed its name officially to The Biograph Company, recognizing the already popular appellation. The films themselves had long been referred to simply as "Biographs."

Griffith began the month with an adaptation from an author said to have been his favorite, Charles Dickens. The film was *The Cricket on the Hearth,* and it featured a newcomer, Violet Mersereau, in the principal ingénue role. The cast included Herbert Prior, Linda Arvidson, and Owen Moore. Two other new faces had been added to the company, Clara T. Bracey, a character actress, and another ingénue, Stephanie Longfellow.

Mary Pickford

Toward the end of April, a young Canadian actress came to the studio looking for work. Her name was Gladys Smith and she, along with a younger sister and brother, under the firm guidance of a strong-willed mother, had started from Toronto, Canada, in pursuit of an acting career. Gladys used the stage name Mary Pickford, which had been assumed at the request of David

Belasco, the theatre director-producer. He had been her last employer, in *The Warrens of Virginia,* a successful melodrama by William C. DeMille. Pickford was her mother's middle name. In the family for a time, however, the first name remained Gladys. Her associates at the time remember calling her "Mary" during this period, but she signed the register of the Caudebec Inn, on a location trip during the summer of 1909, as "G. Pickford."[3] Mary herself recalled that it took her mother a long time to get used to the "Mary."

Mary Pickford was already an actress of considerable experience. After her father's death when she was four, her mother had attempted to support the family with a small candy store, but the store failed, allegedly when baby brother Jack fed the store's stock to the dog. Mary's mother, who had theatrical ambitions herself, then tried out for Valentine's Stock Company in Toronto. The family always claimed that it was Mary who suggested that she would be right for the baby part in the show. The manager was amused, hired her, and the Mary Pickford career began.

Mary and her family had passed from one stock company and touring company to another from that point until April 1909, when she arrived at the Biograph studio. Terry Ramsaye's probably apocryphal account of the first meeting between Griffith and Mary Pickford had Mary tiptoeing up to a hatchet-faced keeper of the reception room at the Biograph studio:

"I want to see Mr. Griffith."
"Mr. Griffith is busy, he will not see anybody—"
The secretary looked up and into the wistful smile of Mary.
Griffith, with his mind bent on his work in the studio above, was passing at the moment. He stopped abruptly when he heard an amazing change of tone come into the voice of the woman behind the desk, still addressing the caller—
"—but he might take time to see you, my dear."
Griffith wheeled about. Who could this be that the reception clerk

3 Register of the Caudebec Inn, Cuddebackville, New York. In the possession of Lester C. Predmore, Middletown, New York.

would address so tenderly? What miracle had been wrought? Then Griffith saw Mary. Together they went up the big staircase to the studio.[4]

Mary Pickford's own memories of that first meeting were somewhat different from Terry Ramsaye's movie-script approach. Mary recalled:

As I crossed the marble-floored foyer of the old mansion occupied by the Biograph Studio, a man came through the swinging door opposite me and began to look me over in a manner that was too jaunty and familiar for my taste.

"Are you an actress?" he demanded at once.

"I most certainly am," I retorted.

"What, if any, experience have you had, may I ask?"

"Only ten years in the theatre, sir, and two of them with Belasco," I said icily.

"You're too little and too fat, but I may give you a chance. My name is Griffith. What's yours?"[5]

Edward Wagenknecht recalled Mary's summation of her first impressions of Griffith as a "pompous and insufferable creature." It should be noted that Mary Pickford's remembered impressions of Griffith are at complete variance with the impressions of his other co-workers who have left testaments or comments. They described Griffith as soft-spoken, courtly, a typical Southern gentleman.[6] Mary's own autobiography would lead one to believe that the description she applies to Griffith's behavior would be, perhaps, more accurately applied to her own.

Griffith took Mary to a dressing room, applied some makeup himself, and tested Mary for the principal role in *Pippa Passes*. He was finishing a temperance drama much in the vein of the

[4] Terry Ramsaye's idea of the physical geography of the 11 East Fourteenth Street studio seems to conform more to a movie stereotype of backstage life than to actuality. The main studio was on the first, or entry, floor. Griffith could not be working in the studio above, nor could they ascend the staircase together to the studio. They would have ended in the projection room, perhaps.

[5] Pickford: *op. cit.,* p. 105.

[6] Blanche Sweet, in a taped interview with the author, June 17, 1965, New York, New York.

earlier *The Drunkard's Reformation,* with Tony O'Sullivan, Harry Salter, and a child actress, Adele de Garde. Mary was shown about the studio and then given a brief walk-on role in the picture. This small vignette may well have served as a screen test, for it served no other purpose. It was cut from the final print of the film, *What Drink Did.*

Mary was asked to return the next day. She did and was cast in a small role in *Her First Biscuits,* a split-reel slapstick comedy. Mary was one of the mob of hungry actors who eat a batch of leaden biscuits and proceed to writhe, comically, in pain. Almost the entire Biograph acting company appeared in this short film. The cast included, in addition to Mary, Linda Arvidson, Marion Sunshine, Florence Lawrence, Mack Sennett, Harry Salter, Charles Inslee, John Compson, Mrs. Herbert Miles, Arthur Johnson, and Harry Myers. The film, as was typical of the short comedies, was shot in one day.

A week later Griffith was starting a more ambitious film, *The Lonely Villa,* based on a synopsis submitted by Mack Sennett. Marion Leonard was cast in the leading role, and Mary played one of Miss Leonard's children, along with Adele de Garde. Before he was ready to begin filming *The Lonely Villa,* Griffith used Mary in the role of the daughter in *The Violin Maker of Cremona,* in which Herbert Miles played the role of the cripple-hero, Fillippo. Opposite Mary for the first time was a handsome, young Irish actor, Owen Moore.

The Lonely Villa was a standard melodrama, but it provided Griffith with an opportunity to expand his editing technique of crosscutting, or parallel editing, to produce a last-minute rescue.

Up the road they go at breakneck speed, and during all this time the burglars are working from room to room getting closer and closer to the frightened little family, who are, at the last, standing huddled in the library. Crash goes the door, in leap the sinister dogs, but at the same time in rushes the husband with the police and friends, so the burglars will have ample time to taunt each other with "I told you so."[7]

7 Biograph Bulletin No. 247.

The shots are cut back and forth between the three groups—the burglars, the husband and friends, and mother and children huddled in the library.

Ramsaye relates the story of a momentary difficulty in getting the right effect during the filming of *The Lonely Villa:*

> The work of the robbers at the door was just a shade unconvincing. Griffith was not satisfied and decided on a retake, which was considered rather a wasteful procedure in the motion picture practice of the day.
>
> While the remaking of these scenes was in progress, a stranger found his way as far as the studio door. It was James Kirkwood, just off the road from playing in *The Great Divide* with Henry Miller . . . Kirkwood had wandered into Biograph, looking for his friend Harry Salter, an actor who had become an assistant to Griffith.
>
> Salter introduced Kirkwood to Griffith.
>
> Griffith sized up Kirkwood at a glance.
>
> "Here, put on a beard and get into this scene as one of the robbers."

Kirkwood was reluctant, but Griffith persuaded him to give it a try. Kirkwood joined the robbers in the scene, lending a strong shoulder to the business of breaking in the door, and making his film debut. Sometime later Kirkwood brought an actor friend around to the studio, a former colleague from Miller's *The Great Divide,* Henry Walthall. Both Kirkwood and Walthall became key leading men for Griffith in the next few years, and Walthall played the leading male role in Griffith's epic *The Birth of a Nation.*

Griffith made significant strides in the disjunctive editing of *The Lonely Villa,* not only by crosscutting the three scenes during the "rescue," but by increasing the tempo of the final action through a progressive, though not necessarily linear, shortening of the shots. Griffith also improved on the techniques of gaining suspense through delay. The headlong process of arriving in time for the rescue is temporarily halted through some device. In *The Lonely Villa* this is accomplished by raising a drawbridge in the path of the rescuing automobile. The heroes do, at the last conceivable moment, manage to get through the rising bridge and continue on their way. Although the basic plots and structure of the film melodrama were almost identical with those of the stage, Griffith had found and was polishing a technique, unique to the film, which the stage could never duplicate and which was capable of building suspense far beyond the stage's capability.

Mack Sennett, the nominal author of *The Lonely Villa,* had taken the plot for the film from a newspaper story. He received fifteen dollars from Dougherty for the synopsis, and sent the other Biograph players to read the local newspapers.

Griffith produced thirteen films during May 1909. With the arrival of spring, more location trips were scheduled to New Jersey and Connecticut. According to the Biograph laboratory records, *The Peach Basket Hat* was made in Fort Lee; *The Son's Return* took the company to Leonia and Coytesville, New Jersey; *His Duty, A New Trick,* and *The Way of Man* were made at Edgewater, New Jersey, just below Fort Lee on the edge of the Hudson palisades; *The Message, The Country Doctor,* and *The Cardinal's Conspiracy* were made at Greenwich, Connecticut; and *The Renunciation* was made at Shadyside, New Jersey.

Linda Arvidson recalled these early location trips to New Jersey:

We left our subway at the 125th Street station. Down the escalator, three steps at a bound, we flew, and took up another hike to the ferry building . . . we wondered . . . if we would have time for some nourishment before the 8:45 boat.

A block this side of the ferry building was "Murphy's," a nice clean saloon with a family restaurant in the back . . . we stuffed ourselves until the clock told us to be getting to our little ferryboat . . . we would rush to the ferry, seek our nook in the boat, and enjoy a short laze before reaching the Jersey side. At one of the little inns along the Hudson we rented a couple of rooms where we made up and dressed. Soon would appear old man Brown and his son, each driving a two-seated buggy. And according to what scenes we were slated for, we would be told to pile in, and off we would be driven to "location."

In the studio on the night preceding a day in the country, each actor packed his costume and make-up box and got it ready for Hughie.

Hughie's job, according to Linda Arvidson, was to drive the wagon which transported the costumes, props, camera, and tripods to the location. He would leave well ahead of the company so that the equipment would be there when the company arrived. The prop-wagon driver's full name was Hugh Ford. The "advance man," charged with locating appropriate scenic spots for Griffith's approval, was Miss Gene Gauntier, who later became a prominent screen writer for other outfits, as well as a leading actress for a time at Kalem.

The customary shooting day began early in the morning with the first bright sunlight.[8] Shooting preparations—getting the camera ready, arranging properties—could generally be handled quickly. Johnny Mahr and Bobby Harron were responsible for unloading the property wagon. The actors arrived on location already wearing their makeup. Not a moment of precious sunlight could be wasted. Studio filming, of course, was less rigidly tied to the time of day.

The camera would be set up in some position that offered protection for the cameraman from the hot sun, preferably under the shade of a tree. In the beginning the location of a suitable shady tree often determined the camera angle for a given shot and frequently also determined the background behind the action. Griffith was successful in changing this limiting custom and got the camera moved to the position he wanted even if it meant shifting Bitzer or Marvin out of the shade. To gain his end, Griffith had to resort to subterfuge. On one occasion, he sent one of the prop boys to the village for some bottles of beer, and when the beer arrived, he asked the cameraman to move a little closer to the action, and out of the shade of the tree. The cameraman refused. Griffith then held up a bottle of beer, and much after the manner of moving a horse with a carrot, dangled it promisingly over the spot for the new camera setup. For one bottle the

[8] Lester Predmore, in a taped interview, May 1, 1965, Middletown, New York: "The Company always had an early breakfast, leaving for location as soon as the sun peeked over the hill."

cameraman only looked interested, but for two he promptly moved the camera to the new spot.[9]

Griffith's use of subterfuge to obtain the desired end was a standard part of his technique as director. To enliven a particularly wooden acting performance, he would invent a fictional story that would arouse the actor. If a jealous reaction was required from one of the ingénues and was not forthcoming, he would tell her a tale about her sweetheart's infidelity, tip off Bitzer or Marvin to have the camera ready, and when the girl produced the right feeling of jealousy or outrage, it was captured for the film. According to Bitzer, Griffith would then put his arm around her and confess the falsehood.

Griffith used many pragmatic techniques. As Lillian Gish has recalled, Griffith told his actors:

. . . to watch animals, children, grown people under stress of emotion. We were all made to visit hospitals, insane asylums, death prisons, houses of prisoners to catch, as he put it, humanity off guard so that we would know how to react to the various emotions we were called upon to portray.[10]

Miss Gish also recalled Griffith's rehearsals as arduous and lengthy. He used:

. . . chairs for horses, tables for trains . . . all who happened to be around were pressed into service as actors and to help work out the props.

Griffith made great physical demands upon his actors.

We were made to keep our bodies trained for acrobatic pantomime to be used when the camera was at a distance. Doubles were unheard of in those days and we were called upon to do the most fantastic stunts.

Sometimes the Griffith wiles were worked on the acting company as a whole. It was necessary, during one of the early films,

9 Bitzer: Unpublished notes.
10 Lillian Gish: "D. W. Griffith, the Great American," *Harper's Bazaar*, October 1940.

to clear a path through some tall grass to the door of an old house that was to be used as a background. The heat was almost unbearable, and the entire company had retreated to the shade. No one was ready to take up the shovels and begin making the path, so Griffith walked over to the shovels, picked one up, and started clearing the path himself. After a few moments he paused and casually remarked that it was certainly a lot cooler after some moments of physical exertion. He then began to shovel with greater vigor and, again pausing, repeated his earlier remarks about how delightfully cool it became when he stopped work. The company reacted in the classic manner of Tom Sawyer's friends, mopped their brows, picked up shovels, and followed Griffith's example. The path was quickly cleared, and the actors admitted that it did feel cooler when they ceased their exertions.

On occasion Griffith had to take more direct action to get the proper performance from an actor. One of his demonstrations led to the departure of Charles Inslee, the actor who played the gypsy in *The Adventures of Dollie*. Griffith took over to show how a fight scene should be staged. Inslee lost his temper during the exchange of demonstration blows and, taking a vicious swing, hit Griffith on the jaw. Griffith retaliated with a blow that knocked Inslee to the floor. Bitzer managed to record part of the fight on film, but Inslee decided that he had had enough of Griffith and Biograph.

In a later picture during this period, Griffith used the shock approach to get a reaction from Mae Marsh. He stationed a member of the company behind the set with a double-barreled shotgun loaded with blanks. The cameraman had been cautioned to be ready. At the right moment the gun was fired, and Miss Marsh registered the shocked surprise Griffith had aimed for.

Before getting ready to shoot a scene, Griffith would gather the actors around him while he outlined the nature of the scene. Since Griffith did not work from a script, there was no way for the actors to know in advance what the director had in mind, or even what the story was about. Griffith would tell the story, describe the action, and answer questions. Then he would ask them to take their places to begin filming.

Griffith's greatest asset in working with his company was an infectious enthusiasm. The actors would be swept away by his confidence and energy. He viewed the task at hand always as one of great significance. Every picture, as it was being filmed, was considered a potential masterpiece. He exhibited great patience, and the members of the company were treated with courtesy and kindness. His rare outbursts of temperament were apparently calculated to achieve some immediate directorial effect. His usual manner was to speak softly and to work with the actors as individuals, coaching each one in his or her performance, then assembling the results into a whole, with a minimum of attention to the company as a unit. Because the Biograph acting company functioned in much the same manner as a resident theatrical company, Griffith knew the talents and temperament of each of his actors and could take full advantage of each individual's capabilities.

When working at the Fourteenth Street studio, Griffith would often walk out of the studio, leaving the actors with instructions to work out a bit of business by themselves. After a time, he would return and pass on their efforts, selecting those points which were valid and rejecting any excesses. In one of the early studio films, the scene called for a group of friends at a bachelor party the night before a wedding to offer a toast to the future bridegroom. The set had been painted to look as elegant as possible because the actors were supposed to represent the cream of society. It had been studded with rented palms, the set builder's idea of luxury, and the actors were stationed about the set in rented dress suits. Some of the suits fitted and, as often happens with costumes, some did not. Arthur Johnson, who probably would have looked handsome in a canvas bag, managed to look urbane, debonair, and completely at ease. His suit seemed to fit better than anyone else's. At the other end of the fitting scale were Tony O'Sullivan and Mack Sennett, the first overweight in an underweight suit, the other cadaverous in a suit much too large. The actors felt awkward, and the sense of society camaraderie that Griffith wanted was not achieved. He announced to the cast that it was their problem to work out, and left the studio for the projection room upstairs. As he left, he promised that if they managed to get the proper atmosphere in the scene, he would go to the front office and ask for a five-dollar raise for them all. As soon as Griffith was out of sight, Billy Bitzer attempted to get things moving by arranging the actors in poses imitating those of the lobby dwellers he had observed in the Hoffman House, a fashionable New York hotel. Somehow it did not work. But then one of the actors suggested that they work out a special college yell to be shouted as they raised their glasses in the toast. When Griffith returned, the company was ready to play the scene. They began by lifting Owen Moore, who was playing the bridegroom, to their shoulders, carrying him across the room, and depositing him on top of a table. Then they raised their glasses, half turned toward Griffith at the camera, and shouted with great enthusiasm:

> "Biograph!
> Hah! Hah! Hah!
> Ten Dollars,
> Ten Dollars,
> Rah! Rah! Rah!"

The scene worked, Bitzer captured it on film, and Griffith kept his word. He interceded with the front office for the raises. The base pay for these actors went from five dollars a day to ten. However, other evidence would seem to indicate that extras, and even minor players, were paid only five dollars a day throughout 1910. Griffith also made deals, even on a weekly basis, with some of the players.

It would be too much to assume that all the actors who worked for Griffith were impressed with him or his methods. Those who did not like him were undoubtedly among those who performed in a picture or two and then left. Most of the people who worked for Griffith did so for long stretches of time, and if they left for a while, they reappeared later, and a large nucleus of performers remained with Griffith during his entire five years with Biograph and even after.

Griffith did not use a star system. The hero in today's film might well be cast as the villain in tomorrow's, or just as an extra in the background. The ingénues frequently donned heavy make-up and shawls to appear in character parts. Griffith did try, however, to keep the major roles within type. The young members of the company did not play old-age roles in the foreground of the films. Griffith's casting was not based on a system of favorites. Even the stars of the future—Mary Pickford, Lillian Gish, Mack Sennett, and Lionel Barrymore—were not treated in any special fashion. Mary Pickford was cast not only as a bright-faced ingé-nue named "Little Mary" but also as a dark-complected Indian maiden. Mary always thought that she was cast as an Indian because her eyes photographed dark, whereas the other girls' eyes photographed light. In 1909, she was teamed with Billy Quirk, an aging, married juvenile, to play in a series of adolescent comedies beginning with *The Son's Return*. This series was popular, but Griffith made only a few in the series.

In the spring of 1909, the principal romantic leads were still being assigned to Florence Lawrence, and occasionally to Steph-anie Longfellow or Linda Arvidson. Griffith was casting his wife increasingly in intermediate, "mother" roles, however. Marion Leonard was the other player of "mother" roles. The old ladies were being portrayed by Mrs. Herbert Miles and Kate Bruce, with Jeannie MacPherson playing toothy spinsters. Harry Salter, Mack Sennett, Tony O'Sullivan, and Frank Powell were the vil-lains, or sometimes the police, and any of the leading men not cast in the hero's role were added to the villains' roster. The male leading roles were taken by Owen Moore, Henry Walthall, James Kirkwood, and Arthur Johnson. The juvenile contingent, male, depended upon Billy Quirk, Bobby Harron, and for a brief time Johnny Tansey. The children were usually played by Gladys Egan, Adele de Garde, Mary Pickford, and Jack Pickford. Griffith used girls more frequently in his films than boys, particularly if a small child was called for. Later he was to disguise Frank Powell's son, Baden Powell, as a girl in a number of pictures. In one series, however, he did use a young lady named Edna Foster in a boy's role. This was not unusual casting, even in the theatre of the day. Jack Pickford, for example, had once been booked with his sisters in a play in New York as "Edith" Pickford.

Cuddebackville

In June, Griffith decided that the hot, muggy weather in New York was not conducive to filmmaking, and he decided to take part of the company to a country location that had been recommended by J. J. Kennedy, Biograph's president—Cuddebackville, New York. Cuddebackville was in the Orange Mountains of New York State, just a few miles north of Port Jervis, on the New York–New Jersey border. J. J. Kennedy had stayed at a charming little inn located just above the old Delaware and Hudson Canal, called the Caudebec Inn, which during the summer months was popular with New York businessmen and politicians.

On June 26, Griffith finished up a short comedy, *Jones' Burglar*, in the morning. After lunch, Frank Powell, who was now assisting Griffith as well as acting, rounded up the company and started them out for the ferry at 125th Street. The company was very excited about the prospects of some time in the mountains. They thought of the trip as a vacation with pay.

After the ten-cent ferry ride to Weehawken, the company took the train, the Ontario and Western, to Summitville, just beyond Middletown, New York. The branch line, two trains a day, ran through Port Jervis and then on to Cuddebackville. It was a half-day trip from New York.

The company arrived on the evening of June 26, 1909, and checked in at the Caudebec Inn. They came in at a small railroad station about a half mile from the inn, and most of them walked up the hill to the hotel farm from the station. George Predmore, the owner of the inn, brought Griffith, Mary Pickford, and one or two others up to the hotel in his big, red Thomas Flyer.[11]

One member of the company, Frank Powell, perhaps acting as manager, signed everyone into the inn register. On this first trip to Cuddebackville, the group consisted of Griffith, Billy Bitzer and his wife, Florence Lawrence, Harry Salter, James Kirkwood, Owen Moore (spelled "More"), Henry Walthall, a Mr. Russell, Mr. Shafer, Mr. Stanhope, Tony O'Sullivan (spelled "Sullivan"), Mr. Martin, Mary Pickford, her sister Lottie Smith, Billy Quirk and his wife, Mr. Smart, Johnny Mahr, Bobby Harron, Young Deer and his wife, Miss McCloy, Henry Behrman, Stanner E. V. Taylor, Gladys Egan, Miss Mullen, Arthur Johnson, and Mack Sennett. Alfred Paget joined them the following Thursday, July 1, after breakfast.[12]

As the Thomas Flyer pulled up in front of the Caudebec Inn, with the rest of the company trudging up the hill behind, their hostess, Mrs. Predmore, stood on the inn's big front porch waving her apron in welcome and saying, "Glad to see you come!" When the company left, she stood there again, calling, "Glad to see you go!" The scene was repeated every time the company arrived or departed during the next two summers.

On the few occasions when Henry Marvin came to check on the work, he took a different route, the Erie railroad to Otisville. He would then telephone the inn and Mr. Predmore would drive over in the Thomas and pick him up. Marvin would look around, stay for supper, and then depart.

The Caudebec Inn was a large summer hotel (small by city standards), with three floors including the main floor, and a number of outbuildings. It could hold approximately eighty guests at capacity, but this included some guests sleeping on cots

11 Predmore: *op. cit.*

12 Register of the Caudebec Inn. Paget was the only late arrival on this trip, although it became the custom on subsequent trips for the actors to come as needed, and to return to New York when their jobs were finished.

in the halls. It had been built primarily to serve the boaters on the old Delaware and Hudson Canal, which ran through the heart of town, a few hundred yards below the inn. Griffith and his wife were always assigned the best front bedroom. Linda, however, was not with Griffith on this first trip. She had gone to Louisville, Kentucky, to visit Griffith's family. The Pickfords were assigned the room across from the Griffiths. Since Mary's mother did not accompany them to Cuddebackville, this arrangement may have been made so that Griffith could keep an eye on them. Some of the men were given single rooms, but most doubled up, and in some instances as many as four men were assigned to a room.

The physical and geographical nature of Cuddebackville to some extent dictated the kinds of stories Griffith could film there. There were several scenic features that would add unusual touches to the backgrounds: the old canal; the Neversink River passing through the hills; impressive rocky cliffs; river rapids; a large pond in a wide place beneath one of the canal dams called "The Basin"; and in the near vicinity there were several stone buildings dating back to colonial days, in reasonably good states of repair. (Most of the features are still visible today [1970]. The town was named after a colonial soldier, Major Cuddeback, but the Predmores had preferred to use an earlier French form of the Cuddeback name for their inn; hence the Caudebec Inn.)

After a day of preparation and location scouting on Monday, Griffith began work on the first Cuddebackville film, *The Mended Lute*, Tuesday morning, June 28. Biograph (Bulletin No. 263) called this film "A stirring Romance of the Dakotas." Much of it was shot on the banks of the Neversink River, and a small Indian village was constructed for a set. The cast featured Owen Moore, Florence Lawrence, and James Kirkwood. Considerable authenticity of detail was achieved by using a real Indian couple, Young Deer and his wife, as technical experts. The Indian costumes, headdresses, and equipment have a highly realistic look. The feature attraction of the picture was a canoe chase filmed on

"The Basin," as well as on the Neversink. It should be noted that this picture was entirely about Indians. There were no characters representing the whites.

A second Indian picture followed—*The Indian Runner's Romance*—which was started on the second day and filmed alternately with *The Mended Lute*. The second picture featured Arthur Johnson as a villainous cowboy, James Kirkwood as the Indian hero, and Mary Pickford as an Indian girl. The plot is once again a standard melodrama, but with the difference that the villains are all white, the hero who saves his Indian beloved from their hands is an Indian, and the Indian triumphs in the final chase and fight.

On they gallop, the Indian fighting furiously, until at last the cowboy drops lifeless from the saddle. Drawing the horse up, the Indian dismounts and releases the terror stricken squaw, whom he takes tenderly back to his wigwam.

In preparation for the filming of these two pictures, Mrs. Young Deer would teach the company authentic Indian dances in the inn dining room after supper. Young Deer checked the bows, arrows, and other props and costumes.

In the morning, after an early breakfast, the company set out for the location. The props were carried in a wagon driven by young Lester Predmore, the innkeeper's oldest son, who used his own horse, Jerry, and earned some extra summer money. Bobby Harron loaded the wagon with the properties needed for the day, while Johnny Mahr, the other property boy, helped Bitzer with the camera. (All the Cuddebackville pictures were photographed by Bitzer.) Another team, pulling a hay wagon, carried the actors to the site, this wagon driven by Elton Cuddeback, a descendant of the village's founder. Griffith and a chosen few were driven in the Thomas. For *The Mended Lute* the Indian village set was built in the Oakland valley about four miles from the inn, on the banks of the Neversink.

The company would work until noon, and about an hour

would be allowed for lunch. The lunch period was never extended because Griffith could not afford to waste the sunlight. Sandwiches were brought out from the hotel to the company, but Griffith would usually be driven back to the hotel for lunch and a conference with Bitzer away from the distracting chatter of the group. Even before the hour was up, Griffith had returned to the location and was ready for work.

In the evening, after Mrs. Young Deer's dancing lessons, Griffith would retire to work out the plans for the next day's shooting, and the company was free to occupy themselves as they saw fit. There were no planned recreational facilities at the Caudebec Inn, although a handsomely appointed mission bar in the front of the inn was well patronized. The other principal time wasters were card games, gentle games in the dining room, and poker in a small building across the road from the inn, next to the icehouse. The building in which the poker game was held was the town polling place and was appropriately dubbed "Tammany Hall." When bad weather prevented filming, the card games continued all day.

The company stayed at Cuddebackville until July 4. *The Indian Runner's Romance* was finished on July 3. Griffith wrote to his wife in Louisville:

Dear Linda:

Well, I am back in New York. Got back at twelve o'clock last night . . . I have accounts to make out for eight days, imagine that job, can you?

Haven't had my talk with Mr. Kennedy yet, as I have been away, but expect to on Tuesday or Wednesday as soon as I can see him. Lost six pounds up in the country, hard work, if you please . . .

And then I want to go back to that place again and take you this time because it's very fine up there. I am saving a great automobile ride for you—if I stay. . . .

The last "if" was in reference to Griffith's renegotiation of his contract with Biograph. Griffith did work out a new contract with Kennedy and signed it in August. The principal change was a raise in the commission, from one-twentieth of a cent to one-tenth for each linear foot of positive film sold that had been made under Griffith's supervision. The minimum salary guarantee of a hundred dollars remained.[13]

Back at the studio, while conducting the negotiations, Griffith directed six pictures. The most ambitious was *The Sealed Room,* a Renaissance drama with Mary Pickford, Henry Walthall, Marion Leonard, Arthur Johnson, and George Siegman, which owed much of its basic plot to Poe's *The Cask of Amontillado.* Marion Leonard played a queen in love with a troubador. The king, Arthur Johnson, seals the pair in their tower love nest. Henry Walthall played the luckless troubador. Mary Pickford was an extra. The picture was finished on July 23, and on the twenty-sixth, Griffith and company returned to Cuddebackville for a second stay.

This time Mrs. Griffith went along. Linda recalled being met by George Predmore in the red Thomas, and she promptly dubbed it "The Red Devil." Her impression of the Caudebec Inn was:

Caudebec Inn was no towering edifice—just a comfy place three stories high, with one bathroom, a tiny parlor, rag-rugged, and a generously sized dining-room whose cheerful windows looked upon apple orchards. It was neat and spotlessly clean.

The first film on the schedule at Cuddebackville was *1776,* or *The Hessian Renegades,* a drama of the American Revolution, for which Griffith was able to draw on the extensive research he'd done for his 1907 play, *War.* The initial problem was finding a suitable location. Griffith needed a colonial house, and so George Predmore introduced Griffith to a wealthy landowner near Cuddebackville named Goddefroy. Griffith was warned that Mr. Goddefroy had no use for automobiles and most modern inven-

---

[13] Contract between Griffith and The Biograph Company, August 31, 1909, signed "Lawrence W. Griffith" and "J. J. Kennedy, for The Biograph Company," in possession of the Film Library of The Museum of Modern Art.

tions, or ideas, but he did have an authentic colonial stone house on his property. Goddefroy took an instant liking to Griffith and gave the company carte blanche to film on his estate. Goddefroy even supplied the horses for *1776,* since the Biograph horses had not been shipped to Cuddebackville as yet. Goddefroy asked Griffith:

> "Have you seen the old stone house down below?"
> . . . "Why, why, no."
> "Come along and I'll show you. Maybe you can use it."
> . . . Just built for us was the old stone house that had been on the place so long that no one knew when it had been built.

Griffith composed *1776* with medium close shots, cutting the actors frequently at the knees. A look at the location today suggests that if he had used longer shots some inappropriate background might have intruded. Necessity was probably the reason for the tight composition, and the results are more effective, more immediate, and less static pageant than if longer shots had been used.

1776 was followed by a short comedy, 211 feet, featuring Mary Pickford and called *The Little Darling,* filmed at the Caudebec Inn itself, except for one scene at the train station.[14]

Griffith returned to the Civil War theme with the third picture at Cuddebackville, *In Old Kentucky.* It was a story of two brothers separated by the war, one fighting for the Confederacy and one for the Union. The big scene was the homecoming of the defeated brother, ragged and footsore, to a party at the old plantation in honor of the successful brother's return home as a war hero. Bulletin No. 276 states:

> Reaching the portals he gets a glimpse of the festive scene on the inside, and sorrowfully starts away, but old Uncle Jasper espies him and drags him in . . . The mother folds her lost boy to her heart, and

14 Lester Predmore's description of a film directed by Mack Sennett at Cuddebackville seems to coincide with the description of this short film. There is no corroborating evidence, however.

George (the other brother) with the Union flag thrown over his arm stretches forth his hand to his brother, who with the tattered colors of the Confederacy held affectionately to his breast, receives the warm grasp, typifying the motto of Kentucky "United we stand, divided we fall."

Griffith was to direct a similar scene of the defeated Confederate returning home, one of the most touching scenes in any film, in *The Birth of a Nation.* The same actor, Henry Walthall, played the returning veteran in both films.

Griffith came back to the Indian theme with *Comata, the Sioux,* with James Kirkwood once more playing the Indian hero. Linda Arvidson played the hapless Indian girl who goes to live with a white cowboy, bears a child, and then is deserted. She reclaims her baby at the end of the picture, but both perish as they return to their homeland in the "Black Hills." Once again Griffith depicted the white man as the villain, the Indians as the hero and heroine.

The company returned to New York on August 11. A short melodrama, *The Children's Friend,* was filmed at Sea Breeze and Edgewater, New Jersey, and a more ambitious drama, based on George Eliot's *Silas Marner* and called *The Broken Locket,* followed at Edgewater, with Frank Powell, Kate Bruce, and Mary Pickford.

"Pippa Passes" and Lighting

A major picture remained to be finished in New York before Griffith took the company back to Cuddebackville for more outdoor work in August. The film was *Pippa Passes,* based on the poem by Robert Browning. Griffith had wanted to make this film for a long time. He had tested Mary Pickford for the role of Pippa when she first came to Biograph. Mary did not get the role, however. Griffith cast Gertrude Robinson. Linda Arvidson recalled: "David thought Mary had grown a bit plump; she no longer filled his mental image of the type."

The story of *Pippa Passes* required that the film be constructed in four separate sections, labeled Morn, Noon, Evening, and Night. Each episode was to be separated by a shot of Pippa singing her song. (This structure is almost identical with the general scheme of Griffith's giant *Intolerance,* 1916, which also was divided in four sections, separated by shots of Lillian Gish rocking a symbolic cradle.) A major problem was to achieve lighting effects that would give the mood of each of the four sections. Griffith explained to Bitzer the kind of effects he wanted, and Bitzer protested that he did not see how they could be made. Griffith then turned to Arthur Marvin and had Marvin execute an idea that he, Griffith, had had.

He figured on cutting a little rectangular place in the back wall of Pippa's room, about three feet by one, and arranging a sliding board to fit the aperture much like the cover of a box sliding in and out of grooves. The board was to be gradually lowered and beams of light from a powerful Kleig shining through would thus appear as the first rays of the rising sun striking the wall of the room. Other lights stationed outside Pippa's window would give the effect of soft morning light. The lights full up, the mercury tubes a-sizzling, the room fully lighted, the back wall would have become a regular back wall again, with no little hole in it.

Linda Arvidson reported that most of the Biograph people were highly skeptical, except for Arthur Marvin. But their doubts faded away when they saw the results in the projection room.

At first the comments came in hushed and awed tones, and then when the showing was over, the little experiment in lighting effects was greeted with uncontrolled enthusiasm.

Pippa Passes achieved another distinction. It was the first motion picture to be reviewed by *The New York Times.* The anonymous *Times* reviewer wrote (October 10, 1909):

Pippa Passes is being given in the nickelodeons and Browning is being presented to the average motion picture audiences, who have received it with applause and are asking for more.

This achievement is the present nearest-Boston record of the reformed motion picture play producing, but from all accounts there seems to be no reason why one may not expect to see soon the intellectual aristocracy of the nickelodeon demanding Kant's *Prolegomena to Metaphysics* with the *Kritik of Pure Reason* for a curtain raiser.

Since popular opinion has been expressing itself through the Board of Censors of the People's Institute, such material as "The Odyssey," the Old Testament, Tolstoy, George Eliot, De Maupassant and Hugo has been drawn upon to furnish the films, in place of the sensational blood-and-thunder variety which brought down public indignation upon the manufacturers six months ago. Browning, however, seems to be the most rarified dramatic stuff up to date. . . . That the demand for the classics is genuine is indicated by the fact that the adventurous producers who inaugurated these expensive departures from cheap melodrama are being overwhelmed by offers from renting agents. Not only the nickelodeons of New York but those of many less pretentious cities and towns are demanding Browning and the other "highbrow" effects.

The reaction within the employee group to *Pippa Passes* was probably a factor in Kennedy's desire to settle the new contract with Griffith. The contract was signed, of course, before the public reaction to the picture was known, since *Pippa Passes* was not released until October 4.

Griffith returned with the acting company to Cuddebackville for the third time in 1909 on August 21. This time the company included Mr. and Mrs. Griffith, Arthur Johnson, Marion Leonard, Kate Bruce, Edith Haldeman and her little boy, Gertrude Robinson, James Kirkwood, Frank Powell, Stanner E. V. Taylor, Billy Quirk, Owen Moore, Billy Bitzer, Eddie Shelton, and Arthur Marvin. The size of the cast for the projected pictures had increased, so a second contingent arrived on the twenty-fourth, including a Mr. Cortez, Bobby Harron, William Beaudine, Johnny Mahr, Smart, George Nichols, Tony O'Sullivan, Landers, Gibbs, Foote, "Big" Jim Evans, and Guy Hedlund. The Caudebec Inn was full. Guy Hedlund, a newcomer, found himself assigned to a cot in the hall.

Despite the size of the company, this stay was a short one. Only one picture was fully completed at Cuddebackville, *Leather*

Stocking, freely based on the James Fenimore Cooper stories. Griffith filmed the exteriors for another film, *Fools of Fate,* before the company returned to New York on August 30.

The last film in August was a short drama called *Wanted, A Child,* only 296 feet. According to Bulletin No. 279, the plot concerns a family with too many children, living on the edge of poverty. They constantly complain about having too many mouths to feed, but when faced with an offer by a wealthy relative to take some of the children off their hands, reply:

Dear Brother: Me and my wife have thought over your kind letter. At first we were going to send you all our children, but we find we are too poor to spare one. . . .

—rather reminiscent of Mary Griffith's early struggles to keep her fatherless family together in Louisville, Kentucky.

Griffith directed eleven films in September. Location trips were made again to Greenwich, Connecticut, for *The Little Teacher,* in which Mary Pickford played the young school teacher faced with an unruly group of students and Arthur Johnson was the stalwart surveyor who comes to her aid against Billy Quirk, the chief troublemaker. Other trips were made to Atlantic Highlands, Gallilee, Edgewater, Fort Lee, and Englewood, New Jersey.

The Gallilee excursion took Griffith to a small fishing village, now absorbed by Sea Bright, New Jersey, and a return to a story of unrequited love on the shore of a fishing community. Linda Arvidson, once again was the lonely figure gazing out to sea, waiting for her loved one's return. Bitzer's photography was particularly crisp, and the environment at Gallilee gave Griffith a striking background for the film. Griffith chose the picture's title, *Lines of White on a Sullen Sea,* from a poem by William Carleton. The other actors in the cast were George Nichols, Dorothy West, Charles West, James Kirkwood, and Dell Henderson.

There had been a major defection from Biograph upon the return from Cuddebackville. Florence Lawrence and Harry Salter had been secretly negotiating with Carl Laemmle, the founder of the Independent Motion Picture Company, known as "IMP," and when J. J. Kennedy discovered this they were dismissed from Biograph. Laemmle's film company was outside the Edison Licensee group, the Motion Picture Patents Company, and warfare had erupted both in the courts and on the film locations. The issue was still the camera, and the Motion Picture Patents Company was attempting to seize the illegal cameras being used by the independents.

For a Biograph player to negotiate with Laemmle was a form of trading with the enemy. After their dismissal, Florence Lawrence and Harry Salter did not reappear until April 2, 1910, when Laemmle announced that "The Biograph Girl" was now an "IMP." Salter was announced as the distinguished director who would continue to be responsible for Miss Lawrence's film successes. Salter had been a Griffith assistant, but there is no record that he ever directed a film at Biograph. Miss Lawrence had achieved one noteworthy thing by changing her affiliation. She was now billed with her own name, no longer under Biograph's cloak of anonymity. The Lawrence defection to what must have seemed greater personal recognition was probably not lost on the remaining members of the Biograph acting company. Florence Lawrence and her husband had been popular with the group. But Griffith was not particularly discommoded. The acting company was now operating in such fashion as to be completely independent of any one actor or actress. Each character category was staffed in depth, and Griffith's practice of alternating casts kept any one player from being too important. The constant factor was Griffith himself.

The last film in September 1909 was *The Light That Came,* a reworking of the Cinderella story. The homely sister falls in love with a blind musician. When the musician's sight is about to be restored, she worries that he will not love her. In the last shot, however, the musician does ask for the homely sister, providing the standard happy ending. The production was apparently hampered by the small sets in the Fourteenth Street studio. Consequently, Griffith used rather close shots, with the actors framed at the knees.

Ten films were completed in October. Griffith directed *Nursing a Viper,* a story of the French Revolution, with Arthur Johnson as a French aristocrat sympathetic to the revolutionists. Griffith returned to this setting in his later career with the memorable *Orphans of the Storm.* In both films, he clearly declared for the republicans against the *ancien régime.*

In mid-October, Griffith directed a film based on a story by Mark Twain, *The Death Disc,* set in Cromwellian England. George Nichols, Linda Arvidson, Gertrude Robinson, Jeannie MacPherson, James Kirkwood, and "Big" Jim Evans were in the cast. The persecuted family of the film were Roman Catholics suffering under the iron rule of a tyrannical Cromwell. The story seems to parallel in many respects the French Huguenot episode in *Intolerance,* except that the religions are reversed and the family in *The Death Disc* is saved at the end of the film.

Griffith ended the month of October with the production of *Through the Breakers* (Bulletin No. 901). Marion Leonard and James Kirkwood play pleasure-loving parents who neglect their small child, Adele de Garde, for a gay round of parties and cards. The child becomes ill and dies. The husband deserts the wife, but:

> At the grave of the child we see the poor woman, with bruised heart, breathe forth prayers of contrition, when the husband drawn by the same impulse, approaches. Softened by the same grief they are reunited, each blaming themselves for their own sorrow.

Griffith used crosscutting for contrast in the film, showing the mother enjoying herself at the ball, contrasted with the sick child at home. Griffith concluded the film with the couple walking out of the scene toward and past the camera. Griffith also attempted further lighting effects, using some sidelighting in the manner of *The Drunkard's Reformation,* but it is not as successful, primarily because the shots are not composed as effectively.

By the end of October 1909, Griffith had made a fundamental change in staging. The actors no longer entered a scene from the right or left as if still working on a stage, but rather from behind the camera, and they exited toward and past the camera. This form of exit, particularly, enabled Griffith to move the actor from a medium shot into a closeup within the confines of a single shot.

The number of Griffith films declined in November to nine. For the first time since Griffith took over in 1908, with the exception of the Sennett-directed comedy at Cuddebackville, another director was added to the Biograph roster. Griffith's company manager and principal actor of businessmen roles, Frank Powell, was given an opportunity to direct. Powell directed a comedy, *The Day After,* in which a very young Blanche Sweet plays the spirit of the New Year. Powell used Blanche Sweet again in his second Biograph film, *All on Account of the Milk,* made the first week in December, with Blanche playing a serving maid who changes places with her mistress, Mary Pickford. Griffith had wanted to use her when she first appeared at Biograph. He had tried her out, but Linda Griffith stated that "finding her so utterly unemotional, he dismissed her saying, 'Oh, she's terrible.'"

After *Through the Breakers* and a short comedy, *In a Hempen Bag,* Griffith turned to a synopsis based on Frank Norris's novel *The Pit,* called *A Corner in Wheat.* Frank Powell was cast in the leading role, an unscrupulous commodities trader who successfully corners the wheat market. His maneuver at the exchange drives the price of wheat up, raising the cost of bread for the consumer and ruining the wheat farmers. Griffith opened the film with a strong documentary-like scene showing two farmers behind their horse, walking toward the camera from a long shot to a closeup, sowing their wheat. This single shot might well have been a prize one for any of the Department of Agriculture documentary filmmakers of the thirties. Griffith depicts the farmer's decline from the first shot showing prosperity to an identical shot at the end of the film showing only the younger farmer sewing his wheat. The old farmer and the horse have vanished. The wheat tycoon does suffer symbolic retribution when he trips at the grain elevator during a triumphal tour with his society friends, falls into a pit, and drowns under a torrent of grain, his grasping hand, opening and closing, disappearing last. Griffith used his crosscutting technique in this film for much more than suspense or a chase. He used it continually to contrast and comment upon the increasing poverty of the poor and the thoughtless affluent celebrations of the rich. The two stories are frequently intercut. In one instance, Griffith followed a shot of the poor on a bread line being turned away when the bread gives out, with a shot of the tycoon at a sumptuous banquet being served by liveried retainers just as a triumphant toast is proclaimed.

Griffith employed another technique of film storytelling here— the carefully planted detail that passes almost unnoticed but is reintroduced as a vital factor in the film's denouement. In the first shot of the grain pit, Griffith shows a coil of rope in the foreground. Later it is this carelessly placed coil of rope (deliberately placed by Griffith) that trips the speculator and sends him tumbling to his death.

The rapidity with which one-reel films could be made and released offered Griffith an opportunity to turn out a strictly topical film. In mid-November he filmed a situation comedy, *A Trap for Santa Claus,* and had it released on December 20, in time for the Christmas holidays.

In *The Rocky Road,* directed by Griffith at the end of November, he used another last-minute rescue. This time the rescuers were attempting to stop a wedding. The techniques employed are considerably inferior to those in the earlier *A Corner in Wheat,* and Griffith used no crosscutting to lend suspense to the rescue.

In December, however, Griffith used crosscutting to heighten suspense in the concluding moments of *Her Terrible Ordeal,* when Florence Barker, the heroine, is locked in a large safe. (The device of the safe is later used in *The Usurer.*) The general execution of this picture is also inferior to *A Corner in Wheat,* however. Griffith seems to have appeared as an extra in the background of a railway-station shot.

With the addition of Frank Powell to the directorial staff, the number of comedies directed by Griffith declined. Powell took over the direction of the lighter films. Linda Arvidson recalled that the title of the first film directed by him was *His Duty,* but no record of a film by that title seems to exist. All indications would point to *The Day After* as Frank Powell's first film. The records do indicate that Griffith directed the entire output for Biograph from the departure of Wallace McCutcheon in June 1908 until late November 1909, a total of 188 films through November 27. Some thirty-five films during 1910 were not directed by Griffith, and apparently most of these were handled by Frank Powell. One of the Powell-directed pictures included Thomas Ince in the cast. Ince never worked under Griffith's direction, but his wife, Eleanor Kershaw, was a member of Griffith's company and Ince later became Griffith's principal rival as a film producer.

Another of the Powell films was based on a scenario by Mary Pickford, *May and December,* which Mary had confidently sold to Griffith for fifteen dollars.

Surveying his squatters one day, Mr. Griffith announced he needed a split or half-reel.

"Anybody got a story in mind?" he asked.

Three or four of us dashed for paper and pencil and were scribbling like mad. During my first weeks at Biograph I had quite unashamedly sold Mr. Griffith an outline of the opera *Thais* for $10. This time I ventured a plot of my own, and to the great annoyance of the men he bought it.

The picture was purchased, but Griffith turned the Pickford script over to Frank Powell to direct.

Griffith made another sermon on the evils of card playing, *The Last Deal,* in December. Griffith used tight medium-close shots of the poker game, over the backs of some of the players, with their shoulders framing the shot, crosscut with shots of the wife praying at home. Griffith also used a closeup and a change of camera position in mid-scene when the husband, played by Owen Moore, leaves the poker game after losing all his money. Griffith, still forced to limit his scope by the size of the studio and the set, concentrated even more than ever in telling his story in close, tightly composed shots. The camera was still operating head-on into the setting, probably from the rolling dolly, so that there is little variety in camera angle.

Griffith directed eleven films in December, and four more during the first week and a half of January 1910. A few new faces had been added to the company. Frank Grandin appeared in his first picture, *The Duke's Plan,* at the end of December. The other new faces included Lucille Lee Stewart, who later became Mrs. Ralph Ince; Ruth Hart, later Mrs. Victor Moore; and Charles Craig. Craig first appeared in *The Rocky Road* and then played the leading role opposite Mary Pickford in *The Englishman and the Girl.* This film comedy revolved around a group of amateur thespians who were putting on a production of *Pocahontas.* Griffith was perhaps drawing on his experiences with the Virginia Centennial pageant.

Griffith directed 151 pictures during 1909, an average of twelve to thirteen pictures a month. The content followed much the same pattern as during the half year in 1908. The Indian picture in which the red man was a heroic figure standing against the venal white man was represented by *Comata, the Sioux, Leather Stocking, The Redman's View.* Griffith's interest in the Civil War was represented by *In Old Kentucky* and *The Honor of His Family.* The American Revolution was represented once, with *1776, or The Hessian Renegades,* and the French Revolution by *Nursing a Viper.* Griffith made one film set in his native state of Kentucky, *The Mountaineer's Honor,* with Arthur Johnson and Mary Pickford as the lovers. Period films in non-American settings were *Nursing a Viper, The Death Disc, The Cloister's Touch* (set in vague Renaissance period), and *The Duke's Plan* (seemingly French Cavalier, perhaps the reign of Louis XIII). The other films were set in contemporary frameworks.

Griffith continued his interest in filming scenarios based on literary works and had used the writings of James Fenimore Cooper, Robert Browning, William Carleton, George Eliot, and Mark Twain.

The first review of an individual film by *The New York Times* was accorded Griffith's *Pippa Passes*. This film marked a successful experiment with a four-part form and mood lighting.

The editorial technique of crosscutting had been strengthened in the chase sequences and had been successfully used in parallel editing in *A Corner in Wheat* to make a strong social comment.

IV

1910: California

The year 1910 began with the completion of *The Englishman and the Girl;* two films on location at Coytesville, New Jersey—*The Final Settlement* and *His Last Burglary;* and a studio film, *Taming a Husband.* The last was the story of a neglected wife who enlists the aid of her girlfriend to set things right. The setting was late eighteenth century, which made somewhat more believable the girlfriend's donning of male garb to become a pretended lover. The climax of the picture involves an imminent duel between the disguised girl and the husband very reminiscent of the scene in Shakespeare's *Twelfth Night.*

On January 14, Griffith began a film in the New York studio, called *The Newlyweds,* with a cast that included Alfred Paget, Florence Barker, Tony O'Sullivan, Mack Sennett, and W. Christie Miller. Arthur Johnson was the hero, a confirmed woman-hater, who is mistaken for a new bridegroom.

Griffith, never happy with cold weather (according to Bitzer), had been bombarding the front office with requests to take the company to California for winter filming. Griffith's arguments, based on his personal knowledge of California, finally gained them the permission. Work was stopped on *The Newlyweds,* with plans to finish the picture in California. The company selected to make the trip included Frank Powell, in charge as company manager, and Marion Leonard, Florence Barker, Mary Pickford,

Dorothy West, Kate Bruce, Eleanor Hicks, Dell Henderson and his wife, Florence Lee, Mr. and Mrs. George Nichols, Henry Walt-hall, Billy Quirk, Frank Grandin, Charles West, Mack Sennett, Arthur Johnson, William "Daddy" Butler, W. Christie Miller, Tony O'Sullivan, Alfred Paget, Jack Pickford, the cameramen Arthur Marvin and Billy Bitzer, the scenic artist Eddie Shelton, and the property boys Bobby Harron and Johnny Mahr. Only a few people had been left behind. Jeannie MacPherson was one, and she cried when her name was not announced.

The Griffiths proceeded ahead of the company, accompanied by R. H. Hammer, the new corporate secretary of the Biograph Company. Everyone was looking forward to the train trip across the country. Linda Arvidson described it:

> Four luxurious days on luxurious trains before we would sight the palms and poinsettias that were gaily beckoning to us across the distances.
>
> The company departed via the Black Diamond Express on the Lehigh Valley, which route meant ferry to Jersey City. A late arrival in Chicago allowed just comfortable time to make the California Limited leaving at 8 P.M.
>
> The company was luxurious for just three days.
>
> It was only Mr. R. H. Hammer, my husband, and myself who had been allotted four full days of elegance. We *de luxe'd* out of New York via the Twentieth Century Limited.

Jack Pickford, then thirteen, was not scheduled to make the California trip. Mary Pickford related how his inclusion was in fact a last-minute, trainside decision. Mary, now seventeen, was making the trip without her omnipresent mother, sister, and brother, but as she boarded the train, young Jack threw a tantrum and demanded that he be allowed to go. Mary protested that Jack was not packed or prepared, but Mother Pickford indulged Jack and told Mary that she must take him along. The train began to pull out of the station with Mary standing on the steps, still protesting. But her mother picked Jack up and deposited him on the slowly moving train, calling, "Look after your sister,

Johnny!" Jack took this command very seriously and throughout the California sojourn continually warned Mary about associating with this or that man.

The departure was hectic in other respects too. Arthur Johnson and Charles West arrived hatless, breathless, and not so fresh from an all-night party. Owen Moore had refused to go to California without a ten-dollar raise, and Griffith had turned him down. Moore was there to say goodbye to Mary Pickford, still hoping that Griffith would change his mind about the raise, but Griffith did not. Mother Pickford made a last-minute attempt to hold up Griffith for a raise for Mary. Griffith said no, and Mrs. Pickford threatened to keep Mary in New York. Griffith coolly informed her that he had Gertrude Robinson standing by to take Mary's place. At that, Mary climbed aboard without the raise.

The company arrived in Los Angeles by way of San Bernardino, where each member of the company had been presented with a free bouquet of flowers, fragrant carnations. R. H. Hammer suggested that the ladies in the company stay at the Alexandria Hotel at Biograph's expense until they secured suitable quarters for themselves.

The Biograph Company was not the first motion-picture company to arrive in California. The first film team consisted of two men, Francis Boggs and Thomas Persons, employed by Selig. They had arrived late in 1907 and produced California's first film, a one-reel version of the durable *The Count of Monte Cristo*. Another of the independent film companies in California, a fly-by-night outfit called the New York Motion Picture Company, was headed by two former bookmakers, Bauman and Kessel (who later became Mack Sennett's partners in Mutual-Keystone). Bauman and Kessel had left New York because of interference with their operations, allegedly by thugs hired by the Motion Picture Patents Company and J. J. Kennedy, and settled in a studio converted from an abandoned grocery store, on the outskirts of Los Angeles, in 1909.

First California Studio

Griffith arrived in Los Angeles about January 20. His first action, assisted by a Mr. Grey, the advance man for Biograph, was to secure the rental of a loft in which to store properties, and a vacant lot for outdoor filming, at the corner of Grand Avenue and Washington Street, next to a lumberyard and a ball park.

Mary Pickford has described this first Griffith California studio:

Our stage consisted of an acre of ground, fenced in, and a large wooden platform, hung with cotton shades that were pulled on wires overhead. On a windy day our clothes and curtains on the set would flap loudly in the breeze. Studios were all on open lots—roofless and without walls, which explains the origin of the term "on the lot." Dressing rooms being a non-existent luxury, we donned our costumes every morning at the hotel. Our rehearsal room was improvised from a loft which Mr. Griffith rented in a decrepit old building on Main Street. A kitchen table and three chairs were all there was of furniture. Mr. Griffith occupied one of the chairs, the others being reserved for the elderly members of the cast. The rest of us sat on the floor.

Linda Arvidson added:

A stage had to be rigged up where we could take "interiors," for while we intended doing most of our work "on location," there would have to be a place where we could lay a carpet and place pieces of furniture about for parlor, bedroom—but not bath.

. . . Our stage, erected in the center of the lot, was merely a wooden floor raised a few feet off the ground and about fifty feet square, of rough splintery wood, and when we "did" Western barrooms-*au naturel* —it was just the thing.

Although Mary Pickford mentioned the absence of dressing rooms, Linda Arvidson recalled "two small adjoining dressing rooms for the men . . . then similar ones for the women." She also recalled that for very large casts a dressing tent was erected.

Griffith's first filming in California was of the final exteriors for *The Newlyweds*. Two days after the completion of this film, and while the outdoor stage was still being built, Griffith took part of the company to the San Gabriel Mission to make his first all-California film, *The Thread of Destiny*. The old Spanish missions provided a romantic new environment for stories that were still much the same melodramas that Griffith had made in New York and Cuddebackville.

While filming *The Thread of Destiny*, it was necessary for Bitzer to photograph inside the mission. The pulpit was lit by the slanting rays of the sun; the rest of the church was dimly lit. The results—the scene had not been expected to turn out—were excellent and Griffith's ideas on lighting received further reinforcement.

The second film with a distinctly California theme was a historical romance, *In Old California,* with Marion Leonard playing the Spanish señorita and Frank Grandin the handsome young lover who becomes governor of California. The film was made within the boundaries of what came to be known as Hollywood. This was three years before Cecil B. DeMille went west to shoot *The Squaw Man* (1913), sometimes claimed as the first Hollywood motion picture.

The company now settled into a routine not too dissimilar from their New York routine. Trips to various suitable points for exterior work alternated with interior shooting on the Los Angeles "lot." *The Man* was partly filmed in the Sierra Madre Mountains. *The Converts* took the company back to San Gabriel. *Faithful* was made in Hollywood. *The Twisted Trail* entailed a return to the Sierra Madre. *Gold Is Not All* was made at Pasadena, and *A Rich Revenge* at Edendale. *A Romance of the Western Hills* was filmed both in the Sierra Madre and at Pasadena. *Thou Shalt Not* was made at Pasadena, and *The Way of the World* on another trip to the San Gabriel Mission.

Griffith broke the routine of locations by selecting a synopsis based on a Charles Kingsley poem, "The Three Fishers," as his next production. Griffith called it *The Unchanging Sea* and took the company to the beach at Santa Monica and to Port Los

Angeles for the filming. The picture was actually another variant on the Enoch Arden story. The husband was lost at sea and then miraculously washed up on a foreign shore. The grieving wife and small baby daughter wait for his return, gradually growing older. On his island, the husband also grows older, his beard getting longer and longer. Griffith indicated the transitions in time by repeating a shot of the wife and daughter stepping out of their cottage. Each time, Linda Arvidson, as the wife, had aged her makeup, and the place of the baby daughter was taken by an older girl, Mary Pickford.

Griffith used very careful composition in *The Unchanging Sea,* repeatedly contrasting vertical figures with the broad horizontal sweep of beach and sea, and introducing the element of motion within the frame by moving a single figure diagonally across the composition. The shots were held for a long time, giving a very slow pace overall, but the parallel editing between the husband and his family was smoothly executed. Once again Griffith made use of the circular design he had used so effectively in *A Corner in Wheat,* repeating, at the end of the picture, the initial shot of the husband and wife silhouetted against the sea.

At the end of March, Griffith took the company to the mission at San Juan Capistrano to make *The Two Brothers,* with Billy Quirk, Marion Leonard, Kate Bruce, Mary Pickford, and W. Christie Miller in the principal roles. The company left Los Angeles on March 24 in a two-car special, with an extra car attached as a combination baggage car and horse car.

The train arrived in Mission City sometime after midnight on the twenty-fifth in a pouring spring rain. March was going out in California like the proverbial lion. The special was shunted onto a siding and the company waited impatiently for the storm to end, but the rain continued. After a while everyone decided to make a dash for the hotel through the rain. It rained for three days, and each day of rain Griffith would prowl the lobby, darting glances out of the front windows and questioning Bitzer about the prospects for clearing so they could begin filming.

Griffith was not the only member of the company staring out of the hotel windows. The rest of the group were as anxious to quit their cramped quarters in the hotel. On the last day of rain, there was an impressive diversion as the company watched an Indian funeral procession passing by their windows on the way to services in the mission.

The following day the weather cleared. The actors prepared to assume their roles in the film, the first scene of which involved a religious parade, with the actors dressed in borrowed ecclesiastical vestments. A large crowd of Spanish-Americans had gathered to watch the "movie peecha" actors, and as the scene opened, after a rehearsal, the crowd began to grow sullen, resenting what must have seemed a mockery of the previous day's funeral. The resentment built as the parade moved toward the mission. The crowd suddenly broke and rushed the actors, aiming their fury particularly at W. Christy Miller, the elderly character actor, who, in his role as the priest, was carrying a cross. At this onslaught, the actors broke and ran for the safety of the hotel. From the window there they could see the local parish priest attempting, without success, to calm the angry crowd. The mob advanced on the hotel, until finally the hotel proprietor came out on a balcony overlooking the street and spoke to the mob in Spanish. He apologized for the actors, explaining that they had not been mocking the funeral procession. After much shouting back and forth, an agreement was reached. The crowd would be mollified if some of the "cowboys" in the Biograph company would put on an exhibition of riding and roping. The "cowboys" were invited to begin by riding a bronco selected by the mob. Fortunately, Griffith had hired some real cowboys to double in the riding shots; he certainly could not have sent any of his Eastern, "drugstore cowboys" out to perform. The leader of the real cowboys was Art Acord, an experienced rodeo performer, and he quickly volunteered to ride the horse chosen by the crowd. The ride was successful, and the other cowboys put on an informal exhibition of rodeo tricks in riding and roping. The crowd's hostility was converted into enthusiasm, and Griffith was able to resume filming.

The next to last film of the first California season was an ambitious adaptation of Helen Hunt Jackson's *Ramona,* the same story in which Griffith had appeared as an actor. The exteriors were filmed at Peru, California, and Camulos in Ventura County, about seventy miles from Los Angeles. Mary Pickford again played an Indian maiden. The rights for the film had been secured for a hundred dollars, an unprecedented sum when the average price paid for a scenario was twenty-five dollars. Mention was made in the Biograph Bulletin, for the first time, of a special arrangement with a publisher, Little, Brown & Company, for the rights. Biograph also issued a special brochure about the film. Griffith made full use of the long vistas available in California by having Bitzer make a number of panoramic shots with the actors as only tiny parts of the total composition. The theme of the picture was the same theme Griffith had used in his other Indian pictures. As the Bulletin stated: "It most graphically illustrates the white man's injustice to the Indian."

Griffith directed a final film in California before the return to New York, *Over Silent Paths,* at the San Fernando Mission. Linda Arvidson described the old mission as follows:

Mission atmosphere got under the skin; so we determined on San Fernando for *Over Silent Paths,* an American desert story of a lone miner and his daughter who had come by prairie-schooner from their far-away eastern home.

San Fernando mission was twenty-two miles from Los Angeles, with inadequate train service, and the dirt road, after the first winter rains had swelled the "rivers" and washed away the bridges, was often impassable by motor.

The desertion and desecration of the picturesque place was complete. For more than two hundred years the hot sun and winter rain had beat upon the Mission's adobe walls. . . . A few Japs were living in the one habitable room—they mended bicycles. We were as free to move in as were the swallows so thickly perched on the chapel rafters.

Griffith finished shooting the picture on April 6, 1910, and the company began the four-day trip back to New York. The group had been in residence for a little more than three months, and twenty-one films had been completed.

Work began again at Fourteenth Street on April 21, with Griffith directing Frank Powell and Stephanie Longfellow in *The Impalement*. Powell had been busy in California as the director of the comedy unit, but Griffith continued to use him as an actor. The return to New York meant a return to the former routine of shooting the interiors for pictures in the Fourteenth Street studio and making location trips to various spots in New Jersey and Connecticut for the exteriors. Fort Lee, New Jersey, as the nearest location, was still the most frequently used. The Eastern stories were still much the same mixture of temperance dramas, Civil War stories, and melodramas in which mother and child, or a young girl, were menaced by tramps or robbers, to be rescued at the last moment.

Mary Pickford made a last comedy with Billy Quirk, *Muggsy's First Sweetheart,* in May, but she was now more often cast by Griffith as a romantic young woman than as an awkward adolescent.

In July, Griffith directed a melodrama called *The Usurer,* with George Nichols playing a villainous moneylender. In many ways this film echoed the earlier *A Corner in Wheat.* Griffith crosscut from shots of the moneylender enjoying himself at a party to shots showing the effects of his usury on a series of victims. Retribution comes to the moneylender when he is accidentally locked in his giant safe overnight and suffocates in the midst of his hoarded wealth. This parallels the torrent of wheat in *A Corner in Wheat.* Additional suspense, however, was given to the last episode by crosscutting shots of missed opportunities for rescue.

Cuddebackville Again

Griffith finished his 248th film, *The Sorrows of the Unfaithful,* with beach scenes at Atlantic Highlands, New Jersey. Once again

he booked the Caudebec Inn in Cuddebackville for another summer season in the Orange Mountains. Just before the company's
departure, Griffith filmed some interior scenes for *In Life's Cycle,*
with Charles West and Stephanie Longfellow, at Fourteenth
Street, and then finished the exterior shots at Cuddebackville.

The group arrived at the Caudebec Inn on July 20, 1910, to be
greeted by Mrs. Predmore on the porch waving her apron and
calling, "Glad to see you come!" The basic company for this
second summer in Cuddebackville included Mr. and Mrs. Griffith,
once again in the front bedroom; W. Christie Miller; Vernon
Clarges; Mr. and Mrs. Bitzer; Henry Walthall; Johnny Mahr;
Bobby Harron, now signed into the register as "Mr. Harron";
Alfred Paget; Edith Haldeman and her son, who worked in only
one film, *Wilful Peggy,* and left on July 22; Gertrude Robinson;
Stephanie Longfellow; Kate Van Buren; Mr. and Mrs. George
Nichols; Douglas Joss; Mr. and Mrs. Dell Henderson; Kate
Bruce; Mabel Normand, who returned to the city after *Wilful
Peggy*; Claire MacDowell; Dorothy Davenport; the Misses Kibbe
and Hulme, also engaged only for *Wilful Peggy*; Mack Sennett;
Billy Quirk; Frank Grandin; Arthur Marvin; Eddie Dillon;
Herbert Yost; Jack Pickford; Henry "Pathé" Lehrman; "Big"
Jim Evans; Griffith's sparring partner and trainer, Spike Robin-
son; Guy Hedlund, engaged only for *Wilful Peggy*; and George
W. Morris. A number of extras were also brought along to fill
out the casts.

This was the largest company Griffith had worked with on one
location. The proximity to New York, however, meant that
actors who were not needed could be sent back to the city, and
any necessary replacements could be quickly obtained.

One of the actors making the trip to Cuddebackville as an
extra was a little man named Henry Lehrman. Lehrman had
joined the company the previous year and, despite the fact that
very little employment was thrown his way, hung on tenaciously.
His particular favorite was Mack Sennett, and they had roomed
together in the Alexandria Hotel in Los Angeles during the

California trip. Lehrman had first appeared, looking for a job, complete with a thick French accent and an obviously manufactured story about being a leading director for Pathé, the French film company. A more believable story was that he had been a streetcar conductor on the Fourteenth Street line and had become enamoured of the actors he transported to the Biograph studio. Griffith saw through his story but let him hang around, occasionally casting him in a small part, and dubbing him "Pathé." Lehrman had an antic sense of comedy which fitted very well with Mack Sennett's, and when Sennett left Biograph for his own operation at Keystone, he took "Pathé" Lehrman with him as a comedy director. During his tenure at Biograph, "Pathé" Lehrman was the company "character." Mack Sennett remembered Lehrman's first screen appearance:

The scene called for French soldiers to capture a three-story building, rescuing some damsel in distress. Lehrman immediately distinguished himself. He not only ran into the building with the other extras, but suddenly appeared on the roof—and leaped into space.

The fall would have splattered an ordinary man like a scrambled egg, but Lehrman lit on his backside, rolled twenty feet, bounced, and came up grinning weakly.

Griffith was indignant.

"You were not on camera!" he hollered.

"I was just rehearsing," Lehrman said. "I'll do it again." And he did.

The second film at Cuddebackville was *Wilful Peggy,* based on *The Country Cousin* and featuring Mary Pickford, Gertrude Robinson, Claire MacDowell, and Kate Bruce in a story about Ireland in the eighteenth century. Mary Pickford recalled how impromptu action was frequently incorporated into a film, with an example from this picture. Mary had objected to Griffith about being continuously cast as "wishy-washy heroines."

"I'd like to give this mother of mine in the picture a good shake when she orders me to marry a man old enough to be my grandfather."

"Well, why don't you do it, Pickford?" said Griffith. "I've no objection."

So poor Kate Bruce, my cinema mother, was grabbed by her cinema daughter and thoroughly shaken. Mr. Griffith eyed the episode approvingly and then went up to Kate.

"What would you do in real life if a sixteen year old girl shook you?"

"I'd grab her and spank her good and proper," replied Kate.

"Well, what are you waiting for?" said Mr. Griffith. "Go ahead and do it!"

"If you two think I'm going to submit to this nonsense you're very much mistaken," I said, and I took off and ran around an apple tree, with Kate Bruce chasing me till she accidentally stumbled and fell, whereupon I ran back, sat down and kissed her, and we put our arms around each other. Both the chase and the little embrace remained in the film.

Next Griffith began shooting a romantic drama with Henry Walthall and Gertrude Robinson, *A Summer Idyll*, on July 26 and 27, but then switched to begin *The Modern Prodigal*, which cast Jack Pickford in a major role. The son of the Caudebec Inn proprietor, Lester Predmore, was allowed to graduate from driving the prop wagon into a supporting role. Lester coaxes Jack into swimming in the millrace. (The effect of a millrace was created by releasing the water from the dam at The Pond long enough to simulate "white water.") Young Predmore realizes what he has done and runs for help at the village store. An escaped convict, passing by, rescues Jack from the water, only to be caught by the sheriff. The convict is allowed to escape again by the sheriff's wife as a reward for saving the boy. The convict was played by Guy Hedlund, moving up from extra roles. The sheriff was James Kirkwood, and his wife was played by Kate Bruce, who fulfilled Griffith's subtitle for the film, "One Good Turn Deserves Another." Lester Predmore was delighted to receive his pink slip for five dollars for his work as an extra.

Griffith was using more new faces in the company. He deliberately sought out new actors, believing that the public might be a little tired of the "California faces." One of the new actors was Joseph Graybill, who displayed a technique and ability in rehearsal that made the other leading men jealous.

Evenings at the Caudebec Inn were spent much as they had been the previous summer. Some new features had been added. W. Christie Miller entertained the more sedentary in the parlor with his Shakespearean readings. In the dining room, with the lights lowered, Guy Hedlund held séances. He would place his wife, the medium, under hypnosis and then treat the handholders to an exhibition of table tapping and knocking. One evening the tapping seemed to come from directly overhead. The séance was being held at midnight, and the mysterious overhead tapping came from Griffith's shoe banging on the floor for silence.

In addition to the dining-room sessions, Hedlund led midnight expeditions to the local cemetery, where conditions were just right for spoofing the younger members of the company.

"Big" Jim Evans had gathered the poker players together in Tammany Hall, across from the inn. There was a brief attempt to carry on a crap game, but Griffith wandered in, was displeased, and put a stop to the game. The poker games were tolerated. Griffith himself would often drive the Pickfords and the Bitzers in the Predmore car down to Port Jervis, on the New Jersey border, for an evening at one of the local country inns. "Big" Jim would take advantage of Griffith's absence to change the poker game into a personal version of three-card monte, at which he was an expert. His reputation for slickness and professionalism at cards managed, however, to keep the old hands from joining in.

The Goddefroys had welcomed the company back for the second season, although Mr. Goddefroy tasked Griffith with ruining the local wage scales. The Goddefroys were always visiting the locations in their horse and trap, and since they brought the company fresh milk and boxes of apples and pears, they were doubly welcome. Mr. Goddefroy made an even greater hit by bringing the group a special beverage when they were laboring in the hot sun. He mixed Bass's Ale and ginger ale in a milk pail, over a large block of ice. This refreshing drink Goddefroy called "shandygaff." The company willingly stood in line to drink the "shandygaff" out of tin dippers.

If the day's work had been successful, with all weather conditions favorable, Griffith would celebrate, upon returning to the inn, by standing a round of drinks in the mission bar. Billy Bitzer was usually good for a second round.

The company returned to New York at the end of July, but almost immediately a small group set out for the Delaware Water Gap to film the exteriors for *Rose O'Salem-Town*, a story about the Puritans of New England. In this film the good Indians, once again, help the hero win the girl. This picture was followed by *The Oath and the Man,* another drama of the French Revolution, filmed in Paterson, New Jersey. *The Iconoclast* was made at the Fourteenth Street studio as part of *Examination Day at School.* This last film was then finished in Westfield, New Jersey.

On August 28 the company again left for Cuddebackville. Griffith had started a Western film, *The Chink at Golden Gulch,* in the studio. The exteriors were finished at Cuddebackville, using the general store overlooking the pond and canal. (Although somewhat altered in exterior appearance, the general store still exists in much the same capacity in Cuddebackville today.)

Another Indian film, *The Broken Doll,* came next at Cuddebackville. Griffith attempted to start tears flowing profusely with this picture. A little Indian girl who has never known an affectionate word is given a doll by a white child.

This act of kindness, the first the poor child had ever experienced, so overwhelms her with gratitude that she is at a loss to know how to express it.

. . . one (of the Indians) is cruelly assassinated by a drunken (white) rowdy. The Indians, vowing vengeance, return to the reservation with the lifeless brave. A council of war is held, during which the little one appears with the doll in her arms. One of the Indians seizes this image of a white baby and hurls it over the bank, and when the girl climbs down she finds it hopelessly broken. Heart-crushed, the little one buries it in true Indian fashion, and as she is prostrate before the tiny pyre she hears the noise of the war dance. Hastening to the scene she realizes the grave danger of her first and only friends, and runs off to warn them.

. . . [the Indians] meet with powerful resistance at the village . . . and are driven off. Everyone is loud in their praise for the little Indian child and are anxious to know her whereabouts. Alas, they will never know, for the little one, wounded during the conflict, has just enough strength to reach the little grave where she falls, making it a double one, and her pure soul parts with the little body sacrificed upon the altar of gratitude.—Bulletin No. 3745

The company on this final trip to Cuddebackville in 1910 consisted of the Griffiths, Billy Bitzer, Frank Powell, George Nichols, Dell Henderson, Charles West, Frank Grandin, William Butler, Tony O'Sullivan, Eddie Dillon, Jack Dillon, Guy Hedlund, Spike Robinson, "Pathé" Lehrman, Mack Sennett, Charles Craig, "Big" Jim Evans, Alfred Paget, Arthur Marvin, W. Christie Miller, William Beaudine, Bobby Harron, Johnny Mahr, Gertrude Robinson, Mary Pickford, Lottie Pickford, Jeannie MacPherson, Dorothy Davenport, Kate Bruce, Claire MacDowell, Jack Pickford, Gladys Egan, and Abe Kelly. There were also three extras, registered as Jimmy, Frank, and Sam. It was Gladys Egan who played the Indian child in *The Broken Doll.*

In New York again, Griffith maintained his usual pace, directing seven pictures during September. Another Civil War film was on the September roster, *The Fugitive,* and Griffith used several new faces in the picture: Lloyd Carlton, an Australian, also Lucy Cotton and Lucy Cahill, along with the regulars Kate Bruce, Edward Dillon, Dorothy West, Dorothy Davenport, and Edwin von der Butz, known simply as Edwin August.

Eight pictures were completed in October, including another with Mary Pickford as an Indian maiden—*The Song of the Wildwood Flute*—and one of Griffith's Indian advisors, Dark Cloud, in the cast. Griffith also directed an elaborately costumed production of *The Golden Supper,* a Renaissance drama based on a poem by Tennyson. There was also an anti-Czarist film about

Russia, *Waiter No. 5,* which included shots of the starving poor in Russia oppressed by the Czar's tyrannical police.

At the beginning of November, Griffith embarked on an ambitious project which met with some opposition from the Biograph front office. He began two films simultaneously on November 5, each of which told an episode in the same story—*His Trust* and *His Trust Fulfilled.* Dougherty wrote in the Bulletin:

His Trust is the first part of a life story, the second part being *His Trust Fulfilled* and while the second is the sequel to the first, each part is a complete story in itself.

In every Southern home there was the old trusted body servant, whose faithful devotion to his master and his master's family was extreme to the extent of even laying down his life if required.—Bulletin No. 3778

The first reel concerns the charge given to the servant (played by Wilfred Lucas, an actor friend of Griffith's from his stock-company days) to protect the soldier's wife, child, and home while he is fighting with his regiment in the Civil War. The husband is killed in battle, and friends bring the widow his sword, which is hung above the mantel. The house catches on fire, and the old servant remembers his trust and, dashing to the burning house, first saves the child and then returns to the house to save the colonel's sword. He takes the homeless widow and child to his own small cabin and stays on the doorsteps to guard over them.

The second reel starts four years later. The war is over. The child has grown up and wishes to pursue a higher education at the seminary. It is the faithful servant's savings that keep her there. When his savings give out, he is tempted to steal to help the girl, but he cannot bring himself to commit a crime. His faithfulness is observed by an English cousin of the girl's, and the cousin takes over the financial burden. The girl meets the cousin and they become engaged and marry.

Old George at a distance views the festivities with tears of joy streaming down his black but honest cheeks, and after they depart for their new home, he goes back to his cabin, takes down his master's saber and fondles it, happy in the realization that he has fulfilled his trust.—Bulletin No. 3779

It was Griffith's intention to release the two reels as a single picture, double the length of current films. Henry Marvin objected on the grounds that the audience's attention could not be held for as long as twenty minutes. Marvin's opinion prevailed, and the film was released in two parts. It was not until Griffith's departure from Biograph that the film was released as he had originally desired. By that time, longer films had become standard.

In November, Griffith made *Winning Back His Love*. This picture shows that Griffith was still turning out studio potboilers without any significant use of the new techniques employed in his more ambitious films. He did move the camera closer for the climactic shots, but the total is slow-moving and pedantic.

Another November film was *The Two Paths*. This was also a studio potboiler, but it does afford a slight parallel with Griffith's *Intolerance*. The heroine is shown twisting her fingers in her dress, to indicate tension. In *Intolerance,* Griffith has Mae Marsh twist her fingers in a similar manner during the trial sequence of the modern story. Griffith also repeated his firelight effect in *The Two Paths*. The cast included Charles West, Linda Griffith, Marion Leonard, and Donald Crisp.

The need to grind out films without any particular attempts at quality is represented in December by *Lily of the Tenement,* with George Nichols, Arthur Johnson, and Dorothy West. Griffith used only two sets. The actors make very stagy entrances and exits, and the camera work is perfunctory.

By December 20 Griffith had completed a total of 288 films. He made eighty-six films during 1910, sixty-five fewer than in 1909. Griffith was, of course, no longer responsible for the entire Biograph output. He had turned comedy over to Frank Powell, and Mack Sennett had been initiated into the directorial ranks. Griffith had asked for and carried out longer rehearsals before filming, and he had taken the Biograph company on a long cross-country trip to California which involved not only travel but the setting up of a new studio.

Griffith's interest in many of his previous themes continued unabated. He made Indian films, both in the 1909 manner and with the addition of the scenery in southwestern California. The Spanish-Mexican themes that had interested him in 1908 were still evident, as witness his use of authentic mission scenery in California. The Civil War was treated in a number of pictures, and there was the usual scattering of costume epics based on segments of European history, including the Renaissance and the French Revolution.

The films with a Spanish theme were *The Thread of Destiny, In Old California, The Way of the World, The Two Brothers,* and *Ramona.* The films with an Indian theme, which would also include *Ramona,* were *A Romance of the Western Hills, A Mohawk's Way, Rose O'Salem-Town, The Broken Doll,* and *The Song of the Wildwood Flute.* The Civil War was the theme in *In the Border States, The House with Closed Shutters, The Fugitive, His Trust,* and *His Trust Fulfilled.* Films with a historical theme included *The Call to Arms,* a drama set in the Middle Ages and filmed at Lambert's Castle in Paterson, New Jersey, and *Wilful Peggy, The Oath and the Man, The Golden Supper,* and *Heart Beats of Long Ago.*

Because of the California trip, there were films with a general Western background in 1910, including *The Man; The Twisted Trail; A Rich Revenge,* filmed in a California oil field; *The Gold Seekers,* set in the days of the 1849 gold rush; *Over Silent Paths; Unexpected Help,* another film in the California oil fields; and *That Chink at Golden Gulch.*

By 1910, Griffith had strengthened and extended the use of crosscutting to show parallel action, or disjunctive editing, notably in *The Usurer.* The technique was now standard practice.

Griffith made even greater use of natural scenery as an element in overall film design, using the long shot and the extreme long shot effectively in *Ramona*. He made use of extremes in natural lighting, filming, in the California mission, interiors without artificial light, though still following the practices he had established in *Pippa Passes* in 1909.

In 1910, too, Griffith made the first attempt to expand into the two-reel picture with *His Trust* and *His Trust Fulfilled*.

Griffith's birthplace at Lagrange, Kentucky, as drawn by himself. This "reconstruction" of a home that did not exist when he made the drawing (in 1914) bears a resemblance to the "little Colonel's" home in *The Birth of a Nation*. Below, left: Colonel Jacob Wark Griffith, his father. Right: Lawrence Griffith as a young actor.

Linda Arvidson (Mrs. D. W. Griffith) and her husband, in their only joint film appearance, *When Knights Were Bold,* a Biograph film of Griffith's pre-directorial period of early 1908.

The Biograph studio at 11 East Fourteenth Street, New York, where Griffith directed the major Biograph films from the summer of 1908 until October 1913.

FORM NO. 1326   **BULLETIN No. 151. RELEASED July 14, 1908**

THE ADVENTURES OF DOLLIE

HER MARVELOUS EXPERIENCE AT THE HANDS OF GYPSIES

LENGTH, 713 FEET.   **PRICE, 14 CENTS PER FOOT.**

One of the most remarkable cases of child-stealing is depicted in this Biograph picture, showing the thwarting by a kind Providence of the attempt to kidnap for revenge a pretty little girl by a Gypsy. On the lawn of a country residence we find the little family, comprising father, mother and little Dollie, their daughter. In front of the grounds there flows a picturesque stream to which the mother and little one go to watch the boys fishing. There has come into the neighborhood a band of those peripatetic Nomads of the Zingani type, whose ostensible occupation is selling baskets and reed ware, but their real motive is pillage. While the mother and child are seated on the wall beside the stream, one of these Gypsies approaches and offers for sale several baskets. A refusal raises his ire and he seizes the woman's purse and is about to make off with it when the husband, hearing her cries of alarm, rushes down to her aid, and with a heavy snakewhip lashes the Gypsy unmercifully, leaving great welts upon his swarthy body, at the same time arousing the venom of his black heart. The Gypsy leaves the scene vowing vengeance, and the little family go, back to the lawn, where the father amuses little Dollie with a game of battledore and shuttlecock. During the game the mother calls papa to the house for an instant. This is the Gypsy's chance, for he has been hiding in the bushes all the while. He seizes the child and carries her to his camp where he gags and conceals her in a watercask. A search of the Gypsy's effects by the distracted father proves fruitless and the Gypsy with the aid of his wife gathers up his traps into his wagon, placing the cask containing the child on the back. Down the road they go at breakneck speed, and as they ford a stream the cask falls off the wagon into the water and is carried away by the current. Next we see the cask floating down the stream toward a waterfall, over which it goes; then through the seething spray of the rapids, and on, on until it finally enters the quiet cove of the first scene, where it is brought ashore by the fisherboys. Hearing strange sounds emitted from the barrel, the boys call for the bereft father, who is still searching for the lost one. Breaking the head from the barrel the amazed and happy parents now fold in their arms their loved one, who is not much worse off for her marvelous experience.

No. 3454   **CODE WORD—Reverso**

Produced and Controlled Exclusively by the

American Mutoscope & Biograph Co.

11 East 14th Street, New York City.

PACIFIC COAST BRANCH,   312 California Street
                                       Los Angeles. Cal

Licensees { Williams, Brown & Earle.   Kleine Optical Company.
                 Society Italian "Cines"   Great Northern Film Company.
                 American Mutoscope & Biograph Company.

We will protect our customers and those of our licensees against patent litigation in the use of our licensed films.

The Biograph handbill for the first film Griffith directed.

Three shots from *The Adventures of Dollie,* showing the gypsy (Charles Inslee) and his wife abducting the child; Arthur Johnson as the father, and Linda Arvidson as the mother.

G. W. Bitzer, Griffith's cameraman, in a formal self-portrait (note his hand pressing the button behind his back), presented to G. V. Predmore

Tolstoy's *Resurrection,* directed by Griffith in 1909, with Florence Lawrence, Arthur Johnson, and Clara T. Bracey. Note the trademark, "AB" (for American Biograph), in center.

Top: *In Old Kentucky* (1910), one of the many Civil War films directed by Griffith while at Biograph. Mary Pickford is at the far left, the Union soldier at center is Owen Moore, Henry Walthall is the Confederate soldier, and Kate Bruce is at far right.

Bottom: Griffith (with bare arm, center) directing a Western, *The Stage Rustler*. The cowgirl at left is Gene Gauntier, and the figure in profile third from left is Mack Sennett.

A rare photo of the Biograph company at Caudebec Inn in 1911. Mrs. Bitzer is seated in the rear of the Thomas Flyer, Griffith (hand to mouth) is facing Mary Pickford, and Young Deer is on the porch.

Bitzer's postcard says: "Dear Mr. Predmore: Want to thank you for your kindness in driving me to Otisville (gratis) last week. Expect to be up with the Indians in a couple of weeks . . . We are going to do a big war picture at Fort Lee this week (August 23, 1911). Then an easy one, then Cuddebackville. Anything I can do for you, you know the number, 11 E. 14th. G. W. BITZER." *Photos courtesy of Lester Predmore.*

The Caudebec Inn register for July 20, 1910, with the second line reading: "Mr. and Mrs. Griffith, Biograph Co." Note "Norman" for Mabel Normand, three lines from bottom, in the list on this page that ends with Mary Pickford and Claire MacDowell.

Top: A 1910 photo of the little railroad depot at Cuddebackville, New York. Bottom: A scene from *The Little Darling,* using the depot as background (note the wooden shutter), in which Arthur Johnson, Mary Pickford, and Mack Sennett (wearing top hat) appeared. *Courtesy of the Library of Congress.*

Top: *The Mended Lute* (1910), one of several Indian films directed by Griffith. It was filmed at Cuddebackville. James Kirkwood is at left and Florence Lawrence at right.

Bottom: Mary Pickford writes from Toronto on November 2, 1909: "Mr. Predmore, Dear Sir: Your letter at hand. I thank you kindly for the check. I was worried to know how to make up for the loss of five dollars. You are very kind, Mr. Predmore, to trust me and take my word but I asure (*sic*) you, your trust has not been misplaced. Thanking you again, I am yours truly, MARY PICKFORD."

Top: *The Musketeers of Pig Alley* (1912), a realistic Biograph film set on the Lower East Side of New York City. Lillian Gish at left, Dorothy Gish center.

The New York Hat (1912), written by Anita Loos, was Mary Pickford's last Biograph film. Here she is shown with Lionel Barrymore.

Top: With Bitzer at the camera, Griffith is directing Henry Walthall in this publicity shot photographed in June 1913.

Bottom: One of Griffith's last Biograph films, *Man's Genesis*, with Wilfred Lucas, Mae Marsh, and Robert Harron.

Griffith directing a film in Hollywood, during his last weeks at Biograph in 1913. The actors are Dorothy Gish and W. E. Lawrence; Mae Marsh is watching them, Donald Crisp is watching Griffith, and the prop man couldn't care less.

Bottom: The new (1913) Biograph studio in the Bronx, showing the glass-enclosed studio on the roof. Griffith did very little work in this building, mainly the interior scenes of *Judith of Bethulia,* his last Biograph film.

Two scenes from *Judith of Bethulia*. The exterior shot shows Lillian Gish, Kate Bruce (behind pole), Blanche Sweet, and Mae Marsh. The interior shot shows Henry Walthall as Holofernes and Blanche Sweet as Judith. The storming of Bethulia in this film was a preview of Griffith's epic siege of Babylon, in *Intolerance*.

Griffith's announcement of his departure from Biograph in an advertisement in *The New York Dramatic Mirror,* December 3, 1913.

V

1911: The Two-Reeler

Chilly weather in December 1910 reminded Griffith of the advantage of filming in California. The reservations were made and after the Christmas holidays the company once again boarded the train for California. The 1911 California group included Blanche Sweet, Wilfred Lucas, Dell Henderson, Claire Mac-Dowell, Stephanie Longfellow, Florence Barker, Florence La-Badie, Mabel Normand, Vivien Prescott, Dorothy West, Grace Henderson, Kate Toncray, Kate Bruce, Jeannie MacPherson, Gladys Egan, Frank Powell, Edwin August, Charles Craig, Mack Sennett, Joseph Graybill, Charles West, Donald Crisp, Guy Hedlund, Alfred Paget, Eddie Dillon, Jack Dillon, Spike Robinson, Frank Grandin, Tony O'Sullivan, "Big" Jim Evans, and George Nichols. The wives of George Nichols, Frank Powell, Dell Henderson, and Billy Bitzer were also included. Newcomers to the company in the fall of 1910 were Donald Crisp, who had been writing poetry for *The Smart Set* magazine, and Florence Barker and Joseph Graybill.

Some familiar names and faces were missing from the Biograph roster. Marion Leonard and her husband, Stanner E. V. Taylor, the author of *The Adventures of Dollie,* had been hired by Reliance Films. Henry Walthall, James Kirkwood, and Arthur Johnson had also accepted Reliance offers. Griffith was sorry to see Johnson go, but his first leading man had become increasingly unreliable.

Mary Pickford and her family—mother, sister, and brother Jack—had left Biograph in December. Carl Laemmle, the head of an independent production company, IMP, which had raided Biograph once before for Florence Lawrence and Harry Salter, began secret negotiations with the Pickfords late in 1910. Mother Pickford conducted the negotiations, with Laemmle offering to double Mary's salary. Mary herself was going through an emotional crisis as a result of a secret love affair with Owen Moore, an affair that had been furthered at Cuddebackville while Mary was out from under her mother's watchful eyes. In the midst of the negotiations, Mary married Moore secretly, early in January, in Jersey City, New Jersey, dressed in an oversized sealskin coat and unaccustomed high heel shoes borrowed from her mother without her mother's knowledge. Meanwhile, Mother Pickford had accepted Laemmle's offer, and Mary left the Biograph Company. Despite the higher salary, Mary was dissatisfied with IMP, and Owen Moore was never able to get along with Mother Pickford.

One outcome of Mary's departure, and a definite gain for her, was the publicity that followed her change of employer. Now Mary's name became associated with her films, as Laemmle attempted to sell pictures with Mary Pickford as a star. Her salary at IMP was $175 a week, and this too was well publicized, encouraging some of the players at Biograph to ask for more money. Wilfred Lucas demanded, and received, $150 a week to accompany Biograph to California. This was the highest salary Biograph had paid up to this time. Blanche Sweet, on the other hand, signed for only $40 a week.

California, Second Trip

The company arrived in California just after the new year. Accommodations were arranged, and the group was ready to begin work with Griffith on January 5, 1911.

The first California film in 1911 was *Fisher Folks*. Griffith took the company to the same location at Santa Monica where he had filmed *The Unchanging Sea* the previous year. In fact, much of the film was an attempt to repeat the success of the earlier film. *Fisher Folks* told the story of a young crippled girl, played by Linda Arvidson, who falls in love with a handsome young fisherman, played by Wilfred Lucas. The fisherman takes advantage of her infatuation and marries her to revenge himself on the village flirt. The usual difficulties at sea separate the newlyweds for a year, and during the separation a baby is born. Finally the fishing vessel returns and the husband goes back to his wife. Cora, the village flirt, tries to come between them, but her schemes fail in the face of the crippled wife's "forgiveness and love." Cora is left "transfixed with rage on the sands."

The company found some changes in the outdoor studio, now at Georgia and Girard Streets in Los Angeles. The rough-boarded stage of the first season had been replaced with one made of smooth boards, and the size had been almost doubled. In addition, muslin scrims, light diffusers, were operated on an overhead trolley system, and a telephone had been installed on stage. Offices, dressing rooms, and a projection room had been built into a one-story building. The actresses had dressing rooms in the rear of the building, opening directly on the stage. Two large, black automobiles, rented on a monthly basis, were stationed at the studio gate, waiting to take the players on location. For the first time the dressing rooms had makeup tables, mirrors, lockers, and running water.

After completing *Fisher Folks,* Griffith trotted out another temperance drama, *Her Daughter,* with Florence Barker and Edwin August in the principal roles. The key description was:

An inordinate desire to drink made this man the beast he is, for his early life must have been exemplary, or he could not have been the father of a girl of such fine character.—Bulletin No. 3789

His next film, *The Lonedale Operator,* was in the traditional formula of the girl menaced by bandits, with Blanche Sweet as the heroine. The cast included Frank Grandin, Wilfred Lucas, and Charles West. Blanche played the role of the daughter of the railroad telegrapher. The film begins as she is bringing her father his lunch. She pauses for a brief dalliance with her boyfriend, a railroad engineer, and then proceeds to the station, where she finds that her father does not feel well and she agrees to take over his post for the rest of the day. Her father warns her that the payroll is due that afternoon on an incoming train. The train delivers the payroll on time, but it also delivers a disreputable pair of hoboes who climb out from under the last car, where they have been "riding the rods." The tramps spot the delivery of the payroll and plan to rob the girl as soon as the train has left. The rest of the film is concerned with the attempts of the tramps to break into the station and steal the payroll while Blanche frantically attempts to telegraph the next station down the line for help. The basic plot is quite similar to that of *The Lonely Villa,* but Griffith's editing is considerably improved. Greater suspense is created through deliberate delays in getting out the message for help and through better control of the rhythm of the crosscutting. Griffith intercut shots of Blanche in semi-closeup at the telegraph key with medium shots of the operator asleep at the other end. The shots are shortened for increased tempo as the tramps put their shoulders to the outer doors, Blanche telegraphs, and the other telegrapher goes on sleeping. When this device is exhausted, Griffith has the other telegrapher wake up and receive the message. Outside his station, Blanche's boyfriend, the smiling engineer, is standing beside his idling engine, and the message for help starts him out to the rescue behind the thundering engine. The tempo of cutting continues to increase with a shortening of the duration of each shot. The action is also speeded up as the tramps redouble their efforts to break in, using a bench as a battering ram. Griffith mounted a camera on the train's coal car to focus on the scene in the train's cab and heightened the sense of action by showing the blurred scenery flying past the train. External shots show the train steaming around bends and on the straightaway. Blanche swoons over her telegraph key as splinters fly off the inside door to the office; the robbers have succeeded in breaking through the outside door. The train rushes around another bend.

. . . when the thieves finally break into the room they find it in almost absolute darkness as the girl has thoughtfully turned out the light and by the gleam of the moonlight that penetrates the darkness they see the girl's outstretched arm and hand holding a streak of dangerous looking steel directed full in their faces which forces them to cower in the corner.—Bulletin No. 3797

Blanche holds the tramps at bay with what appears to be a silver pistol. Then the hero engineer and his fireman burst into the room, brandishing revolvers for the final rescue. An extreme closeup reveals the "gun" in Blanche's hand is a small monkey wrench. The tramps are chagrined but gallantly doff their hats to the lady.

Griffith directed only five films in January and six in February. His production was now not much more than one film a week. During February new locations were used at Monte Vista for *The Broken Cross,* and three trips were made to Santa Monica, where the company headquartered at the Wentworth Hotel for *The Spanish Gypsy,* for *Madame Rex,* based on a scenario written by Mary Pickford, and for *His Mother's Scarf.* The group journeyed into the Sierra Madre for *A Knight of the Road,* based on an idea supplied by Dell Henderson, with Frank Powell and Dorothy West heading the cast.

There were only five pictures on the Griffith schedule for March. *How She Triumphed* was made in Pasadena, with Blanche Sweet, Vivien Prescott, and Joseph Graybill. A covered-wagon Western, *In the Days of '49,* was made in Eaton Canyon, about a wife who falls in love with a dashing gambler. Claire MacDowell played the wife, and Dell Henderson made an over-weight but lively gambler. *The Two Sides* and *The New Dress* were both filmed at San Gabriel. The latter film was a modern Mexican story, with Wilfred Lucas playing "Jose," the hero, and

Dorothy West playing "Marta," the heroine. Kate Toncray played a shopkeeper who sells Jose a dress for his wife. Jose gets drunk at a roadside inn and gives the dress away. Without the dress, Marta goes mad, but with the advent of Jose's baby her sanity is restored.

"Enoch Arden" in Two Reels

On March 24, 1911, Griffith began his most ambitious project up to that time, another two-reel film based on his old favorite, *Enoch Arden.* This was the second time Griffith had made a film based directly on Tennyson's poem, but he had used elements of the story in several seaside films. The previous film directly taken from the poem had been *After Many Years.*

Griffith directed both pictures in four days, shooting with a cast that included Wilfred Lucas as the husband, Frank Grandin, Linda Arvidson, Florence LaBadie, Bobby Harron, Jeannie Mac-Pherson, and Grace Henderson. Both reels were shot at Santa Monica in the same settings Griffith had used in other films that season, including *Fisher Folks.*

In this new version of *Enoch Arden,* Griffith introduced each of the characters at the beginning of the film with a vignette shot showing the character isolated on the screen. The first shot of the actual story was a beautifully backlighted silhouette of the villagers bidding the sailors goodbye. Billy Bitzer related how this backlighting effect had been one of the happy accidents of some early experimentation. It was known that shooting directly into the light would turn any near object into a silhouette, but no way was known to relieve that harsh effect. Bitzer had playfully shot some footage of Mary Pickford and Owen Moore seated at a table, with the light shining directly at the camera. When the footage was developed, their faces were sufficiently lit by the reflected light from the tabletop to counterbalance the strong light from the sun. Bitzer had expected to throw this footage away, but in the projection room Griffith remarked on the beauty of the shot. To try to duplicate it, at Griffith's request, Bitzer began using reflectors, and it was just such reflectors that were now in use in *Enoch Arden*.

The spirit of improvisation was still very much with the company. The fishing shack lent them for a dressing room for the actresses became "Annie's" bridal home. The men used an abandoned horse car that had been anchored in the sand. George Nichols had returned from San Francisco with the costumes from Goldstein & Company, which had supplied the costumes for *Ramona* the previous year.

In this film, Griffith changed his method of indicating the passage of time. Instead of showing it cinematically, he inserted titles. The actors did, however, use progressively older makeup, and Bobby Harron and Florence LaBadie substituted as the older children during the second half. A number of the shots in the film were almost exact duplicates of earlier shots for *The Unchanging Sea*.

The Biograph home office attempted to release *Enoch Arden* one reel at a time. They did permit the film to be advertised as "Part One" and "Part Two," and the exhibitors began by showing the film on successive days, part one on Monday and part two on Tuesday. But audience demand soon caused the picture to be shown as a single unit.

Enoch Arden became the first two-reel motion picture to be exhibited as such by a producing unit in the Motion Picture Patents Company group. Longer projects such as J. Stuart Blackton's *The Life of Moses,* made in the fall of 1909, had a total of five reels, but each reel was released as a separate picture and there was no intention that they should be combined. Blackton had also made a three-reel version of *Uncle Tom's Cabin* that same year, but this, too, was intended for single-reel release. These early films were closer in concept to the later serials than to the multi-reeled feature film. Also in 1909, P. P. Craft, with the famous "Buffalo Bill" Cody, had joined John P. Harris of Pittsburgh—the man who invented the name "nickelodeon," according to Terry Ramsaye—and Harry Davis in producing a three-

reel picture, *The Life of Buffalo Bill*. This film was directed by
Paul Panzer, a recruit from Vitagraph, an independent. (Panzer
later became more famous as the villain in *The Perils of Pauline*,
with Pearl White.) The film had been a decided financial success:
Craft and his partners divided a $50,000 profit. The independent
filmmakers had beaten Griffith in the race for longer pictures, but
Griffith's film *Enoch Arden* had greater impact because it was
shown in the licensed facilities of the Motion Picture Patents
Company throughout the country. Under instructions from the
home office, Griffith returned to one-reel productions for a time.
In April he directed seven films. *The White Rose of the Wilds*
was made in Rubia Canyon outside Los Angeles. *The Crooked
Road* used the lumberyard near the studio for a background. The
gypsy story, an old favorite, was again brought out for *A Romany
Tragedy*, and *A Smile of a Child* meant another trip to the Went-
worth Hotel in Santa Monica. A new beach background at
Redondo was used for *The Primal Call*, but its successor, *The
Jealous Husband*, was made partially at Santa Monica.

   The Crooked Road was a sentimental romantic melodrama
without any particular distinction in plot. Griffith enhanced the
story, however, by using even closer shots than were typical at this
time. The actors were generally photographed from the thighs
up, and in a few shots they were framed at the waist. Griffith used
one closeup, a shot of the heroine's wedding ring on her hand,
to clarify a crucial detail in the story. Griffith also used shots of
Frank Powell's baby son, Baden, for effect. The baby cooperated
with a natural charm, only slightly marred by his interest in the
camera. There was apparently not too much concern with details
of costume at the time: Griffith permitted the father to be shown
wearing the same suit "three years later."

Lionel Barrymore

   In May 1911, Griffith hired a new young actor who was a
member of one of the United States' great theatre dynasties, the
Drew-Barrymore family. The young actor was Lionel Barrymore,

and Griffith cast him for the first time in *Fighting Blood*. This was one of the few times when Griffith made a standard Western, with Indians attacking a white cabin for no apparent reason. Lionel was the first of his family to make films, although both his brother John and his older sister, Ethel, already a prominent stage star, were to end their careers in motion pictures. Barrymore recalled his encounter with Griffith late in 1910:

The movies were in low esteem . . . little more than nickelodeon performances, one-reelers with no sense of direction and certainly no art. I went down to 11 East Fourteenth Street to call on D. W. Griffith, whom I had met at lunch, and offered myself as a motion picture actor.

Griffith was not encouraging.

He looked me up and down, peering over that fine, cantilevered nose of his, and he said:

"I'm not employing stage stars."

"I'm not remotely any such creature," I said. "I will do anything. I mean absolutely anything. Believe me, I'm hungry. I want a job."

"All right," said Griffith, "we'll put you on. . . ."

The first opportunity to use Barrymore's acting services did not occur until after the company moved to California.

As the number of Griffith-directed pictures decreased, the slack in the production schedules was picked up by Griffith's former assistants, now promoted to full-fledged directors. Mack Sennett had joined Frank Powell as a comedy director, and Powell was now making standard melodramas using the Griffith "last-minute rescue." Griffith still held tight supervisory reins. His approval was needed for both stories and the use of the acting company. Some of the players interested Griffith far less than others, and these rejects gravitated in many instances to Sennett. Among the coterie surrounding the new comedy director were Mabel Normand, Fred Mace, Ford Sterling, and "Pathé" Lehrman.

The closing film of the 1911 California season was another Western, *The Last Drop of Water*. Linda Griffith recalled:

We set up camp in the San Fernando desert—two huge tents, one for mess, with cook and assistants who served chow to the cowboys and extra men. Two rows of tables, planks set on wooden horses, ran the length of the tent—there must have been at least fifty cowboys and riders to be fed hearty meals three times a day. The other tent contained trunks and wardrobe baskets, and here the boys slept and made up.

Griffith used eight prairie schooners for the desert caravan around which the film was built, plus a generous contingent of soldiers, Indians, dogs, chickens, and horses, and one cow. The climax of the picture is the rescue of the remnants of the caravan by the U. S. Cavalry. The cast included almost the entire Biograph complement: Blanche Sweet, Charles West, Bobby Harron, Dell Henderson, W. Christie Miller, Jeannie MacPherson, Joseph Graybill, and William Butler.

Griffith completed only four pictures in May 1911. The company returned to the East the last week in May, the departure being delayed once by the old bugaboo of the early filmmakers, static on the film. Light streaks ruined the last shots, and the company had to reassemble on location and shoot the scenes over again before they could catch their train.

Bobby the Coward was the first film on the schedule when Griffith began work in New York again on June 1. Bobby Harron was given the leading role, with Joseph Graybill, Jaque Lenor, and Guy Hedlund supporting as "street thugs." Bobby Harron was still in charge of props, but Griffith was finding more and more use for him as an actor. The pattern of work in New York resumed the old routine, interiors filmed in the Fourteenth Street studio and exteriors in various nearby locations. Griffith filmed *A Country Cupid* in Westfield, New Jersey, and *The Ruling Passion* at Bayonne. *The Rose of Kentucky* pretended that the tobacco fields outside Hartford, Connecticut, were in Griffith's home state, and then Griffith finished this film in Coytesville, New Jersey. *The Sorrowful Example* was done at Fort Lee, *Swords and Hearts* at Coytesville, *The Stuff Heroes Are Made Of* at Lynbrook, Long Island, *The Old Confectioner's Mistake* at Fort Lee, *The Eternal Mother* at Coytesville, and *Dan the Dandy* in Fort Lee.

The company Griffith was using in New York included Guy Hedlund, Joseph Graybill, Edwin August, Blanche Sweet, Gladys Egan, Claire MacDowell, Charles Mailes, Wilfred Lucas, Dorothy West, Frank Grandin, W. Christie Miller, W. C. Robinson, Marion Sunshine, Grace Henderson, Mabel Normand, Dell Henderson, and Charles West. One new face added to the company in principal roles was that of Edna Foster. Griffith switched his sometime formula of little boys playing girls and cast Edna Foster in a series of roles as a boy.

Cuddebackville and Three Cameras

When *Dan the Dandy* was finished, Griffith and the company departed for Cuddebackville. This proved to be the last visit for the Biograph group to the Caudebec Inn. Griffith arrived and registered alone; he and his wife, Linda Arvidson, had separated during the stay in California. (Griffith and Linda Arvidson remained married, although separated, until February 28, 1936, when Griffith was granted a divorce in Kentucky under a law granting divorce to parties separated five years. Linda Griffith continued to receive a large percentage of D. W. Griffith's earnings until the end of his career in the thirties. She offers no hint of difficulties throughout her book about the early days, and definitely leaves the impression that she was a member of the Biograph acting company through 1912. The divorce records indicate, however, that both parties agreed that the separation took place in 1911.)

The company that checked in at the Caudebec Inn for the last time included Mabel Normand, Claire MacDowell and her husband Charles Mailes, Kate Bruce, Gladys Egan, Billy Bitzer, Wilfred Lucas, Edwin August, one of the Dillons, Joseph Graybill, Charles West, Alfred Paget, William Butler, "Big" Jim Evans, Guy Hedlund, Donald Crisp, Gertrude Robinson, Dark Cloud and his wife, "Pathé" Lehrman, Fred Mace, Mack Sennett, William Beaudine (who had replaced Johnny Mahr in the property department), and a number of riders for the Indian and

Western films. The group arrived with a special railroad car filled with horses for these films.

The first film at Cuddebackville in 1911 was a romantic drama, *The Revenue Man and the Girl,* with Dorothy West and Edwin August in the leading roles. This was another film about Kentucky mountaineers, cast in a familiar pattern. Dorothy West was a moonshiner's daughter who falls in love with the handsome revenue man, Edwin August.

The horses and riders were scheduled for the second picture at Cuddebackville, *The Squaw's Love,* another film about Indian life. The Biograph Bulletin subtitled the picture "An Indian Poem of Love in Pictures." The story, as related in the Bulletin, was a simple one:

White Eagle is betrothed to Silver Fawn before leaving for a hunting trip. Gray Fox, his friend, loves Wild Flower, the chief's daughter, but when he asks her father's sanction, he is exiled for his presumption, the chief ordering him to be taken off to the wilds and deprived of his firearms. Starvation would have been his fate, had not White Eagle happened along. To aid his friend, White Eagle promises to bring Wild Flower to him, and when Silver Fawn sees White Eagle stealthily leave the camp with Wild Flower, she imagines her lover false. She follows, and creeping up behind, hurls Wild Flower over into the stream, from which perilous plight she is rescued by Gray Fox, who is escaping in a canoe from a gang of drunken Indians who have seized him. The chief, however, had ordered death for the fugitives, and after the meeting of the four and an explanation given, they make good their escape only after Wild Flower has swum under the canoes of their pursuers and ripped them with a knife, causing them to sink.

Dorothy West played Silver Fawn, Mabel Normand was the chief's daughter Wild Flower, and Griffith cast his technical advisor, Dark Cloud, as the Indian hunter White Eagle.[1]

Griffith, with Bitzer's assistance, had planned a special scene for this picture which necessitated using more than one camera-

[1] Lester Predmore recalled the role of Silver Fawn being played by Marion Leonard, but Miss Leonard had left Biograph the previous year and her name does not appear on the register.

man. A new cameraman, P. Higginson, had been hired the previous March to take over the duties of photographing the comedy unit under Powell's direction. Arthur Marvin had made his last film, *Priscilla's Engagement Ring,* on February 11, 1911, and had died not long after. Now Higginson was brought to Cuddebackville to assist Bitzer on *The Squaw's Love.* The special scene was the fight between Silver Fawn and Wild Flower on a cliff high above the Neversink River. Griffith planned to use three cameras to film the fight scene, because Mabel Normand was to be pushed over the cliff and was to execute a back dive into the river below. The third camera was manned by Bobby Harron. Mabel Normand did the dive perfectly on the first try, was rescued from the chilly water, wrapped in blankets, and driven off to the inn for a reviving round or two in the mission bar.

On August 3, 1911, the company departed for New York with their special railroad car full of horses and never returned to Cuddebackville. Griffith apparently planned to come back later in the fall, because Bitzer wrote a postcard to George Predmore on August 23, 1911:

Expect to be up with the Indians in a couple of weeks. Anything I can do for you, you know the number is 11 East 14th Street. We are going to do a big war picture at Fort Lee this week, then an easy one, then Cuddebackville.[2]

The "big war picture" referred to in Bitzer's postcard was *The Battle,* another Civil War film. Griffith had made a number of Civil War pictures centering on intimate stories of the war and its aftermath, but the war itself had not been particularly emphasized. Now Griffith undertook the staging of a battle. The Biograph Bulletin outlined the story:

In the days of '61 how many brave soldiers were urged to deeds of valor and heroism by thoughts of "the girl he left behind." This story

[2] Bitzer, in a postcard sent to George Predmore at the Caudebec Inn, from New York City, August 23, 1911. In the possession of Lester Predmore, Middletown, New York.

tells of the transforming of a pusillanimous coward into a lion-hearted hero by the derision of the girl he loved. The battle takes place outside her home, and he, panic-stricken, rushes in, trembling with fear, to hide. She laughs in scorn at his cowardice and commands him to go back and fight. Her fortitude inspires him and he manages to rejoin his company before his absence is noticed. Ammunition is low and somebody must take the hazardous journey to procure more from another regiment, which he volunteers to do. This undertaking cannot be described, for the young man faces death at every turn. The most thrilling part of his experience is where the opposing forces build bonfires along the road to menace the powder-wagon.

The cast included Blanche Sweet, Bobby Harron, Charles West, Donald Crisp, and Spottiswoode Aitken. The battle scenes, using artillery, were staged and photographed in a style bearing a considerable resemblance to Griffith's later work in *The Birth of a Nation*.

Griffith had directed six pictures in August and six in September. The six pictures completed in October were all filmed close to the Fourteenth Street home studio, with journeys for locations only to Fort Lee and Coytesville, New Jersey. Six more films were made in November, and six in the final month of the year.

Griffith began *Through Darkened Vales* at the end of September, finishing it in October. He had the actors make exits toward the camera, walking into semi-closeups as they passed the camera, and he used a considerable number of medium-close shots, cutting the actors at the waist. The story is typically melodramatic: Blanche Sweet loses her eyesight as the result of the explosion of a chafing dish, and her lover, Charles West, goes blind from overwork while supporting her. Charles uses his savings for Blanche's eye operation, and the lovers are united in the concluding shot.

In October, Griffith used some effective crosscutting for suspense in *The Miser's Heart*. The exteriors of real New York tenements give a documentary realism to part of this story. Griffith also used a number of jump cuts.

Also in October, Griffith directed *The Failure,* with Dorothy Bernard in the principal role. In this film there is a more complicated blend of closeups, medium shots, and long shots, edited with considerable freedom. Wilfred Lucas, the hero, is fired from his bookkeeping job, loses his society fiancée, and takes a singing job in a saloon, where he is befriended by Dorothy Bernard, a homely dance-hall girl. When Lucas inherits a farm, and with it the chance to redeem himself, he tries to return to his society fiancée, but she rejects him. At the end of the picture, he remembers the little dance-hall girl and brings her to the farm. The last shot shows the two together, walking behind the horse and plow —a scene reminiscent of the opening and closing shots in *A Corner in Wheat.*

One of the November films was *A Terrible Discovery,* in which Griffith used some effective crosscutting during the final chase. The story is a rather silly one, with a gangster disguising himself as an old lady to gain access to the district attorney's house. Griffith has the gangster wield a gimmicky umbrella gun as he seeks revenge.

The second picture in December 1911 was *A Blot in the 'Scutcheon,* based on another poem by Browning. Edwin August played the hero, "Henry, Earl Mertoun," and Dorothy Bernard was the heroine, "Mildred," in this seventeenth-century drama.

Griffith made a strong comment on the ephemeral values of material wealth in another December film, *A String of Pearls.* The real pearls given by a multimillionaire, Dell Henderson, to his film wife, Grace Henderson, are meaningless next to the gift of Christmas savings that poor neighbors make to a young man for necessary medical attention.

The last film Griffith directed in the Fourteenth Street studio was *The Root of Evil,* with Dorothy Bernard and Harry Hyde. It was a routine melodrama about a disinherited daughter left a widow with a small child. Her rich father's unscrupulous adviser attempts to secure the fortune for himself by poisoning the old man's drink. The little grandchild, innocently, imitates his actions, which she has seen by accident, and reverses the poisons. The adviser dies, and the picture comes to a happy ending.

Griffith in 1911 consolidated many of his techniques. He was at last able to carry through his design for a longer picture, with the production of *Enoch Arden* in two really indivisible parts. His previous two-reel film had been easily separated because each story was quite independent of the other, but Griffith carefully made *Enoch Arden* so that the two reels had to be brought together to give a satisfactorily complete story.

Griffith's editorial technique had become smoother, with easy use of crosscutting, not only for suspense but as a standard story-telling device. *The Lonedale Operator* showed Griffith's increased ability to mix medium closeups with medium and long shots. The camera had been made mobile by mounting it on a train. The extreme closeup was used not just for shock value but as the climax of a carefully constructed sequence.

The acting company was further augmented during 1911 with many extras, and Griffith was moving toward more spectacular elements in staging, such as the wagon train encircled by Indians in *The Last Drop of Water,* and the Civil War battle in *The Battle.* As we have seen, three cameras were employed simultaneously to obtain a single spectacular scene in *The Squaw's Love.*

The year 1911 also marked Griffith's last location trip to Cuddebackville and the Orange Mountains. Bitzer and Griffith had asked George Predmore if his young son, Lester, who had become a company favorite, might accompany them to California in January 1912, but Predmore decided that Lester should continue his education instead.

Griffith had signed his fourth contract with Biograph in November 1911. The previous year, in August, he had signed the contract with his stage name and then crossed out Lawrence and substituted, in ink, David. In the 1911 contract he signed for the first time David W. Griffith. His commissions and salary had steadily increased. In 1910 his base salary had been raised to $75 a week, with 1/8 cent for each linear foot of film, and a guarantee of not less than $200 a week. In 1911 the minimum remained the same, but his commission was raised to 1¾ mills for each linear foot of positive film sold or leased. After this contract, Griffith's income totaled about $3,000 a month.

Griffith directed seventy films in 1911, sixteen fewer than in 1910.

VI

1912–1913: Spectacle; Griffith Leaves Biograph

With the Christmas holiday over, Griffith and the acting company
headed once again for California. This time Griffith occupied
his quarters alone. Dell Henderson had taken over the duties of
shepherding the company. Powell, as a director, was entitled to
more consideration. The beginning of January found the company back at the beach in Santa Monica, the location of *Enoch
Arden*. The first film of 1912 was *The Mender of the Nets*, with
Charles West playing "Tom," the young fisherman, and Mary
Pickford, back after her disastrous experience with IMP, as
"Grace," the little net mender. Mary's position with the company
had changed in two respects: she now received the same salary
she had been paid at IMP, and her name was being released in
connection with her films, although it did not appear on the
Biograph Bulletins.

The Biograph acting company had altered considerably since
Mary Pickford last worked for Griffith. She was no longer the
principal ingénue-leading woman with the company. Griffith had
assembled a group of ingénues and used them interchangeably.
They were Blanche Sweet, Dorothy Bernard, Marguerite Loveridge, and for the first time in 1912 Mae Marsh. Mary Pickford
recalled: "I even noticed some resentment when I returned to
Biograph, especially among the girls who had stepped up during
my absence."[1]

[1] Pickford: *op. cit.*, p. 139.

Blanche Sweet played the lead in the second film of January 1912, *Under Burning Skies,* opposite Wilfred Lucas and a new actor, Christy Cabanne. Griffith combined the temperance theme with a desert setting. Blanche, somewhat thinner than in 1911, played the role with a blond wig set in Pickford ringlets.

The third film, *A Siren of Impulse,* had Dorothy Bernard in the leading role, opposite Charles West. Griffith returned to a Spanish theme with this picture, taking advantage of Dorothy Bernard's dark beauty.

In the fourth film, Griffith came back to Mary Pickford, casting her, once more, as an Indian maid. The film was *Iola's Promise,* or "How the little Indian Maiden Paid Her Debt of Gratitude." There had been little change in story content from the previous years. The plot for *Iola's Promise* was typical:

Iola, the little Indian girl, is held captive by a gang of cutthroats, from whose clutches and abuse she is rescued by Jack Harper, a prospector. She is truly grateful to Jack, for she regards him as something different from the white people she had seen. Jack's sweetheart and she are part of a wagon-train headed for his place, and as luck has been against him, he is somewhat gloomy. Iola learns the reason, and promises to help him find gold. He is amused at this and says "Will you?" "Yes." "Cross your heart?" This cross-your-heart action mystifies the little Indian. She thinks it is a sort of tribe insignia and tells her people that "Cross-heart" people are all right. Iola surely pays her debt of gratitude, not only in finding gold, but in giving her life to protect Jack's sweetheart from her own people, who are embittered against all whites.

Blanche Sweet received the casting nod for the next picture, *The Goddess of Sagebrush Gulch,* subtitled "A Story of the Golden West." Dorothy Bernard played Blanche's sister, and Charles West was "Blue-grass Pete," a charming desperado. The climax of the picture has Blanche and a party of miners rescuing Dorothy from a burning cabin. Griffith used a full repertoire of shots in this film: medium closeups, dynamic diagonal entrances, closeups—all intermixed with spectacular scenic shots in the style of *Ramona*. Several closeups were made of Blanche Sweet with her hair backlit by the sun, with the reflector technique to register her face. Camera setups were changed in mid-scene with increasing freedom. Parallel action through crosscutting was used to build suspense in a climactic gun duel, and one shot of a man sliding diagonally down a dust bank, actually moving diagonally across the screen, introduced a new compositional element. The shortening of shots as the climax of the film approaches shows Griffith repeating his earlier editing technique with increased polish and fluidity.

The last picture in January 1912 was *The Girl and Her Trust,* with Dorothy Bernard as the ingénue lead. This film was a re-make of *The Lonedale Operator,* and a comparison quickly shows how far Griffith's editorial and camera techniques have pro-gressed. The story is only slightly altered from *The Lonedale Operator:*

Grace, the operator at Hillville, is apprised of the fact that train No. 7 will bring to her office $2,000, consigned to the Simpson Construction Company. Jack, the station agent, offers to let her have his pistol, while he is away to lunch, but she scorns this, exclaiming "Danger? Why nothing ever happens in this slow place." However, when the train arrives and the money is placed in the strong box, he again prevails upon her to take the pistol, but without success. Two tramps, who have come in on the bumpers, see the bag placed in the box, and regard this as their great opportunity. Waiting until Jack has gone, they break in and make for the box. It is locked and they must have the key, so they try to get the girl, who has locked herself in her office. This failing, they load the box on a hand-car to take it away to blow it open. The girl, meanwhile, has telegraphed for aid, and realizing the tramps' design, rushes out and throws herself in front of the hand-car. The tramps drag her aboard and are off. They are soon pursued by an engine from the next station ahead, and here occurs, without exception, the most thrilling pursuit ever depicted.

Some of Lee Dougherty's hyperbole in describing the chase should be forgiven, for the chase did introduce some innovations. Shots were made with the camera mounted on the front of the handcar, showing the villainous tramps furiously pumping to make their escape. These were intercut with shots of the pursuing engine, made from fixed positions. Additional shots were made from an automobile riding parallel to the handcar and the pursuing train. These last came to be known as "tracking" shots. The editing brought the pursuing train and the handcar closer and closer together, without ever showing them actually in the same scene until the conclusion of the sequence, when a shot from in front of the handcar shows the engine catching up from the rear. After the capture of the tramps by the train's engineer, again played by Wilfred Lucas, who apparently had acquired a knowledge of running a train engine, the last shot ends with the train slowly backing away from the camera into the distance and a partial fadeout. Griffith also used a noteworthy extreme closeup of a hand at a keyhole that furthered the plot. In addition to Dorothy Bernard and Wilfred Lucas, the cast included Edwin August and Alfred Paget as the tramps, and Charles Mailes as Jack, the telegrapher.

Griffith had made six pictures in January 1912, running the gamut of his previous California styles—Indian films, the wagon train, a railroad chase, a seaside drama, and a Spanish drama.

A period drama of the 1830's led the list for February. It was *The Punishment,* with Blanche Sweet as the heroine, a fruit-grower's pretty daughter, who spurns the attentions of the land-owner's son for the love of her peasant sweetheart, Harry Hyde. The nasty landowner, in Beau Brummel cloak and top hat, was played by Christy Cabanne.

Mary Pickford appeared next in February with her black Indian wig as a little Mexican girl in *Fate's Interception.*

Griffith's production pace continued with six pictures in February. *The Female of the Species* was another sagebrush-and-desert story with Claire MacDowell, Mary Pickford, and Dorothy Bernard in conflict over a man. *Just Like a Woman,* with Mary Pickford, Wilfred Lucas, and Charles Mailes, had as background the California oilfields. It was the story of an older man who loves a young girl and sacrifices his wealth for her so that she may marry a young man, only to discover that she loved him all the time. *One Is Business, the Other Crime* was a story of a political bribe, made at the Los Angeles studio, with Edwin August as a noble politician, and Charles West and Blanche Sweet. The last film for February was *The Old Actor,* which featured a newcomer to Biograph, Frank Opperman. Opperman won considerable attention for his portrayal, despite the competition of Mary Pickford and Edwin August.

A Beast at Bay, a chase melodrama, was one of six Griffith films of March 1912. The climax was a race between a train and a racing car, a device Griffith was to use again in the modern-story section of *Intolerance.* The cast of *A Beast at Bay* included Charles Mailes, Frank Grandin, "Pathé" Lehrman, Mary Pickford, and Alfred Paget. The story in the Biograph Bulletin notes that the hero, Jack, is able to

. . . induce the train dispatcher to let them have an engine to pursue the fugitive and the girl. Here follows the most thrilling pursuit ever witnessed—a race between an engine, a touring car and a racing auto.

Various members of the acting company had from time to time sold scenarios to Biograph. Mary Pickford had written several scripts and on at least one occasion had even sold a rival company some scripts rejected by Griffith. One of Griffith's five films for April 1912, *Lena and the Geese,* was made from a plot she sold him. She also had the leading role. It was a simple story and made a rather unremarkable film, except for Mary's execution of a little dance step when she returns with her geese. The coy dance of happiness was used by Griffith for subsequent heroines. There was one other indirect result from *Lena and the Geese.* Sometime after the film was released on June 17, 1912, it was seen by Lillian and Dorothy Gish in a Baltimore theatre. The Gish sisters and their mother were old friends of the Smith family, now the Pickfords. In fact, the Gish girls and their mother had shared an apartment in New York with the Pickfords while both families were looking for employment in the theatre. The Gishes made a note that *Lena and the Geese* had been made by the Biograph Company at 11 East Fourteenth Street in New York City, and they resolved to look up their friend Gladys Smith, who played the lead in the film, when they reached New York. It was this resolution that eventually led them to find employment as regular members of the Biograph company.

The first picture in May was *Man's Lust for Gold,* with William "Daddy" Butler as the hapless claim jumper, and Bobby Harron and Blanche Sweet playing a brother and sister who set out to find the fabled Skeleton Mine. Griffith again made use of the desert scenery at San Fernando.

The second picture in May was one that Griffith had planned for some time. With this film, *Man's Genesis,* originally called *Primitive Man,* Griffith hoped to escape the potboiler trap in which he found himself at the beginning of 1912. Lee Dougherty thought that Griffith was making a mistake. Dougherty was convinced that a picture about cavemen might be done as a farce but not as a serious picture. According to Linda Arvidson:

. . . Mr. Griffith was determined it should be a serious story; and he did it as such, although he changed the animal skin clothing of the actors to clothes made of grasses. For if the picture were to show the accidental discovery of man's first weapon, then the animal skins would have to be torn off the animal's body by hand, and that was a bit impossible. So Mae and Bobby dressed in grasses knotted into a sort of fabric.

Mae and Bobby were Mae Marsh, playing Lilywhite, the heroine, and Bobby Harron in the role of Weakhands. Wilfred Lucas played the villain, Bruteforce. This was Miss Marsh's first important role. She had followed her older sister, Marguerite Loveridge, to Biograph, where Marguerite, actually Margaret Marsh, had been cast for the first time in January 1912 in *The Mender of the Nets.* Mae, still in school, had come to the studio too, and Dorothy Bernard had pointed her out to Griffith, commenting that he should notice the resemblance between Mae and the reigning stage beauty Billie Burke.

A picture scheduled to follow sometime after *Man's Genesis* was *The Sands of Dee,* based on a Charles Kingsley poem. The ingénues of the company all wanted the role, but Griffith decided that it would go to whoever would play Lilywhite in *Man's Genesis.* He had approached Mary Pickford about the role and she replied: " 'I'm sorry, Mr. Griffith, but the part calls for bare legs and feet.' (In those days we even wore stockings and shoes in bathing.)" The role was turned down in succession by Blanche Sweet, Dorothy Bernard, and Mabel Normand. Griffith then announced he was awarding the role to Mae Marsh, and in addition:

. . . for the benefit of those who might be interested that as a reward for her graciousness Miss Marsh will also receive the role of the heroine in *The Sands of Dee.*

The three regular ingénues were thunderstruck. They united in jealous opposition, and even Blanche Sweet's grandmother, a formidable figure, managed to get together over this with her chief rival, Mrs. Pickford. All of them hoped that Mae would fall on her face in *Man's Genesis.* She did not. Mary Pickford commented:

. . . Miss Marsh gave a beautiful performance. Indeed we were all so stirred, we swallowed our pride, and gave her our sincerest congratulations.

But Mary Pickford, for one, began to think that if an untrained girl could outperform veteran actresses in the motion pictures, perhaps she had better consider returning to the stage.

Man's Genesis was billed by Biograph as "a psychological comedy founded upon the Darwinian theory of the evolution of Man." Dougherty's idea that this was a comedy managed to win at least in the Biograph Bulletin.

To introduce the subject, we show an old man telling the story of man to his grandchildren. The story is that of the life of "Bruteforce" and "Weakhands" in the primeval village. The bare fist at this period was the only weapon and, as you may imagine, the law was "might is right." The boy, "Weakhands," stood but small chance against the powerful "Bruteforce" and this condition forced him to exercise his brain, hence it was through his cunning that he managed to win the girl "Lilywhite," for his lack of prowess made him unpopular as a suitor. "Weakhands" and "Lilywhite," however, are beset by dangers at the hands of "Bruteforce" who would break up their little home. It is now that the woe of "Weakhands" is darkest, and he despairs until by accident he discovers a new force. Here the brain becomes active and the first invention, the stone hammer, is evolved, and the first conflict between brains and brawn results in victory for brains.

Griffith made the invention of the stone hammer very easy by providing as props some sharpened, trimmed sticks, and some very peculiar, donut-shaped stones with convenient holes through the center for the insertion of the stick. The grass costumes were considered rather daring, and authentic, but the costume for Mae Marsh, while entirely of grass and leaves, still managed to have the lines of a 1912 dress. Mack Sennett and W. Christie Miller appeared as two incidental cavemen popping in and out of holes in the ground. Charles Mailes played the grandfather, who acts as something of a narrator to begin the film. The picture ended with a nicely handled fadeout.

The film that had the role so coveted by the young ladies of Biograph, *The Sands of Dee,* was the last picture Griffith directed in May. The description hardly indicates, today, what sharpened the girls' interest.

The lines "O Mary, go and call the cattle home, across the sands o' Dee" are undoubtedly the best known of the poet's many gems, and the song has served wonderfully well as the foundation of this production. Mary's mother calls to her to bring the cattle home and as she goes across the sands where the River Dee empties into the sea, she meets her sweetheart, Bobby. Together they drive the cattle home. A happier pair than this lad and lassie was never seen, until one day there came to the sands an artist and, of course, his wonderful skill shown in incorporating her picture in the scene he was painting, amazed her. On the other hand, the artist became quite interested in the girl and she mistook this for love. When Bobby comes to propose she tells him and her parents she is engaged to the artist, but when the girl fails to bring the artist to meet them the stern old father unjustly accuses her and drives her from home. Later, he has cause to repent his hasty action, for "The creeping tide came up along the sand and never home came she."—Bulletin No. 3979

The last film in May 1912 was *Black Sheep,* a modern Western with Charles West, and a new leading man, William Carroll, playing the Mexican villain.

One Indian film, *A Pueblo Legend,* had been made during May. Griffith intended this to be his definitive Indian picture. The company went to Isleta, New Mexico, to use an authentic Indian pueblo as a background. Mary Pickford, once again, played the Indian girl, supported by Wilfred Lucas and Bobby Harron. Griffith and Bitzer used a great deal of the additional footage that went beyond the usual one-reel format to show atmospheric shots of the pueblo and the New Mexican scenery. The results are sometimes strikingly composed, but quite like a travelogue.

At the conclusion of the *Black Sheep* filming at the end of May, the company and Griffith returned to New York. Work out of the Fourteenth Street studio began with *The Narrow Road,* the story of an ex-convict who attempts to go straight, with the help of his faithful wife, but is framed by an evil companion from prison days. Elmer Booth, appearing with Biograph for the first time, played the husband; Mary Pickford was the wife; and Charles Mailes portrayed the evil companion. Harry Hyde played the chief prison guard.

Griffith made only five pictures in June in New York, including *A Child's Remorse,* a film about children endangered by a leaky motorboat, filmed at Greenwich, Connecticut, with Gladys Egan; *The Inner Circle,* a drama about the Mafia, with Adolph Lestina and Mary Pickford; *A Change in Spirit,* a romantic morality tale filmed in Central Park, with Blanche Sweet, Kate Toncray, Henry Walthall, and Charles Mailes. In this last, Blanche Sweet, a protected, innocent rich girl falls in love with a gentleman thief and her love reforms him.

Lillian and Dorothy Gish

Also in June 1912, the two Gish sisters came to Biograph for the first time, looking for their friend Gladys Smith. The receptionist told them that no one by that name worked for the Biograph Company. Lillian insisted that their friend Gladys had played the leading role in *Lena and the Geese.* This produced a reaction and brought forth the guess that their friend must be Mary Pickford. According to Terry Ramsaye:

Mary came down the hall and there was a chatterfest of busy little girls in the hall. As they stood talking, a serious sober-faced man came down the big stairs and walked past with a glance at the trio of young-sters.

"That's Mr. Griffith," Mary whispered awesomely. "He's the director."

They were still talking when Christy Cabanne, then an assistant to Griffith, approached and inquired if Miss Pickford's friends would like to help out in the making of a scene for the picture then in the works.

This was an adventure. They certainly would.

Up in the studio under the green-blue glare of the lamps, Lillian and Dorothy sat in the first row of an audience scene. They had made their start on the screen as extras.

Mary Pickford remembered this first moment somewhat differently.

We were laughing and reminiscing gaily when Mr. Griffith came through the swinging doors into the hall.[2] I beckoned to him and said:

"I want you to meet three of my dearest friends, Mr. Griffith: Mrs. Gish and her daughters, Lillian and Dorothy, and I think they would be lovely on the screen."

[2] Mary Pickford's sense of the geography at 11 East Fourteenth Street was certainly better than Terry Ramsaye's.

"You have courage to introduce me to two such lovely girls," said Mr. Griffith. "Aren't you afraid of losing your job, Mary?"

"No," I said, "because if they can take it from me, it is obviously not my job."

"You'll be sorry," he told me teasingly as he went up the stairs.[3]

Lillian Gish's own version is somewhat less romantic.

My engagement for motion pictures was quite by accident. Years ago Mary Pickford and her mother, and Dorothy, mother, and myself shared an apartment in New York City as a matter of economy. Mary secured an engagement with the Biograph Company and one day out of curiosity I went down to the studio to see her work. Mr. Griffith was directing a picture at the time. He saw both Dorothy and myself and evidently thought we might become successful screen players. We were immediately engaged and so alike were we then that Mr. Griffith asked mother to put a red ribbon on Dorothy's arm and a blue one on mine so that he could tell us apart. It was certainly funny to hear him call for "Red" when he wanted Dorothy and "Blue" when he wanted me.[4]

Linda Arvidson remembered that the Gish girls had come to the studio expressly at Mary Pickford's invitation.

Things were quiet in the theatre and Mary saw no reason why, when they could find a ready use for the money, her little friends shouldn't make five dollars now and then as well as the other extra people.

Lillian and Dorothy Gish just melted right into the studio atmosphere without causing a ripple. For quite a long time they merely extra-ed in and out of the pictures. Especially Dorothy—Mr. Griffith paid her no attention whatever, and she cried because he wouldn't, but he wouldn't so she kept on crying and trailed along.

Regardless of how the first meeting was arranged, whether by accident or, more probably—despite Miss Gish's statement—by design, the Gish sisters had begun their film careers. An examination of the 1912 photographs and films of the two girls would suggest that the business of tying identifying ribbons on the girls

3 Pickford: *op. cit.*, p. 148.
4 Lillian Gish, in *Harper's Bazaar*, October 1940.

was more of a sample of Griffith's psychological handling of young actresses than an actual necessity. The girls bore a strong family resemblance, but they were definitely not twins.

The first regular roles for the Gish sisters were in *An Unseen Enemy,* in July 1912, with a cast including Bobby Harron, Elmer Booth, Harry Carey, and Grace Henderson. In terms of basic plotting and general film design, this was a remake of *The Lonely Villa.* The Bulletin subtitle bears this out: "The terrible experience of two young girls in a lonesome villa."

Elmer Booth, as the brother of the two sisters played by Lillian and Dorothy Gish, locks their small inheritance in the house safe until the banks open in the morning. He then goes to the village on an errand, leaving the girls with the "slattern" housemaid. The housemaid, played by Grace Henderson, attempts to open the safe and, failing, summons a disreputable friend to help her crack the safe. The Gish girls are locked in an adjoining room with a telephone, but when they attempt to reach it, the maid's hand emerges through a stove port in the wall, holding a revolver. Whenever the girls start for the phone, the hand with the gun waves them back, or fires. The girls retreat, cowering, to a corner of the room. Griffith managed to cover up the illogical nature of this business by cutting from closeups of the hand with the gun to medium shots of the girls to long shots of the attempted safe-cracking and back to closeups of the telephone. The girls finally manage to reach the phone and summon help. Then Griffith began the standard crosscutting for the "rescue": shots of the villains, the cowering girls, the rescuers coming in a fast motorcar, the girls, the robbers, etc. The device to slow down the rescue is a bridge that is slowly swinging open. The rescuers manage to make it across at the last moment, and the rescue is effected with Grace Henderson's hand being revealed as "the unseen enemy." The film ends with a partial fadeout.

Griffith completed six pictures in July 1912, beginning with *Friends,* a Western filmed at Coytesville, New Jersey, with Lionel Barrymore, Henry Walthall, Bobby Harron, Harry Carey, Charles

Mailes, and Mary Pickford in the cast. In this film Griffith used several closeups of Mary. When the film was first screened, she was highly critical of her makeup. Lionel Barrymore thought that he was too fat and had better cut out the beer. *So Near, Yet So Far,* a comedy about adolescent love, with Mary Pickford and Walter Miller playing the young would-be lovers, was next. *A Feud in the Kentucky Hills* was made at Palisades, New Jersey, next to Fort Lee, with Henry Walthall playing an older, bad brother, and Walter Miller as a young, gentle brother, and Mary Pickford as an adopted sister beloved of both brothers. *In the Aisles of the Wilds* was filmed along the banks of the Hudson River, with Claire MacDowell, Lillian Gish, Harry Carey, and Henry Walthall.

Griffith made only two films in August: *The One She Loved,* at Fort Lee, with Lionel Barrymore, Mary Pickford, and Henry Walthall; and *The Painted Lady,* with Charles Mailes, Blanche Sweet, and Joseph Graybill. Griffith was negotiating with J. J. Kennedy for a new contract and had asked for stock in The Biograph Company as part of it. Kennedy replied that Biograph had no stock available for issue. Griffith then asked for ten percent of Biograph's profits, whereupon Kennedy stalled the negotiations.

That August, Mack Sennett was also conducting negotiations with the two former bookmakers, Charles O. Bauman and Adam Kessel. Sennett claimed that he owed a bad horse-racing debt to the pair, $100, and that when they tried to collect, he proposed that they finance him in a new comedy motion-picture company. The negotiations were successful. Bauman and Kessel put up $2,500 for the new firm. Sennett, looking up during a stroll, saw the trademark of the Pennsylvania Railroad and named the new film company Keystone. When he left Biograph, he took with him Mabel Normand, Fred Mace, "Pathé" Lehrman, and Ford Sterling as the nucleus of his acting company.

In September Griffith made a film, partly on the streets of New York City, called *The Musketeers of Pig Alley.* Lillian Gish played the young wife who becomes the object of the intentions of a neighborhood gangster, Elmer Booth. Other roles were played by Walter Miller, the husband; Spike Robinson, Griffith's sparring partner; Harry Carey; and Bobby Harron. Biograph advertised the picture as "a depiction of the gangster evil," and it has sometimes been called the first gangster picture, although Griffith had used the same ingredients before. The atmosphere and some of the characterizations are forerunners of the gangster sequences in *Intolerance*. *The Musketeers of Pig Alley* projects a documentary reality with considerable force. The cinematography is crisp and well defined, and the exterior scenes depict an excellent cross section of New York tenement life during the period.

The second and final picture in September 1912 was *Heredity*. Harry Carey played a renegade white trapper who proves false to his Indian bride and his half-breed son. The inevitable retribution is visited on the sadistic father during an Indian attack, and his wife and child return to the safety of the Indian tribe. Jack Pickford played the Indian boy, and Marion Sunshine was the wife. Biograph Bulletins on original issues of Griffith films do not exist beyond this point. Flyers concerning subsequent films, including reissues of Griffith films, begin to appear again in 1914.

In October 1912, Griffith came back to the Civil War theme with *The Informer,* with a cast that included Harry Carey, Mary Pickford, Lionel Barrymore, Henry Walthall, and Lillian Gish.

Griffith made seven pictures in October, a return to something resembling his former pace. These included *Gold and Glitter,* with Lillian Gish, Lionel Barrymore, and Elmer Booth; *My Baby,* with Mary Pickford, Lionel Barrymore, Henry Walthall, Lillian Gish, and Walter Miller; *The Unwelcome Guest,* with Charles Mailes, Jack Pickford, Mary Pickford, Lillian Gish, Claire MacDowell, Elmer Booth, Harry Carey, and Walter Miller; *Pirate Gold; Brutality,* with Mae Marsh, Bobby Harron, and Walter Miller; and *The New York Hat,* with Mary Pickford,

Lionel Barrymore, Lillian and Dorothy Gish, Mae Marsh, Bobby Harron, and Charles Mailes.

Mary Pickford Leaves Biograph

The New York Hat was Mary Pickford's last film for Biograph, and her last film under the direction of D. W. Griffith. She had been negotiating for some time with David Belasco, and the stage producer had made her an offer of the leading role in *A Good Little Devil*. Mary accepted the part readily and then informed Griffith that she was leaving Biograph. Mary recalled that she:

. . . suddenly realized how much [she] would miss [her] beloved Biograph and the guiding hand of this brilliant man.

Mary also remembered that Griffith had tears in his eyes as he said: "God bless you, Mary. I'll miss you very much."

The New York Hat was based on a scenario mailed to Biograph by a sixteen-year-old schoolgirl, Anita Loos. Miss Loos came from a theatrical background. Her father, R. Beers Loos, was the proprietor of a traveling stock company on the West Coast that specialized in melodramas. Anita had not been permitted to act with her father's company, but she had played the role of a boy in a Nance O'Neill production of *The Jewess*. This was the same Nance O'Neill who had been Griffith's employer in 1906. Lee Dougherty had no notion of the age of the author who sent in *The New York Hat,* of course, and Biograph purchased many stories from writers in other cities, so when Griffith liked the story, Dougherty mailed Miss Loos a check for twenty-five dollars.[5]

Mary Pickford played the role of a young, orphaned schoolgirl whose mother has left a small, secret bequest in the hands of the kindly minister, Lionel Barrymore. The minister was instructed to do something to please the daughter. When he notices

[5] Biograph Authors Record book. This record of scripts, production dates, and payments to authors from 1910 to 1915 does not list all films, nor are exact shooting dates given, only the month of production.

that she is enamoured of an expensive New York hat in the window of the local ladies' shop, he secretly purchases the hat for her. The gift of the hat is completely misinterpreted by the local blue-nose gossips, "uplifters," and a scandal is set off. Griffith had used the characterization of "uplifters" before, and they reappear forcefully in the modern section of *Intolerance*. As expected, the innocence of the girl and the minister is finally demonstrated to the penurious father, Charles Mailes, and the town fathers, who have gathered for a final confrontation, when the minister produces the dead mother's letter. The crowning comment is made with a shot showing the enlightened elders leaving Little Mary's house and snubbing the group of gossips gathered on the doorstep. The film was a smooth blend of medium shots, closeups, and intercutting as a regular part of the narration.

Mary Pickford ended her association with Biograph with a farewell party in her Riverside Drive apartment for the entire company on October 25, 1912.

Griffith wound up the last two months of 1912 in a burst of activity. He directed fourteen films, including *The Burglar's Dilemma*, written by Lionel Barrymore; a two-reel production (actually a reel and a half), *Oil and Water;* and a final temperance drama, *Drink's Lure,* in December. The company took the Christmas holidays off and, just before the beginning of the new year, started on the train trip to California.

Griffith had directed 423 films for Biograph by the end of December 1912. The greater part had been one-reel pictures, but his cautious venture into two-reel production had been moderately successful.

Henry Marvin was still not particularly enthusiastic about longer productions, and Marvin was backed in his opinion by J. J. Kennedy. The Biograph bosses apparently felt that the company was doing well enough financially without becoming involved in expensive adventures. Both men were quite willing, however, to encourage others to produce and distribute longer films. They had succeeded in 1912 in helping a combine, calling itself the Engadine Corporation, to get a license for showing the Film d'Art production, *Queen Elizabeth,* starring Sarah Bernhardt and Lou Tellegen. The principals in the Engadine Corporation were Edwin S. Porter, Joseph Engel, and a former furrier but at that time the treasurer of the Marcus Loew theatres, Adolph Zukor.

Under the joint sponsorship of the Engadine Corporation and the stage producer, Daniel Frohman, *Queen Elizabeth* was given a promotional showing on July 12, 1912. It was a four-reel picture but consisted just of twelve shots. In terms of film construction, it was on a par with the average film of 1907–1908, a photographed stage play, and not that of the Griffith films of 1912. By way of contrast to *Queen Elizabeth*'s twelve shots in four reels, *The Sands of Dee* was composed of sixty-eight shots in one reel. There were no closeups, no medium shots in *Queen Elizabeth.* The actors were always shown full-length, and in added footage at the end of the film they came forward and took a stage bow. Despite the antiquated character of the film, Zukor and partners made an immediate profit of over 400 percent, according to Terry Ramsaye.

Despite the fact that they helped obtain a license for the four-reel *Queen Elizabeth,* Kennedy and Marvin were still firmly wedded to the idea that Biograph should keep to the successful one-reel format. As Ramsaye reported it, Kennedy told Griffith:

> The time has come for the production of big fifty thousand dollar pictures. You are the man to make them. But Biograph is not ready to go into that line of production. If you stay with Biograph it will be to make the same kind of short pictures that you have in the past. You will not do that. You've got the hundred thousand dollar idea in the back of your head.

Nevertheless, when Griffith departed for California late in December 1912, he had a verbal commitment to make more two-reel pictures as he thought appropriate. Biograph was willing to go this far, but they made it plain that the home office must approve each project. Undoubtedly, Griffith chafed under this edict. He had long felt that the character of a film should flow from the nature of the story, and it had become obvious to him since *His Trust* and *His Trust Fulfilled* that many stories could not be compressed into the ten-minute framework. This was not the first time that Griffith's plans for outsized theatrical expression had been rebuffed. His play, *War,* had been rejected by Henry Miller because of the large cast and the extensive scenery. Also, Edwin S. Porter had rejected Griffith's script based on *La Tosca* as much too ambitious for the Edison Company.

1913, the Final Year

The basic California company in 1913 consisted of Lillian and Dorothy Gish, Elmer Booth, Harry Carey, Lionel Barrymore, Henry Walthall, Walter Miller, Claire MacDowell, Charles Hill Mailes, Joseph McDermott, Alfred Paget, Kate Bruce, Kate Toncray, Jack Dillon, Mae Marsh, William "Daddy" Butler, Blanche Sweet, and W. Christie Miller. Griffith's assistant director was Christy Cabanne; and Tony O'Sullivan and Dell Henderson had been promoted to directors, in charge of melodramas and comedies respectively. Sennett had left Biograph, of course, and Frank Powell had also found more rewarding opportunities.

Other Biograph players from earlier years were now scattered throughout the industry. Flora Finch, briefly a Biograph player, was a principal comedienne with John Bunny at Vitagraph. Harry Myers was working for Lubin. Florence LaBadie and George Nichols were employed by Thanhouser. George Nichols had become Thanhouser's principal director, on the basis of his association with Griffith and Biograph. Nichols repeated some of Griffith's steps; for example, he took the Thanhouser company to Cuddebackville for filming, undoubtedly remembering the locations from his work with Griffith.

Owen Moore, now separated from Mary Pickford, was playing opposite Florence Lawrence at Victor. Adele de Garde had joined the Vitagraph Company. Edwin August was with Lubin, Vivien Prescott with IMP, Billy Quirk at GEM, and Marion Leonard and her husband, Stanner E. V. Taylor, were at Monopole.

When the acting company left the old studio at 11 East Fourteenth Street after Christmas 1912, The Biograph Company had already started construction of new, modern studios on 175th Street in the Bronx. *Drink's Lure* was the last Griffith film made on Fourteenth Street. The studio had served the company since 1906, when Biograph had abandoned their first rooftop premises, and for seven years had been the home base for the company. Over 570 films were edited and distributed from its studio and offices.

The new studios in the Bronx were described by Linda Griffith as she saw them in 1913:

> The big new studio up in the Bronx was now finished, with two huge stages—one artificially lighted, and one a daylight studio. There was every modern convenience but an elevator.
> . . . From the dressing-rooms a balcony opened that looked down on the studio floor. . . .

But Mrs. Griffith was nostalgic for the old studio:

> . . . Though the last word as to modern equipment, the new studio merely chilled. That atmosphere of an old manse that had prevailed at 11 East 14th Street, did not abide in the concrete and perfect plumbing and office-like dressing rooms at East 175th Street.

The studio in the Bronx was to be completed and ready when the company returned from California.

In January 1913, Griffith directed five films, all one-reel pictures, leading off with *Love in an Apartment Hotel,* based on a synopsis purchased from William Marston, who had given his address as Harvard College, Cambridge, Massachusetts. The cast included Mae Marsh, Edward Dillon, Blanche Sweet, Henry Walthall, Walter Miller, Jack Dillon, Bobby Harron, and Harry Carey. The other January films were *Broken Ways,* with Blanche

Sweet, Henry Walthall, Harry Carey, and Bobby Harron; *A Girl's Strategem; Near to Earth;* and *A Welcome Intruder,* with Claire MacDowell, Charles Mailes, and Charles West.

February 1913 began with *The Sheriff's Baby,* filmed in the San Fernando Valley with Henry Walthall, Lionel Barrymore, Alfred Paget, Kate Bruce, Jack Dillon, Harry Carey, Joseph McDermott, and Bobby Harron. In it Griffith used some short shots in slightly out-of-focus closeups. Three more pictures followed in February: *The Hero of Little Italy,* with Blanche Sweet, Kate Toncray, Charles West, Harry Carey, Charles Mailes, and William Butler; *The Perfidy of Mary,* with Mae Marsh, Dorothy Gish, Walter Miller, and Lionel Barrymore; and *A Misunderstood Boy,* a drama of the gold fields, written by Griffith's assistant, Christy Cabanne, and filmed with Bobby Harron, Alfred Paget, Lillian Gish, Lionel Barrymore, and Charles Mailes.

Griffith topped the one-reel format with the first film of March 1913, *The Little Tease,* which had an extra half reel. This was another drama about Kentucky mountaineers, with Mae Marsh, Bobby Harron, Kate Bruce, W. Christie Miller, and Henry Walthall. Griffith followed this picture with six more one-reel films: *The Lady and the Mouse; The Wanderer; The House of Darkness; Olaf—An Atom,* with Claire MacDowell and Charles Mailes, and with Harry Carey in the title role of Olaf; *Just Gold,* with Lionel Barrymore, Charles West, Alfred Paget, Joseph McDermott, Charles Mailes, Kate Bruce, and Lillian Gish; and *His Mother's Son,* with Jennie Lee, Walter Miller, Bobby Harron, Victoria Forde, W. Christie Miller, and Mae Marsh. Most of these films followed standard formulas. Griffith gave a touch of fantasy to *The Wanderer,* however, which was made with a Spanish theme.

In April, Griffith filmed another two-reel picture, *The Yaqui Cur,* an Indian drama with Bobby Harron, Lionel Barrymore, Kate Bruce, and Victoria Forde. This was followed by *The Ranchero's Revenge,* with Lionel Barrymore, Claire MacDowell, and Harry Carey.

A second two-reel film was produced at the end of April, *The Mothering Heart,* originally titled *Mother Love,* with a first major role for Lillian Gish, specifically tailored for her talents. The film was actually 1,525 feet, the equivalent of a reel and a half, but technically the film had to be shown in two-reel form. Griffith completed six films in April, including the two two-reel films.

May 1913 began with *The Mistake,* in one reel. This was followed by *Her Mother's Oath* and *During the Round-up,* both one reel. The last film in May was *The Coming of Angelo,* an Italian drama, with Blanche Sweet, Charles Mailes, and Walter Miller. *The Coming of Angelo* was finished on May 28, 1913.

During May, Griffith's mind was occupied with future prospects. It was reported in *The Motion Picture World,* a trade paper, that he was having an imposing Western town constructed in the San Fernando Valley for a forthcoming film. The town, it was noted, was going to be "authentic" and three-dimensional. Griffith kept his own counsel. It was his intention, apparently, not to divulge his activities outside the company. Yet even the company was not certain what Griffith was up to. The town under construction was a special setting for a two-reel picture to be called *The Battle of Elderberry Gulch.*

Griffith's personal schedule of production had been announced under a new Biograph policy of permitting limited exploitation of the members of the company. Certain featured players were to be made known to the public for the first time, but it was the directors who were to be accorded the primary publicity. Biograph, it seemed, did not wish to become involved in the burgeoning star system that was sending salaries soaring because of rivalry between companies for certain actors and actresses. It was announced in *The Moving Picture World* that Griffith would be directing the Saturday releases, O'Sullivan the Monday releases, and Dell Henderson the mid-week comedies. This new policy was to take effect in April 1913.

Lee Dougherty, the one-man editorial board at Biograph, announced his resignation at Biograph to accept a position as story editor with Kinemacolor in California. Dougherty knew that the Biograph players were about to return to the East, and he had decided to remain in California. Tony O'Sullivan organized a farewell party for him. O'Sullivan, Bitzer, and Bobby Harron were the last of the pre-Griffith Biograph employees who still remained with the company.

"Judith of Bethulia," Four Reels

Although Griffith was far removed from New York and the openings of new films, he was aware of the new competition from longer films. On April 1, 1913, *Quo Vadis,* an eight-reel film produced by Cines in Italy, began showings at the Astor Theatre in New York City. The film played a total of twenty-two weeks at a top admission price of one dollar and was subsequently exhibited successfully in other large cities. Griffith could not have seen the film before he returned to New York City, but he was aware of its sheer size and magnitude. The details of film productions were now being reported and advertised in a growing trade press, principally *The Motion Picture World,* and also *Photoplay* and *The Dramatic Mirror.*

Blanche Sweet remembers seeing *Quo Vadis* after the company returned to New York, when Griffith's *Judith of Bethulia* (in which she starred) was still shooting in the Bronx studio. Miss Sweet thinks that Griffith may have seen *Quo Vadis,* although she is not certain that he did.

As far as Griffith could judge, there was no reason to be confined within the one-reel, or even the two-reel form, if the nature of the story demanded a longer film. In secret, he began planning a multi-reel picture. Dougherty had purchased a script from Grace A. Pierce of Santa Monica on April 11, 1913, called *Judith and Holofernes,* based on a biblical story from the Apocrypha. Griffith was already familiar with the story as told in play form by Thomas Bailey Aldrich, but the Pierce scenario was the in-

surance against a plagiarism suit. Blanche Sweet told me a copy
of the Aldrich play was present on the set during the filming of
the picture, although it was not followed as a shooting script. It
is likely that Griffith borrowed some details from his memory of
the Nance O'Neill production, and transmitted them to Frank
Woods, who rewrote the Pierce story into a scenario. Griffith
thought of *Judith* as a big film, certainly the equal of *Quo Vadis,*
but just how big it would be, he had not decided. There were
other films to be made first.

Griffith directed two one-reelers in June—*An Indian's Loyalty,*
with Fred Burns, Lillian Gish, Edward Dillon, and Griffith's
Indian adviser, Dark Cloud; and *Two Men of the Desert,* another prospector story filmed in the desert at San Fernando.

At the beginning of July 1913, Griffith made another two-reel
film that undertook to expose the "uplifters." Griffith called the
picture *The Reformers,* or *The Lost Art of Minding One's Business.* Frank E. Woods, the first film critic for *The Dramatic
Mirror,* wrote the script, as he had others for Biograph. The cast
included William Murray, Walter Miller, Charles Mailes, Mae
Marsh, and Bobby Harron. The film was finished on July 6, 1913.

The Western town at San Fernando was ready and Griffith
began filming *The Battle of Elderberry Gulch.* The principal
action concerned an epic battle between attacking Indians and
the pioneers. Linda Griffith commented:

The Battle of Elderberry Gulch was a famous picture of those days.
The star was a pioneer baby all of whose relatives had been killed by
the Indians. During the time the baby's folks were being murdered
another party of pioneers, led by Dell Henderson, was dying of thirst
nearby. With just enough life left in them to do it, they rescued the
baby from its dead relations, staggered on a few miles, and then they,
too, sank exhausted in the sand and cacti.

Another cornucopia sand-storm blew up.

Kind-hearted Dell Henderson, now sunk to earth, had protectingly
tucked the baby's head under his coat. But the tiny baby hand (in the
story, and it was good business) had to be pictured waving above the
prostrate figures of the defunct pioneers, to show she still lived. Other-

wise, she might not have been saved by the second rescuing party, and saved she had to be for the later chapters of the story.

For though in the end of the story the baby became the lily-white Blanche Sweet, it was, as a matter of fact, a tiny, lightly colored, colored baby from a colored foundling home, whom we often used for the photographic value of its black eyes. . . .

Following *The Battle of Elderberry Gulch,* Griffith filmed a two-reel sequel to *Man's Genesis* called by Biograph *In Prehistoric Days.* Griffith referred to the film as *Wars of the Primal Tribes,* and when it was finally issued in 1913 it was retitled *Brute Force.*

During the month of June, Griffith had carpenters at work in Chatsworth Park, Los Angeles, building the settings for his planned biblical epic, now titled *Judith of Bethulia.* The playing area for the film was approximately twelve miles square, and it had taken four weeks to construct the setting of the walled city of Bethulia. Once Griffith got the rehearsals underway, entire squads of extras were transported to the location.

Edward Martin Woolley reported in the first feature article written about Griffith, in 1914:

Before this Mr. Griffith had been engaged for months in searching the libraries of New York and Washington for illustrations and reference books. . . . The result was that his properties down to minute details were correct so far as records made possible. During the making of the picture, it was necessary to show water at the scenes at the well. In repeated rehearsals the water ran out which all had to be imported into the desert. "Send a special train for two barrels," said Griffith. Those two barrels of water cost more than $80, but Griffith would have spent $800 rather than spoil the picture by using imaginary water.[6]

Blanche Sweet was cast as the widow, Judith, who agrees to pose as a courtesan and visit the camp of the Assyrian general, Holofernes, and assassinate him. Holofernes was played by Henry Walthall in a long beard. Others in the huge cast included Lil-

6 Edward Martin Woolley: "The Story of D. W. Griffith, the $100,000 Salary Man of the Movies," *McClure's,* September 1914.

lian and Dorothy Gish, Gertrude Robinson, Kate Bruce, Bobby Harron, Lionel Barrymore, Marshal Neilan, Antonio Moreno, and Thomas Jefferson. Lionel Barrymore recalled:

> I played, let us phrase it, several important parts in Griffith's *Judith of Bethulia,* the first four-reel feature made in America . . . This picture was modeled on the four-part technique Griffith invented for his previous *Pippa Passes,* and was actually the front runner for his masterwork *Intolerance.* I am, therefore, proud to have worked in it; but beyond recalling that Harry Carey was crucified upside down and that I appeared more than once in various disguises, I do not remember much about what I contributed to this work.

Today's viewer probably finds this film much slower and more majestic—perhaps even dull—than many of Griffith's Civil War and Indian films or the "last-minute rescue" melodramas. Edward Wagenknecht has commented: *"Judith of Bethulia* is heavy and ominous from the first scene; it has a rich, brooding splendor of imagination." Louis Reeves Harrison, in his review of the picture in 1914, said:

> A fascinating work of high artistry, *Judith of Bethulia* will not only rank as an achievement in this country, but will make foreign producers sit up and take notice.

Griffith Leaves Biograph

The Biograph front office, however, noticed something else: the film ended up costing somewhat in excess of $36,000 to produce. This was double Griffith's original estimate of $18,000. The mail and wires brought screams of anguish from Henry Marvin. Griffith's contract terms were still technically those of the first contract he'd signed, however, and he was nominally in charge of all matters pertaining to the film. He ignored the complaints about cost and finished the major portion of the film in June. The company finally returned to New York in the first week of July. Griffith planned to finish *Judith* in the new Bronx studios.

Now Griffith was bluntly informed that he was to be made

supervisor of other directors. He would be allowed to finish the filming and editing of *Judith,* at that point approaching six uncut reels, but he was not to begin any new pictures.

Griffith was busy editing *Judith* from the six reels of raw footage to a workable four-reel form, and preparing the titles with Frank Woods. According to Mrs. Griffith:

> Mr. Griffith wanted some special titling for it. He turned it over to Frank Woods, who phrased the captions in the style of language of the day—the first time that was done. However, it proved too much of a strain for the exhibitors, for they afterward fixed the titles up to suit themselves in good old New Yorkese.

J. J. Kennedy and Henry Marvin had negotiated a deal with the theatrical producers Klaw and Erlanger during the spring. Klaw and Erlanger had formed a new outfit called the Protective Amusement Company, and Biograph contracted to film the K & E stage plays as five-reel features for summer showings in the K & E controlled legitimate theatres. Griffith's personal plans for bigger pictures were submerged in the new arrangements. He was doubly unhappy because no one had informed him of the impending deal. Kennedy told Griffith that he was welcome to stay at Biograph and continue making one-reel films but if he wanted to make big pictures he would have to go elsewhere. In addition, Henry Marvin was holding back the release of *Judith of Bethulia* and *The Battle of Elderberry Gulch.*[7]

Once the editing on *Judith of Bethulia* was complete, Griffith spent a little time helping his former assistants direct. But, beginning in September, Griffith began to appear less and less frequently at the studio.

He had been approached during the summer, when news of his estrangement at Biograph got around, by Harry Aitken, the president of a new film-distributing company, Mutual. Aitken

---

[7] Neither film was released until 1914, after Griffith had left Biograph—*Judith of Bethulia* on March 7, 1914, and *The Battle of Elderberry Gulch* on March 28, 1914.

wanted Griffith to join Mutual as an independent producer. Griffith tried to renegotiate his contract with Biograph, but Kennedy would not reconsider his terms. Then Adolph Zukor approached Griffith with an offer of $50,000 a year to direct for him. Griffith refused, much to the relief of Zukor's partners. (Twelve years later, Zukor employed Griffith at a salary of $156,000 a year.) Griffith accepted Aitken's offer instead, probably because of the freedom it offered and because Zukor was committed to a policy much like that of Biograph–K & E. Griffith's break with Biograph was announced in the *Dramatic Mirror* on September 29, 1913, to be effective October 1.

Griffith did not leave Biograph alone. Billy Bitzer had decided to remain at Biograph for the time being, because of its security. (At Griffith's urging, Bitzer finally did leave Biograph in 1914 and was the cameraman for *The Birth of a Nation*.) Griffith now took many of the prominent Biograph players with him. They included James Kirkwood, Bobby Harron, Owen Moore, Blanche Sweet, Lillian and Dorothy Gish, John Dillon, Henry Walthall, Donald Crisp, Edward Dillon, Mae Marsh, Spottiswoode Aitken, Jack Pickford, and George Siegman. Bobby Harron's departure ended a longer association than Griffith's. Lionel Barrymore returned to the stage. Linda Arvidson Griffith, who had separated from Griffith in 1911, now joined Kinemacolor. Of those who remained at Biograph, only the two Griffith assistants who had been made full directors, Tony O'Sullivan and Dell Henderson, were of note.

The end for Biograph was almost in sight. The ambitious Klaw and Erlanger dramas failed to capture the public's interest, and the day of the one-reel picture, except for comedy, was over. Biograph began a decline, slowed only for a brief time in 1915 to 1917 through the reissue of many of the Griffith pictures and some of the Sennett comedies. The delay in releasing *Judith of Bethulia* canceled any uniqueness it might have shown in competition with the films of 1913. In 1914, audiences were being bombarded with promises of even longer pictures. Biograph reissued *Judith* in 1917 in six reels, replacing much of the footage that Griffith had removed when he edited the picture. The title, for the reissue, was changed to *Her Condoned Sin*. Even this attempt to capitalize on Griffith's reputation earned with *The Birth of a Nation* and *Intolerance* failed, and Biograph, which had provided him with the necessary, often arduous, apprenticeship, gradually disappeared as a producer.

VII

Conclusions

On December 3, 1913, an advertisement appeared in *The New York Dramatic Mirror* over the signature of Albert H. T. Banzhaf, styled as the attorney and personal representative of D. W. Griffith. The advertisement stated:

D. W. GRIFFITH

Producer of all great Biograph successes, revolutionizing motion picture drama and founding the modern technique of the art.

Included in the innovations which he introduced and which are now generally followed by the most advanced producers, are: the large or close-up figures, distant views as represented first in *Ramona,* the switchback, sustained suspense, the *fade-out,* and restraint in expression, raising motion picture acting to the higher plane which has won for it recognition as a genuine art.

For two years from the summer of 1908, Mr. Griffith personally directed all Biograph motion pictures. Thereafter as general director he superintended all Biograph productions and directed the more *important* features until October 1, 1913.

The advertisement then listed 151 motion pictures as the personal productions of D. W. Griffith, beginning with *The Adventures of Dollie* and ending with *Judith of Bethulia.* In fact, this constituted about one-third of Griffith's productions during the Biograph period. The advertisement was placed at Griffith's behest as an attempt to make up for the years in which he received no individual recognition for his work, in accordance with Biograph policy.

After the production of *The Birth of a Nation* in 1914, Griffith was acclaimed nationally and, accordingly, the first evaluations and commentaries on his career began to appear. Others now added to the list of Griffith's contributions to the development of the motion picture. Edward Martin Woolley wrote in 1914:

Gradually Griffith evolved principles of position, make-up and lighting and made many curious discoveries that advanced the art. He found it possible to make-up a slight actor so they [sic] looked statuesque on the screen. Today it takes a young man of the student type usually to play the part of a big bestial bully.

His contributions to this newest form of popular appeal are many and far reaching, but by far the most vital of his contributions has been the close-up. The discovery that it was a fundamental mistake to get the whole figure into the picture has been the result of this one contribution from Griffith. The photo actor has a wider range in describing his emotions with his facial muscles than any actor on the legitimate stage ever had. For six years Griffith's conceptions of picture possibilities have been steadily expanding and the end of those possibilities to his mind is not yet in sight. He began when insignificant pantomimes were termed wonderful. A dozen scenes in a blinding flicker of light. Recently he produced a picture of 700 scenes and 7,000 feet of film.[1]

Edward Wagenknecht, after reviewing the extant Griffith films from the Biograph period, commented:

He broke up his scenes into various shots, taking his pictures from different angles and various distances all the way from the extreme long shot to the extreme close-up of a face or a part of a face or some other part of the body . . . or even inanimate objects of dramatic significance . . . He used cross-cutting (the "switchback") for suspense, for contrast, and for reference, and the flashback for remembrance and startling juxtaposition; he even used shots to build up atmosphere and establish

[1] The reference is to *The Birth of a Nation*. Theodore Huff, in his shot analysis of this film, recorded 1,375 shots, exclusive of titles, in twelve reels. The actual première of *The Birth of a Nation* was February 8, 1915, at Clune's Auditorium in Los Angeles. The film was produced, however, in 1914.

the setting, although they might not advance the action in any way. One might say that the Griffith technical devices were most strongly validated by the fact that others *had* used them; if this had not been so, their use would have been freakish and arbitrary on his part. This was the right way to tell a story in film, and Griffith had the wit to discern it. He built on the foundations his predecessors had laid and took up everything of value that they had often accidentally and uncomprehendingly discovered. All this he had deliberately, intelligently manipulated and developed.[2]

Bosley Crowther has noted how Griffith slowly achieved his consummate mastery of the camera:

With his cameraman, G. W. (Billy) Bitzer, he had learned to move his camera around and shoot a scene from more than one angle. He had worked out the use of the close-up. More important, he had developed unusual ways of assembling shots and scenes to build up a narrative continuity with cumulative force. In 1913, his *Judith of Bethulia*, a Biblical drama which was the first American film to run four reels, clearly foretold his epic bent.[3]

James Agee considered that a major Griffith contribution to film was a certain spirit Griffith brought to the editorial process:

. . . there is in every instant, so well as I can remember, the unique purity and vitality of birth or of a creature just born and first exerting its unprecedented, incredible strength; and there are, besides, Griffith's overwhelming innocence and magnanimity of spirit; his moral and poetic earnestness; his joy in his work; and his splendid intuitiveness, directness, common sense, daring, and skill as an inventor, and as an artist. Aside from his talent or genius as an inventor and artist, he was all heart; and ruinous as his excesses sometimes were in that respect, they were inseparable from his virtues, and small beside them.[4]

Albert Fulton has pointed out a basic element of Griffith's art —directing and editing are inseparable functions:

[2] Edward Charles Wagenknecht: *op. cit.*, p. 92.

[3] Bosley Crowther: "The Birth of 'The Birth of a Nation'," *The New York Times Sunday Magazine*, February 7, 1965, p. 83.

[4] James Agee: *Agee on Film* (New York, 1958), p. 316.

Now that the making of motion pictures has become a specialized but diversified process, a director is favored if he is permitted to edit his own films. That part of the process is usually assigned to a specialist in editing. But Griffith . . . was his own editor. It is difficult to imagine how his films could have been edited otherwise, for not only did he shoot his pictures without a prepared script, but only he knew how the parts were to be fitted together.[5]

Griffith had indeed been responsible for the editing of his own films, and he had also relied on improvisation from a plot outline, a synopsis or scenario, committed to memory. There was no detailed shooting script, and there was no theory of editorial process to guide the development of the production.

. . . all his pictures were conceived in detail and carried in his head. The only written words were put down by the cutter, Jim Smith, whose work it was to assemble the film in sequence and cut it through length after all the scenes were taken. Jimmy came to the final rehearsal and would write a synopsis of what was enacted before him to use subsequently in piecing together the story.[6]

It is Lillian Gish who made the foregoing observation, and it is Billy Bitzer who recorded that the cameraman, himself in particular, was frequently responsible for timing and defining the finished scene in rehearsal. In his notes Bitzer has written:

At luncheon, especially on location, D. W. would eat alone, his assistant finding some sequestered spot; alone he would concentrate on the afternoon scenes. He never used a script, I don't remember him ever using one while shooting.

He rehearsed considerable [sic] at the studio and during the rehearsals when nearly final I would appear with a scratch pad and take out my watch for the purpose of timing the scenes. The cast generally knew that the rehearsal was nearly what he wanted when he would say get Billy and we'll time this.

5 Albert R. Fulton: *Motion Pictures: The Development of an Art from Silent Films to the Age of Television* (University of Oklahoma Press, 1960), p. 90.
6 Lillian Gish, in *Harper's Bazaar,* October 1940.

Seymour Stern has summed up Griffith's contributions in an article originally published at the time of Griffith's death in 1948:

Why is the name of D. W. Griffith still a synonym for the "father of film art"? What were the salient contributions which earned him world-wide and enduring fame?

Broadly speaking, his contributions fall into two major categories. First, the technical discoveries and inventions and creative adaptations. Griffith did not invent all the devices which misinformed commentators of later years ascribed to him. The close-up, for example, appeared as far back as the quaint old primitive film, *The Kiss,* in 1895, and in some of the early German primitives, before Griffith entered the field. But he was the first to use the device for [both] dramatic and psychological effect—a contribution that shaped the entire technique of picture making down to the present day. In addition, he himself added a multitude of more advanced methods, all of which have long since become an established part of film technique. Chief among these were the long shot, the vista, the vignette, the eye-opener effect, the cameo-profile, the fade-in and fade-out, the iris, soft-focus, back lighting, tinting, rapid cutting, parallel action, mist photography, and the moving camera.

But far more important than any single one of these devices, or indeed, than all of them taken together, is the second category of Griffith's contributions, the content of the films themselves—i.e., the emotional, dramatic, intellectual and esthetic content, separate and apart from the mechanics of picture-making. For in the sustained acclaim of mechanics and technique, little attention has been paid to this aspect of the director's achievement.

. . . Griffith's versatile and elastic genius found itself at home in a variety of realms of thought and feeling—the social, the psychological, the philosophical, the poetic, and the religious. He stands alone among directors in having demonstrated, not once but many times, the capacities of the motion picture to project something more important and more lasting than mere entertainment.[7]

Parker Tyler has lauded Griffith's expansion of the film's dramatic vocabulary:

From the beginning, Griffith, for instance, never ceased to expand the area of action (even if it meant placing a desk in the center of a large

[7] Seymour Stern: "Griffith, Pioneer of the Film Art," *Introduction to the Art of the Movies,* edited by Lewis Jacobs (New York, 1960), pp. 155–156.

unoccupied area), desiring only to undo the scope of the dramatic spectacle and yet create its mobile details with some leisure. While as an artist remarkably intelligent, he failed to understand the natural possibilities of the camera, in that he assumed it was primarily extrovertive, while it is equally introvertive. He made many technical advances—the close-up, for example, as an accessory to the long shot, and vice versa. Working thus dialectically, this pioneering director added enormously to the dramatic vocabulary of the movies.[8]

Tyler's evaluation owes something to the pronouncements about Griffith by the Soviet film theorists. Jay Leyda in his history of Russian and Soviet film, *Kino,* noted the extensive showing of *Intolerance* in the Soviet Union during the early twenties, and examined the influence on Soviet filmmakers of this and later Griffith films. Sergei Eisenstein wrote:

Griffith primarily is the greatest master of the most graphic form in this field—a master of *parallel montage.* Above all else, Griffith is a great master of montage constructions that have been created in a direct-lined quickening and *increase of tempo* (chiefly in the direction of the higher forms of parallel montage).

The school of Griffith before all else is a school of *tempo.*[9]

Benjamin Hampton observed in 1931:

Griffith proved himself to be a master craftsman. His mind was stored with plots, situations, incidents, and his stage experience had taught him the tricks and the "business" of dramatic expression. As a director, he was daring in the use of his knowledge, never hesitating to try for the unattainable in story of dramatic effect.

Stagecraft was of some value, but Griffith soon found that its limitations were definitely marked. The primary object of the audience in spoken theatre is to *listen;* the mind can not follow the speech of players and fully observe their expressions at the same time.

Griffith's experiments convinced him that the best romantic screen artists would not be found among the famous heroes and heroines of the stage. He must get new material, young people whose youth and

8 Parker Tyler: *Hollywood Hallucination* (New York, 1944).
9 Sergei Eisenstein: *Film Form,* trans. Jay Leyda (New York, 1949), p. 234.

freshness would withstand the hard eye of the movie camera, and whose minds were not set in the rigid traditions of stagecraft; youthful faces, bodies, and minds that he could train into the new technique of the screen.[10]

Lewis Jacobs lent support to one of Hampton's major comments on Griffith:

Griffith perceived what so many producers have since forgotten: in the theatre, the audience listens first and then watches; in the movie palace the audience watches first and then listens.[11]

Griffith himself commented sparingly on the development of his career, and not at all during the Biograph period. In 1921 he said:

I adopted the flash-back to build suspense, which till then had been a missing quantity in picture dramas. Instead of showing a continuous view of a girl floating downstream in a barrel, I cut into the film by flashing back to incidents that contributed to the scene and explained it.

When I first photographed players at close range, my management and patrons decried a method that showed only the face of the story characters. Today the close-up is employed by nearly all directors to bring a picture audience to an intimate acquaintance with an actor's emotions.[12]

Griffith's commentary on his theory of film drama was contained in a defense against criticism that he depicted sin much too realistically, a defense reminiscent of his letter replying to Hector Fuller's dramatic review in 1907:

All drama must of necessity be conflict—battle, fight. How are we to depict the right unless we show the wrong? Unless we show the evils of a vicious past, how are we allowed to be the means of guiding the footsteps of the present generation?[13]

[10] Hampton: *op. cit.,* pp. 52, 87.

[11] Lewis Jacobs: *The Rise of the American Film* (New York, 1939), p. 119.

[12] Griffith: "The Miracle of Modern Photography," *The Mentor,* Vol. 9, No. 6, July 1921, p. 12.

[13] Jean Bernique: *Motion Picture Acting* (Chicago, 1916), p. 199.

The contributions to the development of the motion picture either claimed for himself by Griffith in his advertisement of 1913 or claimed for him by others can be summarized as follows:

1. *The large photo of details.* This is generally called a closeup or closeup shot.

2. *Distant views, the long shot.*

3. *The switchback.* As originally applied by Griffith, this meant the basic technique in crosscutting for parallel action, but he also used the term to mean flashback. This refers to the process of cutting away from one shot to a second shot, or sequence of shots, representing some incident prior to the present time sequence of the film. It was a way of showing a remembered event or the causes of present events.

4. *Sustained suspense.* Griffith was referring to the results of crosscutting for suspense by extending the time of an action by showing more than one parallel event and by introducing delaying elements in the drive for the climax.

5. *The fadeout.*

6. *Restraint in expression.* This might refer primarily to matters of acting style, although Griffith might also have used it to refer to the design of the film as a whole, the use of scenic environment, the use of costume, the use of properties, and perhaps, too, the development of characterizations.

7. *Lighting.* Griffith has been credited with using more naturalistic interior lighting, and for using natural lighting to obtain unusual effects.

8. *Greater variety of camera position and camera angle.*

9. *Unusual manner of assembling shots.*

10. *The establishment of the screen director as the prime creative force in filmmaking.*

11. *The vignette.*

12. *The iris.*

13. *Soft focus.*

14. *Backlighting.*

15. *Tinting.*

16. *Rapid cutting.*

17. *Parallel action.*

18. *Mist photography.*

19. *The moving camera.*

20. *Film content.* Griffith's contributions in content have been in the realm of the emotional, dramatic, intellectual, and aesthetic.

21. *Expansion of the area of action.*

22. *Direct line quickening and increase of tempo.*

23. *Better written stories with more plausible plots.*

24. *The use of young, fresh talent.*

Griffith did not originate the closeup. In almost the earliest moments of motion-picture making, the closeup was the staple of the Kinetoscope and the Mutoscope, as in *Fred Ott's Sneeze,* and *The Kiss* with May Irwin and John Rice. The closeup had been used by Edwin S. Porter in *The Great Train Robbery* as a novel but extraneous shot. Griffith used the closeup sparingly, as a direct adjunct to the development of the action in the story; that is, the wrench in Blanche Sweet's hand in *The Lonedale Operator,* the pistol in *The Fatal Hour,* the poison in *The Medicine Bottle,* Mary Pickford's head and shoulders in *Friends.*

Griffith claimed to have originated distant views, or the vista shot, but this is relative. There were long shots in many films before Griffith. The shot in *The Great Train Robbery* of the bandits running down into the woods is a long shot. Griffith, however, in *Ramona* utilized effectively the tremendous spaces available in California for striking extreme long shots. The Biograph camera, coupled with Bitzer's skills as a photographer, gave a specially noteworthy quality to these shots.

The switchback, or in its variant the flashback, is, it seems, one of Griffith's genuine contributions to the development of the editorial process in films. Its first appearance, to all indications, was in *The Fatal Hour,* Griffith's ninth film. No example of its use for parallel action prior to this film by any producer has been found. With this, Griffith was able to relate two or more actions occurring simultaneously by interweaving shots from both actions, i.e., crosscutting. He reinforced the technique further in his twenty-ninth picture, *After Many Years*. Before that, shots had been connected in strictly chronological sequence, and only one story was told at a time.

Sustained suspense was a direct result of the switchback shot and the consequent parallel editing, or, in Eisenstein's phrase, parallel montage. Griffith did discover that film time, as opposed to real time, could be shortened or expanded. By increasing the number of shots in parallel actions, or by increasing the physical length of the shots, Griffith discovered, he could expand time. Reversing the process and shortening the physical length of shots, eliminating steps in the sequence of action and skipping over real time elements, would contract time. Thus, Griffith could speed up the tempo of a rescue operation, momentarily slow it down, hold off the actual rescue for as long as it seemed necessary to him, and then rush the final action to the climax. The technique of parallel editing did not emerge all at once. Griffith made slow, steady progress in its use in *The Lonely Villa, The Lonedale Operator,* and *Enoch Arden*. But often he would abandon the technique, regressing to an earlier style of editing, as it is obvious from viewing the Griffith Biograph films in chronological order.

The fadeout was used in films prior to Griffith's, although Billy Bitzer and Griffith were both convinced that each had originated the technique. In fact, they had merely applied it as a device for closing a film. None of the fadeouts in the Griffith films of the Biograph period is a complete fadeout, moreover. The screen does not go completely to black, but is only darkened. The fade-in, a reverse process, is not in evidence in any of the extant films of the Biograph period.

The claim that Griffith contributed "restraint in expression" is extremely vague. Griffith was concerned from the beginning of his directorial career with a realistic style of acting, but this was the realism of the late-nineteenth-century stage. As the Biograph films made greater use of medium and close shots, Griffith found it necessary to stop the broad actions of his stage-trained actors. Yet Lillian Gish's comments about the necessity of remaining in trim for acrobatic pantomime in long shots strongly suggests that, when the shot corresponded to the stage view, Griffith had his actors resume the broad acting style of the proscenium theatre. Griffith's increasing emphasis on naturalism in scenery and costume throughout the period might be interpreted as restraint. He generally did not find the excesses of farce comedy as reflected in painted canvas scenery and outrageous properties amusing, or satisfactory for his own films. He did not discourage their use, however, by Sennett and Dell Henderson when they were given directorial responsibility for Biograph comedies, and he did use such scenery and devices in his own films in 1908 and 1909. The indications are, however, that he abandoned these stage techniques as soon as possible, making increased use of real buildings, natural scenery, and authentic properties. *The Fool and the Girl* and *War,* the two plays he wrote before beginning his film career, would indicate that he thought in terms of a broad, sweeping realism beyond the confines of the theatre even before entering the field of motion pictures. Griffith did ask his actors to observe life around them and take from their observations elements of characterization that would be authentic, but he permitted the use of false stage whiskers on minor characters and he was wedded to many of the typical cliché characters of the nineteenth-century stage. Griffith's "restraint in expression" would probably not be so termed today, but in comparison to the work of others during this period, the description is probably fair enough. Blanche Sweet remembers that the company was most impressed with the acting of Henry Walthall. Walthall's quiet style is readily observable in *1776* in 1909, as well as in later films such as *The Battle of Elderberry Gulch* and *Judith of Bethulia.* The restrained manner of Frank Powell in *A Corner in Wheat* should also be noted.

Griffith's concern for lighting was manifest from the beginning of his association with Biograph, and the descriptions of the lighting effects he desired in his plays indicate a sensitivity to realistic lighting prior to this period. Artificial lighting effects were in their infancy in 1908 for the simple reason that the artificially lighted indoor studio was new. Biograph had moved indoors from a rooftop studio only in 1906. The concern in all the early films was with basic illumination, not effect lighting. The effects achieved by Griffith in lighting were new to the film, but the methods of obtaining them were in use in the legitimate theatre. Griffith, it would appear, was attempting to transfer theatrical lighting to the film.

From all available evidence it seems that Griffith did ask in 1908 that a second shot of a scene be taken from a new camera position closer to the actors and that the two shots be edited together into a sequence in *For Love of Gold*. He did ask, cajole, and demand that his cameraman make his shots from the angle which seemed right to him, Griffith, the director. Shots were made by cameramen standing in a river or under the full sun. And in one instance in *The Squaw's Love,* at Cuddebackville, Griffith asked that three cameras be used to record a stunt that could be repeated only with great difficulty. Also, to make certain necessary shots, Griffith had his camera mounted on a train, mounted on a handcar, and mounted on an automobile.

Griffith's development of the editorial process entailed assembling shots in unusual ways for his time. As late as 1912, *Queen Elizabeth,* the Sarah Bernhardt film, still consisted of shots assembled as scenes would be in a play.

Throughout this period, it is evident that Griffith possessed a strong sense of self-dramatization. With the exception of his first wife, Linda Arvidson, none of the members of his company referred to him in any other way than as Mr. Griffith. With the notable exception of Mary Pickford, his actors and actresses remembered him as a kind, thoughtful, but rather aloof and remote gentleman. Even Billy Bitzer found it difficult to relate the story of Griffith's fight with Charles Inslee, because it was so out of character for Griffith.

When Biograph finally began releasing the names of the creative people connected with their films, it was Griffith's name that received the greatest emphasis. Through his advertisement of 1913, and through subsequent publicity, Griffith made the point over and over that the pictures with which he was associated were Griffith pictures. Mary Pickford, for example, appeared in Griffith films; Griffith did not direct Pickford pictures. The films in Mary Pickford's later career, or, for that matter, the films in Lillian Gish's career after she parted with Griffith, were identified with the star, not with the director. Griffith never lost control of his pictures to a star. During the Biograph period, he carefully avoided any casting that might have led to the development of a star. All the actors were cast, in large or small roles, as Griffith saw fit. He exercised to their fullest the responsibilities given to him in his first contract. This control was not new, however, or unusual. Edwin Porter exercised similar control, and so did J. Stuart Blackton. Griffith did not originate the concept of the director as the principal controlling force in making motion pictures; he merely did the first really effective job of publicizing that control.

The vignette shot and its subsequent development into the iris shot appear, on the basis of available evidence, to have been the work of Billy Bitzer, given currency by Griffith's recognition of their usefulness in achieving screen effects. The same must be said for soft focus and backlighting, although accidental examples of both effects occur in films prior to this period. It was Griffith's recognition of their value in the film narrative that was the contribution.

Griffith should not be given credit as the originator of tinting or coloring film, since both techniques were used experimentally almost from the inception of motion pictures. Yet the few original films in the possession of the Museum of Modern Art Film Library would indicate that Griffith employed tinting as a tasteful device, which added to the film's effectiveness. Since few original prints are available of work by other producers, no one can really prove that Griffith contributed anything unusual or even original in this respect.

Rapid cutting and parallel action were outgrowths of the switchback and crosscutting for suspense, as indicated. Griffith's cutting never reached the frenzied peak of Eisenstein's in the twenties, but enough short shots were used to indicate the direction the editorial process might take.

Mist photography was not an observed development during the Biograph period, although Griffith did take advantage of atmospheric effects, to a limited extent, in the last films of the period. *A Pueblo Legend* (1912) was overloaded with such atmospheric photography.

The moving camera can be considered to be a Griffith contribution only in a very limited sense. Shots involving vertical and horizontal movements of the camera have been observed in films of 1898 and 1900, and at least one tracking shot, with the camera moving parallel to another moving object, has been observed in a film of 1898, as noted. Griffith did redevelop these techniques during the Biograph period, using an effective tracking shot in *A Beast at Bay* and another in the Indian fight in *The Massacre*. Griffith was extremely sparing in his use of the moving camera, however. He used it only when there seemed to be no other effective way to present the material.

Griffith's contributions to screen content during the Biograph period must be regarded as minimal. With few exceptions, the plots of his pictures adhered to the formulas of the stage melodrama. Griffith managed to retain "the sweet young girl who is separated from her lover by the machinations of a wicked villain" as a staple of the film story throughout the period. Two exceptions should be noted, however. Griffith's interest in giving a fair and honest presentation of the American Indian was unusual for his time, and it is almost as unusual today. The second exception would be Griffith's concern with the relationship between the poor and the rich. Almost invariably, when the two classes came together in the same film, Griffith portrayed the poor sympathetically and the rich with scorn and derision. Further, he managed to show class contrasts sharply through crosscut images, as for example in *A Corner in Wheat*. He was not afraid to take the side of social reform, yet he held the society do-gooder up to scorn. Griffith's poor could help themselves, but they could not be bought. Sergei Eisenstein was to comment about Griffith:

> In social attitudes Griffith was always a liberal, never departing far from the slightly sentimental humanism of the good old gentleman and sweet old ladies of Victorian England, just as Dickens loved to picture them. His tender-hearted film morals go no higher than a level of Christian accusation of human injustice and *nowhere* [italics mine] in his films is there sounded a protest against social injustice.[14]

Eisenstein could not have been further from the truth. Griffith dealt forcefully with a social issue, reinforcing with striking shots the values retained from the Frank Norris novel. The injustice of the white man toward the Indian was strikingly presented in other films. Griffith also showed the corruption inherent in politics and politicians.

The emotional and dramatic content of the Griffith films of this period was generally that of the stage melodrama, yet he demonstrated that the camera could heighten and extend the realism of these emotions. The intellectual content probably must be judged as elementary. Griffith was not an intellectual. His reactions to drama were emotional, and each of the films examined demonstrates that he was concerned with dramatic relationships rather than intellectual concepts. Griffith did not intellectualize his directorial concepts. He did not write books of film theory, and his terminology was as direct as could be devised. It should also be observed that during the Biograph period he quite literally did not have the time for theorizing, even if he had been so inclined, and he was not.

During this period Griffith did not make any significant contributions to better writing for the films. All his films were made

14 Eisenstein: *op. cit.*, p. 233.

from synopses, mere plot outlines, carried in his head during the actual shooting. Plots were purchased from a wide variety of sources, or Griffith would draw on literature he was personally familiar with. He used a few classic works, filming one picture based on a play by Shakespeare, one based on Tolstoy (*Resurrection*), one on Browning (*Pippa Passes*), and one on Tennyson (*Enoch Arden*). The plausibility of the plots seemed of minor concern to Griffith. Most of his pictures had no more plausibility than the forgotten melodrama he had acted in with the Twilight Revelers.

Griffith did use fresh, young talent, in addition to some not so fresh, older talent. Most of the people who joined the company had had stage experience, although not in the first rank. Griffith's acting company was always well balanced between young, relatively inexperienced actors and experienced character actors. One of his basic character actors, W. Christie Miller, was given recognition in California during the last Biograph season, in 1913, as the second oldest actor in motion pictures.[15] Griffith showed little, if any, partiality for his young players. They were used in a wide variety of roles. On the basis of roles played for Griffith, Mary Pickford might just as easily have become known as "Little Pocahontas" instead of as "Little Mary." Griffith handled his young players with great sensitivity, however, and he had a specific image for them to project, an image combining the most-remembered features of his early loves—long-leggedness, athleticism, and quick wit. That Griffith gave young unknowns opportunities was as much a result of low pay scales and the contempt with which established actors regarded the motion picture as of any specific motivation on his part. Most of the players in the Biograph acting company came to Griffith seeking employment. In that sense only, he "discovered" them. Griffith did not engage in any talent hunts after his initial search for a leading man for *The Adventures of Dollie* produced Arthur Johnson.

15 *The Motion Picture World*, April 9, 1913.

One of Griffith's contributions that has been generally over-looked by film historians and critics is his transfer of the theatre stock-company concept to the film industry. Griffith had himself been a member of such companies, in which each player played many roles. In most instances the company was not built around a star, although Griffith had worked with some stars—Nance O'Neill, for one. But even with a star, the rest of the company was cast with great flexibility. Thus, when Griffith was given the responsibility of managing the acting company for Biograph, as well as directing their films, he used the form of theatrical organization he knew. It probably never occurred to him to engage actors for individual films. Instead, he formed a stock company. Some actors did come and go. When the company went to California, for example, a few actors were left behind, some from personal choice and others like Jeannie MacPherson because of economics. On the whole, however, the Biograph acting company was remarkably stable. Eventually, many of these actors showed a greater loyalty to Griffith personally than to Biograph by following him to Mutual. The cast of Griffith's first completed film after leaving Biograph, *The Battle of the Sexes* (released April 12, 1914), included Lillian Gish, Owen Moore, Donald Crisp, and Bobby Harron. Blanche Sweet and Mae Marsh appeared in Griffith's next film, *The Escape* (released June 1, 1914), along with Moore, Crisp, and Harron. Griffith's third film, *Home Sweet Home* (released May 17, 1914), was almost a reunion film, as it included Henry Walthall and Edward Dillon in addition to Moore, Lillian Gish, Mae Marsh, and Blanche Sweet. Before Griffith's formation of the stock company for films, there was no comparable structure in the industry. Griffith himself had made the rounds of the various companies with headquarters in New York. After Griffith, the stock company became an integral part of the industry, lasting through the twenties, thirties, and forties, until the arrival of television as a competitive force around 1948. Then the large motion-picture producers—Metro-Goldwyn-Mayer, Twentieth Century-Fox, Warner Brothers, Columbia Pictures, and Paramount, along with others—began releasing their contract players.

The nature of Griffith's development of crosscutting for parallel action and suspense has been mentioned. Rhythm in film construction was not a conscious concern for him. Eisenstein was quite right in saying that "the School of Griffith before all else is a school of tempo." But rhythm is an intrinsic factor in any film. Even the worst motion picture establishes some sort of rhythm through the juxtaposition of the various elements that go into it: the degrees of light and shade from shot to shot; the different lengths of the shots; the types of shots—long shots, medium shots, close shots, closeups; and even, within a framework closely identified with Eisenstein and the Soviet film directors, the ideological content. The Griffith films show an increasing awareness of all these elements and the effects that they will achieve if arranged in specific patterns. Griffith establishes a firm and obvious rhythm in *A Corner in Wheat* that is based on the ideological content of each shot. There is more than a dualism in the editing. He not only uses contrasting shots of the speculator and the farmer but also shows the impact of the action on the city dwellers and on the other participants in the grain market.

The repetitive shots in *The Unchanging Sea,* where the camera setup was kept the same but the composition and lighting slightly altered, strongly establish a rhythm but do not basically alter the tempo. Where tempo was a prime consideration, as in a typical "last-minute rescue" sequence, the variation of shot lengths was quite obviously calculated for an emotional effect enhanced by rhythm. Tempo alone could have been achieved by simply shortening each shot until the climax was reached. Griffith varied the shot lengths, however, sometimes lengthening them in the middle of the sequence. The overall effect was an increase in tempo.

In *The Lonedale Operator* Griffith uses sixty-six shots to build the final sequence from the moment Blanche Sweet realizes she is in danger. Griffith enhances the feeling of danger by using a series of short shots, ranging in screen time from one and three-quarters of a second to six seconds. As Blanche tries to summon help with the telegraph, Griffith introduces another series of short shots, ranging from two seconds to five seconds. Then he breaks the rhythm with a long shot, thirteen seconds, of the potential rescuers idling in a distant freight yard. This is followed by a three-second shot of Blanche still trying to summon help. Griffith then devotes ten seconds to showing the tramps successfully breaking down the door. When the rescuers finally learn of Blanche's danger, Griffith picks up the tempo again with another sequence of short shots. He changes the rhythm once during the ride to the rescue, however, by inserting a twenty-four-second shot of the interior of the train's cab—the longest shot in the entire sequence. The last shots then grow progressively shorter: four seconds, three seconds, two and a half seconds, and two seconds. The actual rescue runs for eighteen seconds, followed by slightly more than three seconds for the closeup of Blanche's hand holding the silver wrench, and the closing shot in the film runs for fifteen seconds. As this analysis indicates, Griffith's technique of building suspense involved not only tempo but a fairly complicated rhythmic structure. The shot of the interior of the engine is the longest shot of the film and falls in the middle of the sequence, but its length does not slow down the pace, because of the frantic action within the cab.

Griffith's use of rhythmic structure during the Biograph period was quite elementary, but it does show a strong intuitive sense of visual rhythm at work.

Griffith's contribution to film length is of small importance. He was not the first to conceive of a screen narrative that would require more than one reel. Griffith was the first, as far as can be determined, to insist that a motion picture with more than one reel should be shown continuously as an entity. And he was the first to have this goal realized, with the two parts of *Enoch Arden*. By the time Griffith made *Judith of Bethulia*, his longest film of the Biograph period (four reels), other producers had entered the market with even longer films. It is of little significance to claim that Griffith was the first to make an American film of four reels. In the world of the silent film, in which the language barrier was nonexistent for all practical purposes (titles didn't really count for very much), such a chauvinistic distinction means little. It meant even less in 1913.

Upon his departure from Biograph, Griffith entered into a series of production relationships that still gave him a high degree of personal control over his projects. He became the first of the independent producers, antedating a trend that would not become general until the fall of the major studios in the fifties. Griffith managed, for almost twenty years more, to maintain personal independence in face of the rise of the tightly controlled stock-company structure that he had introduced. His ultimate tragedy has been best stated, perhaps, by the late James Agee:

He lived too long, and that is one of the few things that is sadder than dying too soon.

There is not a man working in movies or a man who cares for them who does not owe Griffith more than he owes anybody else.

Agee's words were written in 1948. The film studios were declining, but they had not fallen. The rise of the independent producer and production was just beginning. It might be argued now that Griffith's tragedy was that he did not live long enough. At seventy-three, he died too soon.

Bibliography

I. UNPUBLISHED MATERIAL

Biograph Bulletins, March 2, 1907, to November 7, 1912.
Biograph Authors' Records, 1910 to 1916.
Biograph Cameraman's Record Book, 1903 to 1912.
Biograph Cameramen's Assignment Book, 1903 to 1912.
Bitzer, G. W. Unpublished notes and conversations. The Museum of Modern Art Film Library, New York.
Byrne, Richard Burdick. "German Cinematic Expressionism," unpublished Ph.D. dissertation, State University of Iowa, 1962.
Chenoweth, Stuart C. "A Study of the Adaptation of Acting Technique from Stage to Film, Radio, and Television Media in the United States, 1900-1951," unpublished Ph.D. dissertation, Northwestern University, 1957.
Gregory, John Robert. "Some Psychological Aspects of Motion Picture Montage," unpublished Ph.D. dissertation, University of Illinois, 1961.
Griffith, David Wark. Unpublished memoir and notes for a projected autobiography. The Museum of Modern Art Film Library, New York.
———. *The Fool and the Girl,* unpublished manuscript play, Rare Books Division, The Library of Congress, Washington, D.C.
———. *War,* unpublished manuscript play, The Museum of Modern Art Film Library, New York.
Highlander, James Lee. "Daniel Frohman and the Lyceum Theatre," unpublished Ph.D. dissertation, University of Illinois, 1960.
Kuiper, John Bennett. "An Analysis of the Four Silent Films of Sergei Mikhailovich Eisenstein," unpublished Ph.D. dissertation, State University of Iowa, 1960.
McCaffrey, Donald William. "An Investigation of Three Feature-Length

Silent Film Comedies Starring Harold Lloyd," unpublished Ph.D. dissertation, State University of Iowa, 1962.

McCray, William Edward. "The Place of Robert Emmett Sherwood in American Drama," unpublished Ph.D. dissertation, School of Education, New York University, 1963.

Predmore, Lester. A taped interview with the author, May 1, 1965, Middletown, New York.

Sanderson, Richard Arlo. "A Historical Study of the Development of American Motion Picture Content and Techniques Prior to 1904," unpublished Ph.D. dissertation, Indiana University, 1961.

Sweet, Blanche. A taped interview with the author, June 17, 1965, New York.

Tyro, John Henry. "A Comparative Analysis of Motion Picture Production Courses Offered in Selected Colleges and Universities in the United States," unpublished Ph.D. dissertation, Indiana University, 1961.

II. BOOKS

Agee, James. *Agee on Film*. New York: McDowell, Obolensky Co., 1958. 432 pp.

Agnew, Francis. *Motion Picture Acting*. New York: Reliance Newspaper Syndicate, 1913. 243 pp.

Arnheim, Rudolph. *Film*. London: Roy Ltd., 1953. 230 pp.

Balazs, Bela. *Theory of the Film*. London: Roy Ltd., 1953. 291 pp.

Ball, Eustace Hale. *The Art of the Photoplay*. New York: G. W. Dillingham Company, 1913. 226 pp.

Bardeche, Maurice and Robert Brassillach. *The History of Motion Pictures*. New York: W. W. Norton and The Museum of Modern Art, 1938. 412 pp.

Barry, Iris. *D. W. Griffith: American Film Master*. New York: The Museum of Modern Art, 1940. 40 pp.

———. *Let's Go to the Movies*. London: Payson & Clarke, 1926. 278 pp.

Barry, Iris and Eileen Bowser. *D. W. Griffith: American Film Master*. Revised edition, 1965. 88 pp.

Bernique, Jean. *Motion Picture Acting*. Chicago: Producer's Service Company, 1916. 252 pp.

Bloom, William J. *Soul of the Motion Picture*. New York: E. P. Dutton & Co., 1924. 248 pp.

Blum, Daniel. *A Pictorial History of the Silent Screen*. New York: G. P. Putnam's Sons, 1953. 265 pp.

DeMille, Cecil Blount. *The Autobiography of Cecil B. DeMille*. Edited by Donald Hayne. Englewood Cliffs, N.J.: Prentice-Hall, Inc., 1959. 348 pp.

Eisenstein, Sergei Mikhailovich. *Film Form*. Translated by Jay Leyda. New York: Harcourt, Brace, Inc., 1948. 279 pp.

――――. *Film Sense*. Translated by Jay Leyda. New York: Harcourt, Brace, Inc., 1942. 282 pp.

Fenin, George N., and William K. Everson. *The Western*. New York: Orion Press, 1962. 362 pp.

Fischer, Edward. *The Screen Arts*. New York: Sheed and Ward, 1960. 184 pp.

Franklin, Joseph. *Classics of the Silent Screen*. New York: Citadel Press, 1959. 255 pp.

Freeburg, V. C. *Art of Photoplay Making*. New York: Macmillan, 1918. 158 pp.

Fulton, Albert R. *Motion Pictures, The Development of an Art*. Norman: The University of Oklahoma Press, 1960. 320 pp.

Goodman, Ezra. *Fifty Year Decline and Fall of Hollywood*. New York: Macfadden, Bartell Corp., 1957. 312 pp.

Griffith, Linda Arvidson. *When the Movies Were Young*. New York: E. P. Dutton Co., 1925. 227 pp.

Griffith, Richard, and Mayer, Arthur. *The Movies*. New York: Simon & Schuster, 1957. 442 pp.

Hall, R. A. *Art of the Silent Motion Picture*. San Juan, Puerto Rico: Privately published, 1939. 176 pp.

Hampton, Benjamin B. *A History of the Movies*. New York: Simon & Schuster, 1957. 442 pp.

Hendricks, Gordon. *Beginnings of the Biograph*. New York: The Beginnings of the American Film, 1964. 78 pp.

――――. *Edison Motion Picture Myth*. Berkeley: University of California Press, 1963. 225 pp.

Huff, Theodore. *A Shot Analysis of D. W. Griffith's The Birth of a Nation*. New York: The Museum of Modern Art, 1961. 62 pp.

Hulfish, David S. *Motion Picture Work*. Chicago: American School of Correspondence, 1913. 182 pp.

Jacobs, Lewis. *The Rise of the American Film*. New York: Harcourt, Brace Inc., 1939. 585 pp.

――――, ed. *Introduction to the Art of the Movies*. New York: Farrar, Straus and Giroux, 1960. 302 pp.

Knight, Arthur. *The Liveliest Art*. New York: Macmillan, 1957. 383 pp.

Lewin, William and Alexander Frazier. *Standards of Photoplay Appre-*

ciation. Summit, N.J.: Educational and Recreational Guides, Inc., 1957. 195 pp.

Leyda, Jay. *Kino.* London: G. Allen & Unwin, 1960. 493 pp.

Lindgren, Ernest. *The Art of the Film.* London: G. Allen & Unwin, 1948. 242 pp.

————. *A Picture History of the Cinema.* London: Vista, 1960. 160 pp.

Lindsay, N. Vachel. *The Art of the Moving Picture.* New York: Macmillan, 1915. 289 pp.

Long, Robert E. *David Wark Griffith, A Brief Sketch of His Career.* New York: The Museum of Modern Art, 1946. 38 pp.

Low, Rachel. *The History of the British Film.* Vol. I & II. London: G. Allen & Unwin, 1948. 448 pp.

Milne, Peter. *Motion Picture Directing.* New York: Falk, 1922. 234 pp.

Montgomery, John. *Comedy Films.* London: G. Allen & Unwin, 1954. 337 pp.

Nicoll, Allardyce. *Film and Theatre.* New York: T. Y. Crowell Co., 1936. 265 pp.

Noble, Peter. *Hollywood Scapegoat.* London: Fortune Press, 1950. 328 pp.

Peters, Jan Marie Lambert. *Teaching about Film.* New York: Columbia University Press, 1961. 120 pp.

Phillips, Henry Albert. *The Photo Drama.* Larchmont, N. Y.: Stanhope-Didge Publishing Co., 1950. 195 pp.

Pickford, Mary. *Sunshine and Shadow.* With Cameron Shipp. New York: Doubleday & Co., 1955. 228 pp.

Powdermaker, Hortense. *Hollywood, the Dream Factory.* Boston: Little, Brown and Co., 1950. 342 pp.

Pudovkin, Vsevolod I. *Film Technique and Film Acting.* Translated by Ivor Montagu. New York: Lear, 1954. 367 pp.

Quigley, Martin Jr. *Magic Shadows.* Washington: Georgetown University Press, 1948. 191 pp.

Ramsaye, Terry. *A Million and One Nights.* New York: Simon & Schuster, 1926. 868 pp.

Rand, Helen Margaret and Richard Lewis. *Film and School.* New York: Appleton-Century, 1937. 182 pp.

Rathbun, John B. *Motion Picture Making and Exhibiting.* Chicago: Charles P. Thompson Co., 1914. 176 pp.

Rideout, E. H. *American Film.* London: Mitre Press, 1937. 346 pp.

Rotha, Paul. *Celluloid.* New York: Longman, Green & Co., 1933. 285 pp.

Rotha, Paul and Richard Griffith. *The Film Till Now*. New York: Funk & Wagnalls, 1950. 755 pp.

Schickel, Richard. *Movies*. New York: Basic Books, Inc., 1964. 208 pp.

Seldes, Gilbert. *The Seven Lively Arts*. New York: Harpers, 1924. 478 pp.

Sennett, Mack. *King of Comedy*. With Cameron Shipp. New York: Doubleday & Co., 1954. 284 pp.

Smith, Albert E., and P. A. Khoury. *Two Reels and a Crank*. New York: Doubleday & Co., 1952. 285 pp.

Spottiswoode, Raymond. *Grammar of the Film*. London: Faber & Faber, 1935. 328 pp.

Stern, Seymour. "The Bankruptcy of Cinema as Art," *The Movies on Trial*. Edited by William Perlman. New York: Macmillan, 1936. 488 pp.

Taylor, Deems; Hale Bryant; and Marceline Peterson. *A Pictorial History of the Movies*. New York: Simon & Schuster, 1950. 285 pp.

Tyler, Parker. *Hollywood Hallucination*. New York: Creative Age Press, 1944. 368 pp.

Vardac, A. Nicholas. *Stage to Screen*. Cambridge: Harvard University Press, 1949. 283 pp.

Vidor, King. *A Tree Is a Tree*. New York: Harcourt, Brace, Inc., 1953. 315 pp.

Wagenknecht, Edward Charles. *The Movies in the Age of Innocence*. Norman: University of Oklahoma Press, 1962. 280 pp.

Watkins, Gordon B., ed. *The Motion Picture Industry*. Philadelphia: The Annals of the American Academy of Political and Social Science, 1947. 236 pp.

Wood, Leslie. *The Miracle of the Movies*. London: Burke, 1947. 352 pp.

III. ARTICLES AND PERIODICALS

"Actorless Theatre," *Current Literature,* November 1909.

"After the Show," *English Journal,* November 1915.

Allen, L. "How a Moving-Picture Show is Written," *Collier's National Weekly,* November 1, 1913.

Arvidson, Linda. Untitled article, *Film Flashes* 1916.

Babin, G. "Making of Motion Pictures," *Scientific American,* July 11, 1908.

Beranger, C. F. "Photoplay—A New Kind of Drama," *Harper's Weekly,* September 7, 1912.

Berry, G. "Budget of the Movies," *Bookman,* August 1914.

"Birth of a New Art," *Independent,* April 6, 1914.

Braverman, Barnet. "Notes on Griffith's Creation of Film Forms," The American Contemporary Gallery, Hollywood, 1944.

Brewer, C. B. "Widening Field of the Moving Picture," *The Century Magazine,* May 1913.

Bush, W. Stephen. "History on the Screen," *The Moving Picture World,* February 22, 1913.

———. "Lecture on Three Reel Production," *The Moving Picture World,* October 7, 1911.

———. "New Functions of the M. P.," *The Moving Picture World,* July 6, 1912.

———. "The Film of the Future," *The Moving Picture World,* September 26, 1908.

"Cinematograph Craze," *Dial,* February 16, 1914.

Cocks, O. G. "Moving Pictures as a Factor in Municipal Life," *National Municipal Review,* October 1914.

Coffin, H. L. "Movies on the Move," *Everybody's Magazine,* October 1912.

Collier, J. "Cheap Amusements," *Charities and the Commons,* April 11, 1908.

———. "Light on Moving Pictures," *Survey,* October 1, 1910.

———. "Film Shows and Lawmakers," *Survey,* February 8, 1913.

"Commentary on Biograph Films," *The New York Dramatic Mirror,* May 1909.

"Conversation with Lillian Gish," *Sight and Sound* (London), Vol. 27, No. 3, Winter 1957.

Currie, B. W. "Nickel Madness," *Harper's Weekly,* August 27, 1907.

"David W. Griffith, the Art Director and His Work," *The Moving Picture World,* November 22, 1913.

"Dehumanizing the Stage," *Current Opinion,* April 1913.

Dunbar, O. H. "The Lure of the Films," *Harper's Monthly Magazine,* January 1913.

Dyer, Peter John. "The Decline of a Mandarin," *Sight and Sound* (London), Vol. 28, 1958–1959.

Eaton, W. P. "Canned Drama," *American Mercury,* September 1909.

———. "New Epoch in the Movies," *American Mercury,* October 1914.

Frohman, Daniel. "Movies and the Theatre," *Women's Home Companion,* November 1913.

Gordon, Henry Stephen. "The Story of D. W. G.," *Photoplay,* July, August, October, November 1916.

Grau, R. "Actors by Proxy: Artists and Managers and the Big Profits of the Record and Film," *Independent,* July 17, 1913.

——. "Fortunes in the Moving Picture Field," *The Overland Monthly,* April 1911.

"Great Plays in the Movies," *Literary Digest,* August 2, 1913.

Griffith, David Wark. "The Miracle of Modern Photography," *The Mentor,* Vol. 9, No. 6, July 1921.

——. "Are Motion Pictures Destructive of Good Taste?" *Arts and Decoration,* September 1923.

——. "Pictures versus One Night Stands," *The Independent,* December 11, 1916.

——. "What I Demand of Movie Stars," *Motion Picture Classic,* February 1917.

——. "The Real Truth about Breaking into the Movies," *Women's Home Companion,* February 1924.

——. "The Motion Picture Today—and Tomorrow," *Theatre Magazine,* October 1929.

——. "How Do You Like the Show?" *Collier's,* April 24, 1926.

——. "An Old Timer Advises Hollywood," *Liberty,* June 17, 1939.

Hamilton, Clayton. "Art of the Moving-Picture Play," *Bookman,* January 1911.

"How Miracles are Performed in Moving Pictures," *Current Literature,* September 1908.

"Illusions of the Cinematograph," *Literary Digest,* May 11, 1912.

Johnston, W. A. "Silent Stage Actors Who Pose for Motion Pictures," *Harper's Weekly,* November 13, 1909.

Jump, H. A. "Social Influence of the Moving Picture," *Playground,* June 1911.

Kallen, Horace M. "The Dramatic Picture versus the Pictorial Drama," *Harvard Monthly,* March 1910.

"Making the Most of Moving Pictures," *Women's Home Companion,* April 1912.

Moses, Montrose J. "Where They Perform Shakespeare for Five Cents," *Theatre Magazine,* October 1908.

"Motion Picture Industry," *World's Work,* May 1913.

"Motion Picture Town," *Literary Digest,* November 23, 1912.

"Motion Pictures," *Mentor,* July 1921.

"Moving Pictures Ad Nauseam," *Review of Reviews,* December 1908.

Moving Picture World, The. All issues, from 1908 to 1914.

Mullelt, M. B. "Greatest Moving Picture Producer in the World," *American Mercury,* April 1921.

Musson, B. and R. Grau. "Fortunes in Films, Moving Pictures in the Making," *McClure's,* December 1912.

"New Methods in Motion Pictures," *Survey*, September 1913.

New York Dramatic Mirror, The. Issues from 1907 to 1914.

New York Times, The. Issues from 1908 to date.

"Picture Plots," *New England Magazine*, December 1912.

"Pictures vs. One-Night Stands," *Independent*, December 1916.

Pierce, L. F. "Nickelodeon," *World To-day*, October 1908.

"Pippa Passes," A review, *The New York Times*, October 9, 1909.

"Plays Without Words," *Scribner's Magazine*, July 1909.

"Portrait," *Current Opinion*, April 1915.

"Portrait," *Ladies' Home Journal*, December 1920.

Pratt, George. "In the Nick of Time, D. W. Griffith and the Last Minute Rescue," *Image*, Vol. 6, No. 3, May 2, 1959.

"Review of New and Important Motion Pictures," *Independent*, April 6 and 27, 1914.

"Shaw's Unqualified Approval of the Cinematograph," *Current Opinion*, August 1914.

Shibuk, Charles. "Cinemania," *Films in Review*, Vol. XI, No. 2, February 1960.

Skolsky, Sidney. Syndicated column, *New York Post*, January 4, 1965.

————. Syndicated column, *New York Post*, April 27, 1959.

Smith, Frederick James. "He Might Be the Richest Man in the World," *Photoplay*, December 1926.

Smither, Nelle Kroger. "A History of the English Theatre at New Orleans, 1806–1842," published Ph.D. dissertation, *The Louisiana Historical Quarterly*, Vol. 28, Nos. 1-2, January–April 1945.

Sterling, Philip. "Billy Bitzer, Ace Cameraman," *New Theatre*, April 1937.

Stern, Seymour. "Griffith, Pioneer of Film Art," *The New York Times*, November 10, 1948.

————. "An Index to the Creative Work of D. W. Griffith," *Index Series*, British Film Institute, Nos. 2, 4, 7, 8, 10, April 1944.

————. "The Griffith Controversy," *Sight and Sound* (London), Vol 7, 1948.

————. "11 East 14th Street," *Films in Review*, Vol. 3, 1952.

————. "The Cold War against D. W. Griffith," *Films in Review*, Vol. 7, 1956.

————. "Biographical Hogwash," *Films in Review*, Vol. 10, 1959.

————. "The Soviet Director's Debt to D. W. Griffith," *Films in Review*, Vol. 10, 1959.

"Sweetness and Light from the Cinematograph?" *Spectator*, August 2, 1913.

Tapley, E. P. "Scenes from Literary Masterpieces," *Journal of Education*, February 5, 1914.

"Terms Used in Production of Non-Theatrical Motion Pictures," *Journal of the University Film Producers Association*, Vol. 12, No. 2, Winter 1960.

Townsend, E. W. "Picture Plays," *Outlook*, November 27, 1909.

"Tricks in Motion Pictures," *Literary Digest*, March 21, 1914.

"Tricks in Motion Pictures," *American Mercury*, July 1913.

"Tricks of the Moving Picture Maker," *Scientific American*, January 26, 1909.

Tully, James. "D. W. Griffith," *Vanity Fair*, November 1926.

Wallin, J. E. W. "Moving Picture in Relation to Education, Health, Delinquency, and Crime," *Pedagogic Seminar*, June 1910.

Walsh, George Ethelbert. "Moving Picture Drama for the Multitude," *Independent*, February 6, 1908.

Waters, T. "Out with the Moving-Picture Machine," *Cosmopolitan*, January 1906.

Willey, D. A. "Theatre's New Rival," *Lippincott's*, October 1909.

Willows, M. "Nickel Theatre and Children," *National Child Labor Proceedings*, 1911.

Woolley, Edward Martin. "$100,000 Salary Man of the Movies," *McClure's*, September 1914.

"Youth, the Spirit of the Movies," *Illustrated World*, October 1921.

Appendices

LIST OF FILMS

The following list presents in compact form the record of films directed by David Wark Griffith while employed by The American Mutoscope and Biograph Company, afterward The Biograph Company, from June 1908 to October 1913.

The films are listed in the order of their production. Dates not enclosed in parentheses are the production dates; dates enclosed in parentheses are release dates. The length of the film is given in linear ~~feet~~ for released films, or, where footage is unknown, the number of reels is given in parentheses (1). The name of the cameraman is given next, then a brief classification of film type, and finally the place(s) of production. The following entry is an example:

> *The Greaser's Gauntlet;* 7.14,15; (8.11;08); 1027; Marvin; (Spanish Action). Studio, Shadyside, N.J.

According to the record, *The Greaser's Gauntlet* was filmed on July 14 and 15 for the year indicated at the head of the group. The film was released on August 11, 1908, in a finished length of 1,027 feet. The cameraman was Arthur Marvin; the film was an action picture in a Spanish setting; and it was filmed at the studio, 11 East Fourteenth Street, and at Shadyside, New Jersey.

1908

The Adventures of Dollie; 6.18,19; (7.14;08); 713; Marvin; (Contemporary Action—Gypsy); Studio, Sound Beach, Conn.

The Redman and the Child; 6.30; 7.3; (7.28;08); 857; Marvin; (Indian Action); Passaic River, Little Falls, N. J.

The Tavern Keeper's Daughter; 7.2,13; (7.24;08); 410; Marvin; (Mexican Bandit Action); Studio.

The Bandit's Waterloo; 7.6,8; (8.4;08); 738; Marvin; (Spanish Bandit Action); Studio.

A Calamitous Elopement; 7.9,11; (8.7;08); 738; Bitzer; (Farce Contemporary); Studio.

The Greaser's Gauntlet; 7.14,15; (8.11;08); 1027; Marvin; (Mexican Action); Studio, Shadyside, N. J.

The Man and the Woman; 7.17,18; (8.14;08); 776; Marvin, Bitzer; (Contemporary Temperance); Studio, Fort Lee, N. J.

For Love of Gold; 7.21; (8.21;08); 548; Marvin; (Thieves—Crime); Studio.

The Fatal Hour; 7.21,27; (8.18;08); 832; Marvin; (Contemporary— Gangster); Studio, Fort Lee, N. J.

For a Wife's Honor; 7.28,30; (8.28;08); 474; Marvin; (Contemporary Domestic Triangle); Studio.

Balked at the Altar; 7.29,30; (8.25;08); 703; Marvin; (Contemporary Farce); Studio, Fort Lee, N. J.

The Girl and the Outlaw; 7.31; 8.2,4; (9.8;08); 835; Marvin; (Western Action); Fort Lee, N. J.

The Red Girl; 8.1,12; (9.15;08); 1014; Marvin; (Mexican Indian Action); Little Falls, N. J.

Betrayed by a Hand Print; 8.6,19; (9.1;08); 833; Marvin, Bitzer; (Contemporary Burglary); Studio.

Monday Morning in a Coney Island Police Court; 8.7; (9.4;08); 414; Bitzer; (Contemporary Farce); Studio.

Behind the Scenes; 8.10,13; (9.11;08); 530; Marvin; (Contemporary Theatre Melodrama); Studio.

The Heart of Oyama; 8.14; (9.18;08); 881; Marvin; (Japanese Romantic Melodrama); Studio.

Where the Breakers Roar; 8.21,25; (9.22;08); 556; Bitzer, Marvin; (Contemporary Seaside Melodrama); Studio, Central Park.

The Stolen Jewels; 8.24; 9.15; (9.28;08); 630; Bitzer; (Contemporary Child Centered Melodrama); Studio, New York Curb Exchange.

A Smoked Husband; 8.26,27; (9.25;08); 470; Bitzer: (Contemporary Domestic Farce); Studio, West 12th Street, New York City.

The Zulu's Heart; 8.28,29; (10.6;08); 776; Bitzer; (South African Action); Cliffside, N. J.

The Vaquero's Vow; 8.31; 9.1; (10.16;08); 805; Bitzer; (Mexican Romance Action); Studio.

Father Gets in the Game; 9.3,4; (10.10;08); 604; Bitzer; (Contemporary Situation Comedy); Studio, Central Park.

The Barbarian, Ingomar; 9.5,8; (10.13;08); 806; Bitzer; (Roman Melodrama Romance); Cos Cob, Conn.

The Planter's Wife; 9.9,10; (10.20;08); 865; Bitzer; (Contemporary Triangle Action); Studio, Little Falls, N. J.

The Devil; 9.12; (10.2;08); 570; Bitzer; (Contemporary Triangle); Studio.

Romance of a Jewess; 9.15,25; (10.23;08); 964; Bitzer; (Contemporary Jewish Melodrama); Studio.

The Call of the Wild; 9.17,25; (10.27;08); 988; Marvin; (Indian Action); Coytesville, N. J.

After Many Years; 9.22; 10.8,10; (11.3;08); 1033; Marvin, Bitzer; (Seaside Melodrama); Sea Bright, Atlantic Highlands, N. J.

Mr. Jones at the Ball; 9.23,24; (12.25;08); 503; Bitzer; (Situation Comedy); Studio.

Concealing a Burglar; 9.26,28; (10.30;08); 663; Bitzer; (Contemporary Triangle); Studio.

Taming of the Shrew; 10.1,7; (11.10;08); 1048; Marvin, Bitzer; (Elizabethan Farce); Studio, Coytesville, N. J.

The Ingrate; 10.2,28; 11.2; (11.20;08); 893; Bitzer, Marvin; (Canadian Triangle Action); Studio, Cos Cob, Conn.

A Woman's Way; 10.3,6; (11.24;08); 676; Marvin; (Canadian Woods Action); Coytesville, N. J., Little Falls, N. J.

The Pirate's Gold; 10.8,10; (11.6;08); 966; Marvin, Bitzer; (17th-Century Action Melodrama); Sea Bright, N. J., Studio.

The Guerrilla; 10.12,14; (11.13;08); 898; Marvin, Bitzer; (Civil War Action); Studio, Coytesville, N. J.

The Curtain Pole; 10.16,22; (2.15;09); 765; Bitzer; (Contemporary Farce); Fort Lee, N. J., Studio.

The Song of the Shirt; 10.19,20; (11.17;08); 638; Bitzer; (Contemporary Shirt Factory Melodrama); Studio.

The Clubman and the Tramp; 10.21,29; 11.16; (11.27;08); 994; Bitzer; (Contemporary Farce); West 12th Street, NYC, Studio.

Money Mad; 10.28; 11.2,16; (12.4;08); 684; Bitzer; (Contemporary Miser Melodrama); Studio.

Mrs. Jones Entertains; 10.31; 11.2; (12.8;08); 635; Bitzer; (Contemporary Situation Comedy); Studio.

The Feud and the Turkey; 11.4,6,17; (12.8;08); 904; Marvin, Bitzer; (Contemporary Kentucky Romance); Studio, Shadyside, N. J.

The Test of Friendship; 11.6,25; (12.15;08); 775; Bitzer; (Contemporary Factory Melodrama); Studio, Hoboken, N. J.

The Reckoning; 11.9,10; (12.11;08); 462; Bitzer; (Contemporary Triangle Melodrama); Studio, Hoboken, N. J.

One Touch of Nature; 11.13,18; (1.1;09); 724; Marvin; (Contemporary Child Centered Melodrama); Studio.

An Awful Moment; 11.19,21; (12.18;08); 737; Marvin; (Contemporary Gypsy Melodrama); Studio.

The Helping Hand; 11.23,27; (12.29;08); 879; Marvin; (Contemporary Melodrama); Central Park, NYC.

The Maniac Cook; 11.25,27; (1.4;09); 533; Bitzer; (Contemporary Child Centered Melodrama); Studio.

The Christmas Burglars; 11.28,30; (12.22;08); 679; Bitzer; (Situation Comedy Contemporary); Studio, 8th Avenue and 14th, NYC.

A Wreath in Time; 12.1,8; (2.8;09); 558; Bitzer; (Contemporary Show Business Farce); Studio, 8th Avenue and 14th Street, NYC.

The Honor of Thieves; 12.4,10; (1.11;09); 681; Bitzer; (Contemporary Crime Melodrama); Hudson Street, NYC, Studio.

The Criminal Hypnotist; 12.8,21; (1.18;09); 626; Bitzer; (Crime Melodrama Contemporary); Studio.

The Sacrifice; 12.11,21; (1.14;09); 438; Bitzer; (Romantic Comedy); Studio.

The Welcome Burglar; 12.11,12,29; (1.25;09); 790; Bitzer; (Contemporary Triangle); Studio, Fort Lee, N. J.

A Rural Elopement; 12.16; (1.14;09); 546; Bitzer; (Romantic Comedy); Coytesville, N. J.

Mr. Jones Has a Card Party; 12.17,23; (1.21;09); 583; Bitzer; (Situation Comedy); Studio, Grand Central Terminal.

The Hindoo Dagger; 12.23,29; (3.11;09); 583; Bitzer; (Mystery Melodrama); Studio, Fort Lee, N. J.

The Salvation Army Lass; 12.26,28; 1.27; 2.18; (3.11;09); 926; Bitzer, Marvin; (Slum Melodrama); Studio, Fort Lee, N. J.

Love Finds a Way; 12.31; 1.4; (1.11;09); 319; Marvin, Bitzer; (Medieval Comedy); Studio.

Tragic Love; 12.28,30; 1.12; (2.11;09); 893; Marvin, Bitzer; (Contemporary Murder Melodrama); Studio, Fort Lee, N. J.

The Girls and Daddy; 12.31; 1.1,14; (2.1;09); 901; Marvin, Bitzer; (Contemporary Child Centered Melodrama); Fort Lee, N. J., Studio.

1909

Those Boys; 1.5; (1.18;09); 342; Bitzer, Marvin; (Contemporary Child Centered Comedy); Studio.

The Cord of Life; 1.6,8,13; (1.28;09); 857; Bitzer, Marvin; (Sicilian-American Melodrama); Studio.

Trying to Get Arrested; 1.13; 2.26; (4.5;09); 344; Bitzer, Marvin; (Contemporary Comedy); Palisades, N. J.

The Fascinating Mrs. Frances; 1.9; (1.21;09); 417; Bitzer; (Contemporary Farce); Studio.

Those Awful Hats; 1.11; (1.25;09); 185; Bitzer; (Contemporary Farce); Studio.

Jones and the Lady Book Agent; 1.12,14,20; (5.20;09); 585; Bitzer; (Situation Comedy); Studio.

The Drive for Life; 1.15; 3.23,30; (4.22;09); 940; Marvin, Bitzer; (Contemporary Automobile Melodrama); Fort Lee, N. J.

The Brahma Diamond; 1.14,19; (2.4;09); 1036; Bitzer; (Contemporary Indian Melodrama); Studio.

Politician's Love Story; 1.18,19; (2.22;09); 526; Marvin, Bitzer; (Contemporary Comedy); Central Park, NYC.

The Jones Have Amateur Theatricals; 1.19,20; (2.18;09); 400; Bitzer; (Situation Comedy); Studio.

Edgar Allen Poe; 1.21,23; (2.8;09); 450; Bitzer; (Mid-19th-Century Melodrama); Studio.

The Roue's Heart; 1.23,24; (3.8;09); 755; Bitzer; (Renaissance Romance); Studio.

His Wife's Mother; 1.25,26; (3.1;09); 523; Marvin; (Situation Comedy); Bleecker Street, NYC.

The Golden Louis; 1.28,29; (2.22;09); 474; Marvin; (French Renaissance Melodrama); Bleecker Street, NYC.

His Ward's Love; 1.29; (2.15;09); 235; Bitzer; (Contemporary Romance); Studio.

At the Altar; 1.30; 2.8; (2.25;09); 972; Bitzer, Marvin; (Italian Melodrama); Edgewater, N. J.

The Prussian Spy; 2.1; (3.1;09); 465; Bitzer; (1870 Franco-Prussian War Melodrama); Studio.

The Medicine Bottle; 2.3,4,10,16; (3.29;09); 472; Bitzer; (Child Centered Contemporary Melodrama); Studio.

The Deception; 2.5,6; (3.22;09); 653; Bitzer; (Contemporary Romance); Studio.

The Lure of the Gown; 2.9,10,18; (3.15;09); 547; Marvin, Bitzer; (Italian Contemporary Romance); Fort Lee, N. J.

Lady Helen's Escapade; 2.10,11; (4.19;09); 765; Bitzer; (Contemporary Romance); Studio, Fort Lee, N. J.

A Fool's Revenge; 2.11,12; (3.4;09); 1000; Bitzer; (Renaissance Melodrama); Studio.

The Wooden Leg; 2.13,19; (3.8;09); 240; Marvin, Bitzer; (Contemporary Tramp Comedy); Studio.

I Did It, Mama; 2.15; (3.15;09); 372; Bitzer; (Child Centered Comedy); Studio.

A Burglar's Mistake; 2.16,18; 3.3,5; (3.25;09); 959; Bitzer, Marvin; (Contemporary Blackmail Melodrama); Studio.

The Voice of the Violin; 2.19,23; (3.18;09); 978; Bitzer, Marvin; (Socialist Bomb Plot Melodrama); West 12th Street, NYC, Studio.

And a Little Child Shall Lead Them; 2.22,24; (3.22;09); 340; Bitzer; (Domestic Drama); Studio.

The French Duel; 2.23; 3.11; (5.10;09); 407; Bitzer, Marvin; (Louis XIII Farce); Studio, Coytesville, N. J.

Jones and His New Neighbors; 2.24,25; (3.29;09); 472; Bitzer; (Situation Comedy); Studio, Perry Street, New York.

A Drunkard's Reformation; 2.25,27; 3.1; (4.1;09); Bitzer; (Temperance Melodrama); Studio.

The Winning Coat; 3.2; (4.12;09); 767; Bitzer; (Louis XIII Action); Studio.

A Rude Hostess; 3.3; (4.8;09); 439; Bitzer; (Comedy Melodrama Contemporary); Studio.

The Road to the Heart; 3.4,5; (4.5;09); 618; Marvin; (Mexican Situation Comedy); Studio.

The Eavesdropper; 3.5,8; (5.3;09); 644; Bitzer, Marvin; (Mexican Romance); Studio.

Schneider's Anti-noise Crusade; 3.8,9; (4.8;09); Marvin, Bitzer; (Contemporary Farce); Studio.

Twin Brothers; 3.10,12; (4.26;09); 437; Marvin; (Contemporary Farce); Studio.

Confidence; 3.12,13,20; (4.15;09); 990; Bitzer, Marvin; (Contemporary Romance); Studio.

The Note in the Shoe; 3.13,16; (5.6;09); 711; (Contemporary Romance); Studio.

Lucky Jim; 3.17; (4.26;09); 502; Bitzer, Marvin; (Contemporary Tramp Farce); Fort Lee, N. J.

A Sound Sleeper; 3.18; (4.12;09); 214; Bitzer, Marvin; (Contemporary Tramp Farce); Fort Lee, N. J.

A Troublesome Satchel; 3.18; (4.19;09); 212; Marvin; Bitzer; (Contemporary Farce); Fort Lee, N. J.

Tis an Ill Wind That Blows No Good; 3.20,24; 4.6; (4.29:09); 876; Bitzer, Marvin; (Contemporary Comedy); Studio.

The Suicide Club; 3.25,26; (5.3;09); 368; Marvin, Bitzer; (Contemporary Farce); Studio.

Resurrection; 3.26,30; 4.23; (5.20;09); 999; Bitzer, Marvin; (Russian Drama); Studio.

One Busy Hour; 4.2; (5.6;09); 279; Bitzer, Marvin; (Contemporary Farce); Studio, Fort Lee, N. J.

A Baby's Shoe; 4.5,6,12; (5.13;09); 999; Marvin, Bitzer; (Roman Catholic Drama); Studio, Central Park, NYC.

Eloping with Auntie; 4.6,7,21; (5.24;09); 614; Bitzer, Marvin; (Situation Comedy); Studio.

The Cricket on the Hearth; 4.8,18,24; (5.27;09); 965; Marvin, Bitzer; (19th-Century Drama); Studio, Fort Lee, N. J.

The Jilt; 4.13,16; (5.17;09); 997; Bitzer, Marvin; (Contemporary Society Temperance Melodrama); Studio, Riverside Drive, NYC.

Eradicating Auntie; 4.15,16,28; (5.31;09); 545; Marvin, Bitzer; (Contemporary Situation Comedy); Studio, Fort Lee, N. J.

What Drink Did; 4.19,28; (6.3;09); 913; Bitzer; (Temperance Drama); Studio, Fort Lee, N. J.

Her First Biscuits; 4.20; (6.17;09); 514; Bitzer; (Contemporary Farce); Studio.

The Violin Maker of Cremona; 4.21,23; (6.7;09); 963; Bitzer; (18th-Century Drama); Studio.

Two Memories; 4.23,27; 5.1; (5.24;09); 318; Bitzer; (Contemporary Tragedy); Studio.

The Lonely Villa; 4.29,30; 5.4,6,14; (6.10;09); 750; Bitzer, Marvin; (Contemporary Melodrama); Studio, Fort Lee, N. J.

The Peach Basket Hat; 5.1,6; (6.24;09); 666; Marvin, Bitzer; (Contemporary Situation Comedy); Fort Lee, N. J., Studio.

The Son's Return; 5.5,7,8; (6.14;09); 993; Bitzer, Marvin; (Contemporary Melodrama); Studio, Leonia, N. J., Coytesville, N. J.

His Duty; 5.10,12; (5.31;09); 429; Bitzer, Marvin; (Contemporary Melodrama); Studio, Edgewater, N. J.

A New Trick; 5.11; (6.10;09); 223; Bitzer; (Contemporary Farce); Edgewater, N. J.

The Necklace; 5.12,27; (7.1;09); 969; Bitzer, Marvin; (Contemporary Melodrama); Studio.

The Way of Man; 5.13,24; (6.28;09); 986; Bitzer, Marvin; (Contemporary Tragedy); Edgewater, N. J., Studio.

The Faded Lilies; 5.15,17; (6.17;09); 481; Marvin, Bitzer; (Contemporary Unrequited Love Tragedy); Studio.

The Message; 5.15,26; 6.1; (7.5;09); 944; Marvin, Bitzer; (Contemporary Child Centered Drama); Studio, Greenwich, Conn.

The Friend of the Family; 5.17,19; (7.15;09); 773; Marvin, Bitzer; (Contemporary Child Centered Triangle); Studio.

Was Justice Served?; 5.20,21,24; (6.21;09); 962; Marvin, Bitzer; (Contemporary Courtroom Melodrama); Studio, Englewood, N. J.

Mrs. Jones' Lover, or "I Want My Hat!"; 5.27; 6.18; (8.19;09); 467; Bitzer; (Situation Comedy); Studio.

The Mexican Sweethearts; 5.28; (6.24;09); 309; Bitzer; (Mexican Romance); Studio.

The Country Doctor; 5.29,31; 6.7; (7.8;09); 942; Bitzer; (Contemporary Child Centered Melodrama); Studio, Greenwich, Conn.

Jealousy and the Man; 5.31; 6.15; (7.22;09); 418; Bitzer; (Situation Comedy); Studio, Fort Lee, N. J.

The Renunciation; 6.2,14,18; (7.19;09); 982; Bitzer, Marvin; (Western Comedy); Studio, Shadyside, N. J.

The Cardinal's Conspiracy; 6.3,4,12; (7.12;09); 999; Bitzer; (17th-Century Romance); Studio, Greenwich, Conn.

The Seventh Day; 6.5,8; (8.26;09); 693; Bitzer; (Contemporary Child Centered Divorce Drama); Studio.

Tender Hearts; 6.7,15; (7.15;09); 693; Bitzer; (Contemporary Country Romance); Greenwich, Conn., Fort Lee, N. J.

A Convict's Sacrifice; 6.10,16; (7.26;09); 977; Bitzer; (Contemporary Prison Child Centered Melodrama); Studio, Fort Lee, N. J.

A Strange Meeting; 6.11,17; (8.2;09); 967; (Contemporary Religious Melodrama); Studio.

Sweet and Twenty; 6.19,21; (7.22;09); 572; Bitzer; (Contemporary Adolescent Comedy); Studio, Greenwich, Conn.

The Slave; 6.22,23; (7.29;09); 998; Bitzer; (Roman Melodrama); Studio.

They Would Elope; 6.24,25; 7.15; (8.9;09); 572; Bitzer, Higginson; (Contemporary Comedy); Studio, Little Falls, N. J.

Mr. Jones' Burglar; 6.26; (8.9;09); 388; Marvin, Bitzer; (Contemporary Situation Comedy); Studio, Coytesville, N. J.

The Mended Lute; 6.28,29,30; 7.2; (8.5;09); 996; Bitzer; (Indian Melodrama); Cuddebackville, N. Y.

The Indian Runner's Romance; 6.29,30; 7.2,3; (8.23;09); 994; Bitzer; (Indian Melodrama); Cuddebackville, N. Y.

With Her Card; 7.7; (8.16;09); 1000; Bitzer; (Contemporary Romance); Studio.

The Better Way; 7.9,10,12; (8.12;09); 990; Bitzer; (Puritan Drama); Studio, Coytesville, N. J.

His Wife's Visitor; 7.13; (8.19;09); 526; Bitzer; (Contemporary Romance); Studio.

The Mills of the Gods; 7.17; (8.30;09); 672; Bitzer; (Contemporary Romance); Studio.

Pranks; 7.19,20,28; (8.30;09); 328; Marvin; (Contemporary Farce); Little Falls, N. J.

Oh, Uncle; 7.22,23; (8.26;09); 292; Bitzer; (Contemporary Farce); Studio.

The Sealed Room; 7.22,23; (9.2;09); 779; Bitzer; (Renaissance Melodrama); Studio.

1776, or The Hessian Renegades; 7.26; 8.2,3; (9.6;09); 965; Marvin, Bitzer; (American Revolution Melodrama); Cuddebackville, N. Y.

The Little Darling; 7.27; 8.3; (9.2;09); 211; Bitzer; (Contemporary Farce); Studio, Cuddebackville, N. Y.

In Old Kentucky; 7.29; 8.3,5,6; (9.20;09); 983; Bitzer; (Civil War Melodrama); Cuddebackville, N. Y.

The Children's Friend; 7.30; 8.12; (9.13;09); 386; Bitzer; (Contemporary Child Centered Comedy); Sea Breeze, N. J., Edgewater, N. J.

Comata, the Sioux; 8.6,7; (9.9;09); 963; Bitzer; (Indian Melodrama); Cuddebackville, N. Y.

Getting Even; 8.9,10,13; (9.13;09); 587; Bitzer; (Contemporary Comedy); Studio, Edgewater, N. J.

The Broken Locket; 8.10,11,19; (9.16;09); 999; Bitzer; (Contemporary Temperance Melodrama); Edgewater, N. J., Studio.

A Fair Exchange; 8.14,23; (9.23;09); 995; Bitzer; (18th-Century Child Centered Melodrama); Studio, Cuddebackville, N. Y.

The Awakening; 8.16,17,20; (9.30;09); 691; Bitzer; (Contemporary Romance); Studio, Edgewater, N. J.

Pippa Passes; 8.17; 21; (10.4;09); 983; Bitzer, Marvin, Higginson; (19th-Century Romance-Fantasy); Edgewater, N. J., Studio.

Leather Stockings; 8.24,25,26,27; (9.2;09); 996; Bitzer, Marvin; (Indian Scout Melodrama); Cuddebackville, N. Y.

Fools of Fate; 8.27,30; (10.7;09); 972; Bitzer; (Contemporary Melodrama); Cuddebackville, N. Y., Studio.

Wanted, a Child; 8.31; (9.30;09); 296; Bitzer; (Contemporary Child Centered Melodrama); Studio.

The Little Teacher; 9.1,3,8; (10.11;09); 982; Bitzer, Marvin; (Contemporary Comedy); Greenwich, Conn., Leonia, N. J., Studio.

A Change of Heart; 9.2,4; (10.14;09); 977; Bitzer; (Contemporary Melodrama); Studio, Greenwich, Conn.

His Lost Love; 9.7,8,10; (10.18;09); 968; Bitzer; (Contemporary Child Centered Melodrama); Studio.

Lines of White on the Sullen Sea; 9.11,18; (10.28;09); 975; Bitzer; (Seaside Melodrama); Studio, Atlantic Highlands, N. J., Gallilee, N. J.

The Gibson Goddess; 9.11,17; (11.1;09); 576; Bitzer; (Contemporary Comedy); Highlands, N. J., Studio.

In the Watches of the Night; 9.13,14,20; (11.25;09); 996; Bitzer; (Slum Melodrama); Edgewater, N. J., Studio.

The Expiation; 9.15,16; (10.21;09); 992; Bitzer; (Contemporary Romance Melodrama); Studio.

What's Your Hurry; 9.21,27; (11.1;09); 403; Bitzer; (Contemporary Situation Comedy); Fort Lee, N. J., Studio.

The Restoration; 9.22; 10.1; (11.8;09); 964; Bitzer; (Contemporary Romance); Studio, Little Falls, N. J.

Nursing a Viper; 9.24,29; (11.4;09); 920; Bitzer; (French Revolution Melodrama); Studio, Englewood, N. J.

Two Women and a Man; 9.25; 10.2,4; (11.15;09); 998; Bitzer; (Contemporary Triangle Vamp); Studio, Fort Lee, N. J.

The Light That Came; 9.30; 10.2,4; (11.11;09); 998; Bitzer; (Contemporary Romance); Studio.

A Midnight Adventure; 10.5,6,8; (11.15;09); 519; Bitzer, Marvin; (Contemporary Comedy); Studio.

The Open Gate; 10.9,12; (11.22;09); 988; Bitzer; (Contemporary Pastoral Romance); Studio, Coytesville, N. J.

Sweet Revenge; 10.11,13; (11.18;09); 471; Bitzer; (Contemporary Romance); Studio, Central Park, N. Y.

The Mountaineer's Honor; 10.14,19,20; (11.25;09); 977; Bitzer; (Kentucky Mountain Romance); Studio, Cuddebackville, N. Y.

In the Window Recess; 10.16,28; (11.29;09); 337; Bitzer; (Contemporary Convict Melodrama); Studio, Fort Lee, N. J.

The Trick That Failed; 10.23; (11.29;09); 645; Bitzer; (Contemporary Romance); Studio.

The Death Disc; 10.26,28; (12.2;09); 995; Bitzer; (Cromwellian Melodrama); Coytesville, N. J., Studio.

Through the Breakers; 10.29,30; 11.1, 10; (12.6;09); 974; Bitzer; (Contemporary Child Centered Melodrama); Edgewater, N. J., Studio.

In a Hempen Bag; 11.2,9; (12.16;09); 455; Bitzer; (Contemporary Melodrama); Studio, Edgewater, N. J.

A Corner in Wheat; 11.3,13; (12.13;09); 953; Bitzer; (Contemporary Social Melodrama); Studio, Jamaica, L. I., N. Y.

The Redman's View; 11.4,6; (12.9;09); 971; Bitzer; (Indian Melodrama); Mt. Beacon, N. Y.

The Test; 11.11,13; (12.16;09); 545; Marvin, Bitzer; (Contemporary Comedy); Studio, Coytesville, N. J.

A Trap for Santa Claus; 11.13,15,16,20; (12.20;09); Bitzer; (Contemporary Comedy); Studio, Fort Lee, N. J.

In Little Italy; 11.17,20; (12.23;09); 956; Bitzer; (Italian Melodrama); Fort Lee, N. J., Studio.

To Save Her Soul; 11.22,27; (12.27;09); 986; Bitzer, Marvin; (Contemporary Religious Romance); Studio, Fort Lee, N. J.

Choosing a Husband; 11.27; (12.30;09); 531; Bitzer; (Contemporary Comedy); Studio.

The Rocky Road; 11.29,30; 12.1,24; (1.3;10); 990; Marvin, Bitzer; (Contemporary Temperance Melodrama); Studio, Hackensack, N. J., Edgewater, N. J.

The Dancing Girl of Butte; 12.2,4; (1.10;10); 984; Bitzer; (Western Comedy); Studio, Edgewater, N. J.

Her Terrible Ordeal; 12.6,9; (1.10;10); 952; Bitzer; (Contemporary Melodrama); Studio, Fort Lee, N. J.

The Call; 12.7,8,10; (1.20;10); 989; Bitzer; (Contemporary Circus Romance); Fort Lee, N. J., Studio.

The Honor of His Family; 12.10,17,18; (1.24;10); 988; Marvin, Bitzer; (Civil War Melodrama); Coytesville, N. J., Studio.

On the Reef; 12.12,14; (1.17;10); 988; Bitzer; (Contemporary Triangle); Studio.

The Last Deal; 12.15,16; (1.27;10); 991; Bitzer; (Contemporary Gambling Melodrama); Studio.

One Night, and Then—; 12.20; (2.14;10); 992; Bitzer; (Contemporary Bohemian Melodrama); Studio.

The Cloister's Touch; 12.20,21; (1.31;10); Bitzer, Marvin; (Monastic Drama); Studio.

The Woman from Mellon's; 12.22,24; (2.3;10); 988; Bitzer; (Contemporary Romance); Studio.

The Duke's Plan; 12.27,28; (2.10;10); 985; Bitzer; (Louis XIII Melodrama); Studio.

The Englishman and the Girl; 12.31; 1.4; (2.17;10); 975; Bitzer; (Contemporary Comedy); Studio.

1910

The Final Settlement; 1.5,8; (2.28;10); 981; Bitzer, Marvin; (Contemporary Temperance Melodrama); Coytesville, N. J., Fort Lee, N. J.

His Last Burglary; 1.7; (2.21;10); 995; Bitzer; (Contemporary Child Centered Melodrama); Coytesville, N. J.

Taming a Husband; 1.10,12; (2.24;10); 986; Bitzer; (18th-Century Comedy); Studio.

The Newlyweds; 1.14,26; (3.3;10); 981; Marvin, Bitzer; (Contemporary Comedy); Studio, Los Angeles, Cal.

The Thread of Destiny; 1.28; (3.7;10); 977; Bitzer; (Mexican Romance); San Gabriel Mission, Cal.

In Old California; 2.2,3; (3.10;10); 991; Bitzer; (Spanish California Melodrama); Hollywood, Cal.

The Man; 2.4,5; (3.12;10); 983; Bitzer; (Contemporary Tragedy); Studio, Sierra Madre, Cal.

The Converts; 2.8,9; (3.14;10); 986; Bitzer; (Temperance Melodrama); Studio, San Gabriel Mission, Cal.

Faithful; 2.10,12,16; (3.21;10); 994; Marvin, Bitzer; (Contemporary Romance); Studio, Hollywood, Cal.

The Twisted Trail; 2.15,18; (3.24;10); 988; Bitzer; (Contemporary Melodrama); Sierra Madre, Cal.

Gold Is Not All; 2.18,19,21,24; (3.28;10); 988; Bitzer; (Contemporary Social Drama); Studio, Pasadena, Cal.

As It Is in Life; 2.22,23; (4.4;10); 981; Bitzer; (Contemporary Child Centered Drama); California Pigeon Farm.

A Rich Revenge; 2.25,26; (4.7;10); 980; Bitzer; (Contemporary Comedy —Oil Fields); Edendale, Cal.

A Romance of the Western Hills; 3.1,2; (4.11;10); 980; Bitzer; (Indian Melodrama); Sierra Madre, Pasadena, Cal.

Thou Shalt Not; 3.3,5,11; (4.18;10); 987; Bitzer; (Contemporary Child Centered Drama); Studio, Pasadena, Cal.

The Way of the World; 3.12,14; (4.25;10); 950; Bitzer; (Religious Drama); San Gabriel Mission, Cal., Glendale, Cal.

The Unchanging Sea; 3.16,17; (5.5;10); 952; Bitzer; (Seaside Melodrama); Santa Monica, Cal.

The Gold Seekers; 3.18,19,21; (5.2;10); 976; Bitzer, Marvin; (1849 Gold Fields Melodrama); Sierra Madre, Studio, Cal.

Love among the Roses; 3.22,23,24; (5.9;10); 983; Marvin, Bitzer; (Fairy Tale Romance); Hollywood, Cal.

The Two Brothers; 3.25,26,29; 4.4; (5.9;10); 993; Bitzer, Marvin; (18th-Century Mexican Romance); San Juan Capistrano, Cal.

Unexpected Help; 3. -; (7.28;10); 968; Bitzer; (Contemporary Oil Fields Melodrama); Cal.

An Affair of Hearts; 3.2,16,17; (5.19;10); 967; Marvin; (Contemporary Comedy); Verdugo, Cal.

Ramona; 3.30; 4.1,2; (5.23;10); 995; Bitzer; (Indian-White Romance); Peru, Cal., Camulos, Ventura County, Cal., Studio.

Over Silent Paths; 4.5,6; (5.16;10); 980; Bitzer; (Western Mining Drama); San Fernando, Cal.

The Impalement; 4.21,23,28; (5.30;10); 987; Marvin, Bitzer; (Contemporary Tragedy); Studio, Stanford, Conn.

In the Season of Buds; 4.27,28; (6.2;10); 990; Bitzer, Marvin; (Pastoral Comedy); Stanford, Conn.

A Child of the Ghetto; 4.29,30; 5.2,4; (6.6;10); 989; Marvin, Bitzer; (Slum Melodrama); Studio, Westerfield, Conn.

In the Border States; 5.3,14; (6.13;10); 990; Bitzer; (Civil War Melodrama); Studio, Delaware Water Gap, N. J.

A Victim of Jealousy; 5.6,7; (6.9;10); 987; Bitzer; (Society Melodrama); Studio.

The Face at the Window; 5.10,14; (6.16;10); 997; Bitzer; (Contemporary Child Centered Melodrama); Studio.

The Marked Time-table; 5.17,18,25; (6.23;10); 996; Bitzer; (Contemporary Melodrama); Studio.

A Child's Impulse; 5.18,26,27; (6.27;10); 994; Bitzer, Marvin; (Contemporary Child Centered Melodrama); Studio, Westfield, N. J.

Muggsy's First Sweetheart; 5.20,27; 6.3; (6.30;10); 982; Bitzer; (Contemporary Comedy); Westfield, N. J., Studio.

The Purgation; 5.24,27,28; (7.1;10); 988; Bitzer; (Contemporary Melodrama); Studio, Westerfield, Conn.

A Midnight Cupid; 6.3,4; (7.7;10); 997; Bitzer; (Contemporary Tramp Comedy); Studio, Coytesville, N. J.

What the Daisy Said; 6.8,9; (7.11;10); 987; Bitzer; (Pastoral Romance); Delaware Water Gap, N. J.

A Child's Faith; 6.7,11; (7.14;10); 986; Bitzer; (Slum Child Centered Melodrama); Studio.

The Call to Arms; 6.1,6,15,21; (7.25;10); 994; Bitzer; (Medieval Melodrama); Studio, Lambert Castle, Paterson, N. J.

Serious Sixteen; 6.8,9,13; (7.21;10); 535; Bitzer, Marvin; (Contemporary Comedy); Delaware Water Gap, N. J.

A Flash of Light; 6.14,16,17; (7.18;10); 998; Bitzer; (Contemporary Romance); Studio.

As the Bells Rang Out; 6.18; (7.21;10); 457; Bitzer; (Contemporary Melodrama); Studio.

An Arcadian Maid; 6.22,23,25; (8.1;10); 984; Bitzer; (Pastoral Melodrama); Studio, Westfield, N. J.

The House with the Closed Shutters; 6.25,27; 7.1,2; (8.8;10); (Civil War Melodrama); Coytesville, N. J., Studio.

Her Father's Pride; 6.28,29,30; (8.4;10); 996; Bitzer; (19th-Century Quaker Drama); Studio, Coytesville, N. J.

A Salutary Lesson; 7.6,8,9; (8.11;10); 980; Bitzer; (Contemporary Child Centered Drama—Seashore); Studio, Atlantic Highlands, N. J.

The Usurer; 7.10,15; (8.15;10); 994; Bitzer; (Contemporary Melodrama); Studio.

The Sorrows of the Unfaithful; 7.12,13; (8.22;10); 994; Bitzer; (Seaside Contemporary Melodrama); Studio, Atlantic Highlands, N. J.

In Life's Cycle; 7.18,21; 8,18; (9.15;10); 997; Bitzer; (Temperance Melodrama); Fort Lee, N. J., Cuddebackville, N. Y.

Wilful Peggy; 7.19,22; (8.29;10); 997; Bitzer; (18th-Century Irish Romance); Studio, Cuddebackville, N. Y.

A Summer Idyll; 7.26,27; 8.1,3; (9.5;10); 991; Bitzer; (Pastoral Romance); Cuddebackville, N. Y.

The Modern Prodigal; 7.28,30; (8.29;10); 992; Bitzer; (Contemporary Child Centered Melodrama); Cuddebackville, N. Y.

Rose O'Salem Town; 8.3,20; (9.26;10); 998; Bitzer; (Puritan Witchcraft Melodrama); Studio, Delaware Water Gap, N. J.

Little Angels of Luck; 8.5,6; (9.8;10); 998; Bitzer; (Contemporary Child Centered Drama); Studio.

A Mohawk's Way; 8.9,12; (9.12;10); 991; Bitzer; (Indian Drama); Delaware Water Gap, N. J.

The Oath and the Man; 8.16,19; (9.22;10); 997; Bitzer; (French Revolution Melodrama); Studio, Paterson, N. J.

The Iconoclast; 8.25,26; (10.3;10); 992; Bitzer; (Contemporary Printshop Melodrama); Studio.

Examination Day at School; 8.23,31; (9.29;10); 991; Bitzer; (Contemporary Comedy); Westfield, N. J., Studio.

That Chink at Golden Gulch; 8.25,31; (10.10;10); 998; Bitzer; (Western Melodrama); Cuddebackville, N. Y.

The Broken Doll; 9.2,7; (10.17;10); 997; Bitzer; (Indian Child Centered Melodrama); Coytesville, Cuddebackville, N. Y.

The Banker's Daughters; 9.8,9; (10.20;10); 989; Bitzer; (Contemporary Melodrama); Studio.

The Message of the Violin; 9.13,14; (10.24;10); 997; Bitzer; (Contemporary Romance); Studio.

Two Little Waifs; 9.16,21; (10.31;10); 997; Bitzer; (Contemporary Child Centered Melodrama); Greenwich, Conn., Studio.

Waiter No. 5; 9.19,22; (11.3;10); 997; Bitzer; (Russian Socialist Melodrama); Studio.

The Fugitive; 9.24,29; (11.7;10); 996; Bitzer; (Civil War Melodrama); Studio, Fishkill, N. Y.

Simple Charity; 9.23,27; (11.10;10); 993; Bitzer, Marvin; (Anti-"Uplifters" Melodrama); Studio, Fort Lee, N. J.

The Song of the Wildwood Flute; 10.1,17; (11.21;10); 996; Bitzer; (Indian Drama); Studio, Fishkill, N. Y., Westfield, N. J.

A Child's Strategem; 10.6,8; (12.5;10); 998; Bitzer; (Contemporary Child Centered Melodrama); Studio, Westfield, N. J.

Sunshine Sue; 10.6,8; (11.14;10); 998; Bitzer; (Contemporary Melodrama); Studio, Westfield, N. J.

A Plain Song; 10.13,17; (11.28;10); 997; Bitzer; (Contemporary Melodrama); Studio, Westfield, N. J.

His Sister-in-law; 10.14,18; (12.15;10); 998; Bitzer; (Contemporary Child Centered Melodrama); Studio, Westfield, N. J.

The Golden Supper; 10.19,29; (12.12;10); 998; Bitzer; (Italian Renaissance Romance); Studio, Greenwich, Conn.

The Lesson; 10.26,28; (12.19;10); 994; Bitzer; (Contemporary Temperance Drama); Studio, Fort Lee, N. J.

When a Man Loves; 10.22,31; (1.5;11); 998; Bitzer; (Contemporary Romance); Studio, Westfield, N. J.

Winning Back His Love; 11.1,3; (12.26;10); 994; Bitzer; (Contemporary Triangle Romance); Studio.

His Trust; 11.5,8; (1.16;11); 996; Bitzer; (Civil War Drama); Fort Lee, N. J.

His Trust Fulfilled; 11.5,18; (1.19;11); 999; Bitzer; (Civil War Drama); Fort Lee, N. J.

A Wreath of Orange Blossoms; 11.7,8,10; (1.30;11); 993; Bitzer; (Contemporary Romance); Studio.

The Italian Barber; 11.13,16; (1.9;11); 993; Bitzer; (Contemporary Comedy); Studio, Fort Lee, N. J.

The Two Paths; 11.19,22; (1.2;11); 992; Bitzer; (Contemporary Melodrama); Studio.

Conscience; 11.22,30; 1.19; (3.9;11); 995; Bitzer; (Contemporary Melodrama); Studio, NYC, Carter-Carnon, Cal.

Three Sisters; 11.26,28; (2.2;11); 997; Bitzer; (Contemporary Romance); Studio.

A Decree of Destiny; 12.2,7; (3.6;11); 995; Bitzer; (Contemporary Romance); Studio.

Fate's Turning; 12.3,6; (1.23;11); 998; Bitzer; (Contemporary Romance); Studio.

What Shall We Do with Our Old?; 12.8,16; (2.13;11); 994; Bitzer; (Social Drama); Fort Lee, N. J.

The Diamond Star; 12.10,12; (2.20;11); 996; Bitzer; (Contemporary Domestic Drama); Studio.

The Lily of the Tenements; 12.14,22; (2.27;11); 996; Bitzer; (Slum Melodrama); Studio.

Heart Beats of Long Ago; 12.19,20; (2.6;11); 997; Bitzer; (14th-Century Romance); Studio.

1911

Fisher Folks; 1.5,7; (2.16;11); 998; Bitzer; (Seaside Melodrama); Santa Monica, Cal.

His Daughter; 1.11,12; (2.23;11); 997; Bitzer; (Temperance Drama); Sierra Madre, Cal.

The Lonedale Operator; 1.14,16; (3.23;11); 998; Bitzer; (Contemporary Railroad Melodrama); Studio, Inglewood, Cal.

Was He a Coward?; 1.23,27; (3.16;11); 994; Bitzer; (Western Melodrama); El Monte, Cal.

Teaching Dad to Like Her; 1.30,31; 2.1; (3.20;11); 995; Bitzer; (Contemporary Romantic Comedy); Studio, Cal.

The Spanish Gypsy; 2.6,8; (3.30;11); 996; Bitzer; (Spanish Romance); Santa Monica, Wentworth Hotel, Cal.

The Broken Cross; 2.9,12; (4.6;11); 1041; Bitzer; (Contemporary Triangle Romance); Studio, Monte Vista, Cal.

The Chief's Daughter; 2.15,16; (4.10;11); 1048; Bitzer; (Indian-White Romance); Studio, San Fernando, San Gabriel, Cal.

A Knight of the Road; 2.17,18; (4.20;11); 1067; Bitzer; (Tramp Comedy); Sierra Madre, Cal.

Madame Rex; 2.21,22; (4.24;11); 1035; Bitzer; (Early 19th-Century Melodrama); Santa Monica, Wentworth Hotel, Old Mill, Cal., Studio.

His Mother's Scarf; 2.23,28; (4.24;11); 1013; Bitzer; (Western Romance); Studio, Santa Monica, Cal.

How She Triumphed; 3.1,4; (4.27;11); 1045; Bitzer; (Contemporary Romance); Pasadena, Cal., Studio.

In the Days of '49; 3.6,16; (5.8;11); 1033; Bitzer; (Covered Wagon Melodrama); Eaton Canyon, Cal.

The Two Sides; 3.12,13; (5.1;11); 1047; Bitzer; (Mexican-American Melodrama); Studio, San Gabriel, Cal.

The New Dress; 3.17,25; (5.15;11); 1032; Bitzer; (Mexican Romance); Studio, San Gabriel, Cal.

Enoch Arden; Part I; 3.24,28; (6.12;11); 1010; Bitzer; (Seaside Melodrama); Santa Monica, Cal.

Enoch Arden; Part II; 3.24,28; (6.14;11); 997; Bitzer; (Seaside Melodrama); Santa Monica, Cal.

The White Rose of the Wilds; 3.31; 4.8; (5.25;11); 1005; Bitzer; (Miner's Children Melodrama); Rubia Canyon, Cal.

The Crooked Road; 4.4,13; (5.22;11); 1025; Bitzer; (Contemporary Temperance Drama); Studio, Lumberyard, Cal.

A Romany Tragedy; 4.11,12; (5.29;11); 1039; Bitzer; (Corsican Gypsy Melodrama); Studio, Lookout Mountain, Cal.

A Smile of a Child; 4.17,18; (6.5;11); 1044; Bitzer; (Fairy Tale Romance); Santa Monica, Wentworth Hotel, Studio.

The Primal Call; 4.19,21; (6.22;11); 1028; Bitzer; (Seaside Romance); Redondo Beach, Studio, Cal.

The Jealous Husband; 4.22,24; (7.10;11); 1030; Bitzer; (Contemporary Triangle Comedy); Studio, Santa Monica, Cal.

The Indian Brothers; 4.28,29; (7.17;11); 1053; Bitzer; (Indian Drama); Lookout Mountain, Cal.

The Thief and the Girl; 5.1,6; (7.6;11); 1069; Bitzer; (Contemporary Reformation Melodrama); Studio, Pasadena, Cal.

Her Sacrifice; 5.4,5; (6.26;11); 1054; Bitzer; (Mexican Tragedy); Santa Monica, Wentworth Hotel, Cal.

The Blind Princess and the Poet; 5.8,9; (8.17;11); (1); Bitzer; (Fairy Tale Romance); Hollywood, Cal.

Fighting Blood; 5.11,17; (6.29;11); 1056; Bitzer; (Indian-Pioneer Action Melodrama); San Fernando, Lookout Mountain, Cal.

The Last Drop of Water; 5.14,20; (7.27;11); 1057; Bitzer; (Covered Wagon-Indian Melodrama); San Fernando-Topango Canyon, Lookout Mountain, Cal.

Bobby the Coward; 6.1,5,9; (7.13;11); 1086; Bitzer; (Slum Melodrama); Fort Lee, N. J., Studio, NYC.

A Country Cupid; 6.5,7; (7.24;11); 1080; Bitzer; (Pastoral Romance); Studio, Westfield, N. J.

The Ruling Passion; 6.10,23; 7.10; (8.7;11); 1073; Bitzer; (Contemporary Child Centered Melodrama); Bayonne, N. J., Studio.

The Rose of Kentucky; 6.13,14,29; 7.5,15; (8.24;11); 1029; Bitzer; (Contemporary Tobacco Field Romance); Hartford, Conn., Coytesville, N. J., Studio.

The Sorrowful Example; 6.23,24; (8.14;11); 1092; Bitzer; (Contemporary Domestic Triangle Melodrama); Studio, Fort Lee, N. J.

Swords and Hearts; 6.27; 7.7,18; (8.28;11); 1030; Bitzer; (Civil War Drama); Coytesville, N. J., Studio.

The Stuff Heroes Are Made of; 6.28; 7.17; (9.4;11); 1031; Bitzer; (Contemporary Child Centered Melodrama); Studio, Lynbrook, Long Island.

The Old Confectioner's Mistake; 7.10,20; (9.7;11); 1023; Bitzer; (Contemporary Child Centered Melodrama); Studio, Fort Lee, N. J.

The Unveiling; 7.13; 8.26,28; (10.16;11); 1035; Bitzer; (Contemporary Mother-Son Melodrama); Studio.

The Eternal Mother; 7.19,22,25; 8.11; (1.11;12); (1); Bitzer; (Contemporary Domestic Triangle); Coytesville, N. J., Studio.

Dan the Dandy; 7.24,27; (9.18;11); 1030; Bitzer; (Contemporary Comedy Drama); Fort Lee, N. J., Studio.

The Revenue Man and the Girl; 7.29; 8.5; (9.25;11); 1034; Bitzer; (Kentucky Mountain Drama); Cuddebackville, N. Y.

The Squaw's Love; 7.31; 8.1,3; (9.14;11); (1); Bitzer, Higginson, Mahr; (Indian Drama); Cuddebackville, N. Y.

Italian Blood; 8.8,11; (10.9;11); 1073; Bitzer; (Domestic Drama); Coytesville, N. J., Studio.

The Making of a Man; 8.14,17; (10.5;11); 1046; Bitzer; (Backstage Drama); Studio, Fort Lee, N. J.

Her Awakening; 8.21,22; (9.28;11); 1050; Bitzer; (Contemporary Moral Drama); Fort Lee, N. J., Studio.

The Adventures of Billy; 8.23,24; 9.2,3; (10.19;11); 1053; Bitzer; (Contemporary Child Centered Melodrama); Studio, Fort Lee, N. J., Westfield, N. J.

The Long Road; 8.30,31; 9.1,5; (10.26;11); 1041; Bitzer; (Slum Melodrama); Studio, Fort Lee, N. J.

The Battle; 9.8,19; (11.6;11); 1135; Bitzer; (Civil War Drama); Coytesville, N. J., Studio.

Love in the Hills; 9.21,23; (10.30;11); 1054; Bitzer; (Tennessee Mountain Drama); Suffern, N. Y.

The Trail of the Books; 9.26,30; (11.9;11); 1084; Bitzer; (Child Centered Tramp Melodrama); Studio, Fort Lee, N. J.

Through Darkened Vales; 9.28,30; 10.2,5; (11.16;11); 1047; Bitzer; (Contemporary Triangle Melodrama); Studio, Fort Lee, N. J.

Saved from Himself; 9.12,16; 10.23,26; (12.11;11); 1037; Bitzer; (Contemporary Domestic Melodrama); Studio.

A Woman Scorned; 10.4,10; (11.30;11); 1084; Bitzer; (Slum Melodrama); Fort Lee, N. J., Studio.

The Miser's Heart; 10.9,4; (11.20;11); 1066; Bitzer; (Slum Melodrama Child Centered); Fort Lee, N. J., Studio.

The Failure; 10.13,24; (12.7;11); 1065; Bitzer; (Rural Romance); Studio, Englewood, N. J.

Sunshine through the Dark; 10.16,24; (11.27;11); (1); Bitzer; (Slum Romance); Studio, Fort Lee, N. J.

As in a Looking Glass; 10.20,25; (12.18;11); (1); Bitzer; (Contemporary Temperance Drama); Studio.

A Terrible Discovery; 11.1,4; (12.21;11); 1207; Bitzer; (Gangster Child Centered Melodrama); Studio, Fort Lee, N. J.

A Tale of the Wilderness; 11.8,13,14,20; (1.8;12); 1125; Bitzer; (Pioneer-Indian Kentucky Melodrama Action); Coytesville, N. J.

The Voice of the Child; 11.9,28; (12.28;11); 1055; Bitzer; (Contemporary Domestic Triangle Melodrama); Studio, Fort Lee, N. J.

The Baby and the Stork; 11.9,22; (1.1;12); 1069; Bitzer; (Contemporary Kidnapping Melodrama); Studio, Westfield, N. J.

The Old Bookkeeper; 11; (1.18;12); 998; Bitzer; (Burglar Melodrama); Studio.

A Sister's Love; 11; (2.8;12); (1); Bitzer; (Domestic Drama); NYC.

For His Son; 11; (1.22;12); (1); Bitzer; (Father-Son Narcotics Melodrama); NYC Studio.

The Transformation of Mike; 12; (2.1;12); 999; Bitzer; (Gangster Reformation Melodrama); NYC Studio.

A Blot on the 'Scutcheon; 12; (1.29;12); (1); Bitzer; (17th-Century Melodrama); NYC and Location.

Billy's Strategem; 12; (2.12;12); 998; Bitzer; (Frontier Child Centered Melodrama); Coytesville, N. J.

The Sunbeam; 12; (2.26;12); 1000; Bitzer; (Child Centered Slum Melodrama); NYC, Studio.

A String of Pearls; 12; (3.7;12); 998; Bitzer; (Contemporary Society Melodrama); NYC, Studio.

The Root of Evil; 12; (3.18;12); 999; Bitzer; (Contemporary Melodrama); NYC, Studio.

1912

The Mender of the Nets; 1; (2.15;12); (1); Bitzer; (Seaside Romance); Santa Monica, Cal.

Under Burning Skies; 1; (2.22;12); (1); Bitzer; (Desert Melodrama); San Fernando, Cal.

A Siren of Impulse; 1; (3.4;12); (1); Bitzer; (Mexican Romance); Cal.

Iola's Promise; 1; (3.14;12); 1056; Bitzer; (Indian-White Romance); Cal.

The Goddess of Sagebrush Gulch; 1; (3.25;12); (1); Bitzer; (Western Romance); Cal.

The Girl and Her Trust; 1; (3.28;12); (1); Bitzer; (Contemporary Railroad Melodrama); Cal.

The Punishment; 2; (4.4;12); (1); Bitzer; (1830's Romance); Cal.

Fate's Interception; 2; (4.8;12); (1); Bitzer; (Indian-White Romance); Cal.

The Female of the Species; 2; (4.15;12); (1); Bitzer; (Desert Melodrama); Cal.

Just Like a Woman; 2; (4.18;12); (1); Bitzer; (Oil Fields Romance); Cal.

One Is Business, the Other Crime; 2; (4.25;12); (1); Bitzer; (Contemporary Political Melodrama); Cal.

The Lesser Evil; 2; 3; (4.29;12); (1); Bitzer; (Shipboard Melodrama); Cal.

The Old Actor; 2; (5.6;12); (1); Bitzer; (Contemporary Drama); Cal.

A Lodging for the Night; 3; (5.9;12); (1); Bitzer; (Mexican-American Romance); Cal.

His Lesson; 3; (5.16;12); (1); Bitzer; (Domestic Triangle); Cal.

When Kings Were the Law; 3; (5.20;12); (1); Bitzer; (18th-Century Melodrama); Wentworth Hotel, Santa Monica, Cal.

A Beast at Bay; 3; (5.27;12); (1); Bitzer; (Contemporary Automobile-Train Melodrama); Cal.

An Outcast among Outcasts; 3; (5.30;12); (1); Bitzer; (Tramp Melodrama); Cal.

Home Folks; 3; (6.6;12); (1); Bitzer; (Domestic Drama); Cal. Studio.

A Temporary Truce; 4; (6.10;12); (1); Bitzer; (Miner-Indian Melodrama Action); Cal.

The Spirit Awakened; 4; (6.20;12); (1); Bitzer; (Farm Triangle Melodrama); Cal.

Lena and the Geese; 4; (6.16;12); (1); Bitzer; (Netherlands Fairy Tale Romance); Cal.

An Indian Summer; 4; (7.8;12); (1); Bitzer; (Contemporary Romance); Cal.

The Schoolteacher and the Waif; 4; (6.27;12); (1); Bitzer; (Pastoral Comedy); Cal.

Man's Lust for Gold; 5; (7.1;12); (1); Bitzer; (Desert Miners Melodrama); Cal. (San Fernando).

Man's Genesis; 5; (7.11;12); (1); Bitzer; (Primitive Man Melodrama); Cal. (Chatsworth Park).

Heaven Avenges; 5; (7.18;12); (1); Bitzer; (Mexican-American Romance); Cal.

A Pueblo Legend; 5; (8.29;12); (2); Bitzer; (Indian Romance); Isleta, New Mexico.

The Sands of Dee; 5; (7.22;12); (1); Bitzer; (19th-Century Romance); Santa Monica, Cal.

Black Sheep; 5; (7.29;12); (1); Bitzer; (Mexican-American Ranch Melodrama); Cal.

The Narrow Road; 6; (8.1;12); 999; Bitzer; (Contemporary Ex-convict Melodrama); NYC.

A Child's Remorse; 6; (8.8;12); 998; Bitzer; (Contemporary Child Centered Melodrama); NYC-Exterior.

The Inner Circle; 6; (8.12;12); 1000; Bitzer; ("Black Hand" Melodrama); NYC, Studio.

A Change of Spirit; 6; (8.22;12); (1); Bitzer; (Contemporary Reformation Romance); NYC, Palisades, N. J.

An Unseen Enemy; 7; (9.9;12); 999; Bitzer; (Contemporary Child Centered Melodrama); NYC, Studio, Fort Lee, N. J.

Two Daughters of Eve; 7; (9.19;12); 1057; Bitzer; (Backstage Child Centered Melodrama); NYC, Studio.

Friends; 7; (9.23;12); (1); Bitzer; (Mining Camp Romance); NYC, Coytesville, N. J.

So Near, Yet So Far; 7; (9.30;12); 999; Bitzer; (Contemporary Romance); NYC-Exterior.

A Feud in the Kentucky Hills; 7; (10.3;12); (1); Bitzer; (Kentucky Mountaineer Romance Triangle); Palisades, N. J.

In the Aisles of the Wild; 7; (10.14;12); (1); Bitzer; (Frontier Trapper Triangle); Passaic River, N. J.

The One She Loved; 8; (10.21;12); 999; Bitzer; (Contemporary Romance Triangle); Fort Lee, N. J.

The Painted Lady; 8; (10.24;12); (1); Bitzer; (Moral Drama); NYC-Exterior.

The Musketeers of Pig Alley; 9; (10.31;12); (1); Bitzer; (Gangster Melodrama); NYC.

Heredity; 9; (11.4;12); 1015; Bitzer; (Indian-Trapper Melodrama); Coytesville, N. J.

Gold and Glitter; 10; (11.11;12); 999; Bitzer; NYC.

My Baby; 10; (11.14;12); (1); Bitzer; NYC.

The Informer; 10; (11.21;12); 1080; Bitzer; (Civil War Melodrama); NYC.

The Unwelcome Guest; 10; (3.15;13); 1004; Bitzer; NYC.

Pirate Gold; 10; (1.13;13); 1000; Bitzer; NYC.

Brutality; 10; (12.2;12); (2); Bitzer; NYC.

The New York Hat; 10; 11; (12.5;12); 999; Bitzer; (Contemporary Romance); Studio, Fort Lee, N. J.

The Massacre; 11; (2.26;13); (2); Bitzer; (Custer's Last Stand Melodrama); Fort Lee, N. J.

My Hero; 11; (12.12;12); (1); Bitzer; (Indian Drama); Studio, Fort Lee, N. J.

Oil and Water; 11; (2.16;13); 1513; Bitzer; NYC.

The Burglar's Dilemma; 11; (12.16;12); 998; Bitzer; (Melodrama); NYC.

A Cry for Help; 11; (12.23;12); 1000; Bitzer; NYC.

The God Within; 11; (12.26;12); 1000; Bitzer; NYC.

Three Friends; 11; (1.2;13); 999; Bitzer; (Western Child Centered Melodrama); NYC.

The Telephone Girl and the Lady; 11; (1.6;13); 1000; Bitzer; NYC, Studio.

Fate; 11; (3.22;13); 1038; Bitzer; NYC.

An Adventure in the Autumn Woods; 11; (1.16;13); (1); Bitzer; NYC.

A Chance Deception; 11; (2.24;13); 998; Bitzer; NYC.

The Tender Hearted Boy; 11; (1.23;13); (1); Bitzer; NYC, Long Island.

A Misappropriated Turkey; 12; (1.27;13); (1); Bitzer; NYC.

Brothers; 12; (2.3;13); 999; Bitzer; NYC.

Drink's Lure; 12; (2.17;13); (1); Bitzer; (Temperance Drama); NYC.

Love in an Apartment Hotel; 12; 1; (2.27;13); 1000; Bitzer; Finished in Cal.

1913

Broken Ways; 1.13; (3.8;13); 1045; Bitzer; Cal.

A Girl's Stratagem; 1; (3.10;13); Bitzer; Cal.

Near to Earth; 1; (3.20;13); 999; Bitzer; Cal.

A Welcome Intruder; 1; (3.24;13); (1); Bitzer; (Kidnapped Child Melodrama); Cal.

The Sheriff's Baby; 2; (3.29;13); 1004; Bitzer; (Desert Child Centered Melodrama); San Fernando, Cal.

The Hero of Little Italy; 2; (4.3;13); (1); Bitzer; Cal.

The Perfidy of Mary; 2; (4.5;13); 1004; Bitzer; Cal.

A Misunderstood Boy; 2; (4.19;13); 998; Bitzer; (Gold Fields Melodrama); Sierra Madre, Cal.

The Little Tease; 3; (4.12;13); (1½); Bitzer; Cal. (Sierra Madre or Lookout Mountain).

The Lady and the Mouse; 3; (4.26;13); (1); Bitzer; Cal.

The Wanderer; 3; (5.3;13); (1); Bitzer; (Desert Fantasy); San Fernando, Cal.

The House of Darkness; 3; (5.10;13); (1); Bitzer; (Psychological Drama); Cal.

Olaf—An Atom; 3; (5.19;13); 1003; Bitzer; (Tramp Romance); Cal.

Just Gold; 3; (5.24;13); (1); Bitzer; (Miners Melodrama); Cal.

His Mother's Son; 3; (5.31;13); (1); Bitzer; (Domestic Drama); Cal.

The Yaqui Cur; 4; (5.17;13); (2); Bitzer; (Mexican-Indian Drama); Cal.

The Ranchero's Revenge; 4; (6.2;13); (1); Bitzer; (Western Melodrama); Cal.

A Timely Interception; 3.31; (6.7;13); 998; Bitzer; (Melodrama); Cal.

Death's Marathon; 4; (6.14;13); 1027; Bitzer; Cal.

The Sorrowful Shore; 4; (7.5;13); (1); Bitzer; Cal.

The Mistake; 5; (7.12;13); (1); Bitzer; Cal.

The Mothering Heart; 4; (6.21;13); 1525; Bitzer; Cal.

Her Mother's Oath; 5; (6.28;13); (1); Bitzer; Cal.

During the Round-up; 5; (7.19;13); (1); Bitzer; (Western Melodrama); Cal.

The Coming of Angelo; 5.28; (7.26;13); (1); Bitzer; (Italian Romance); Cal.

An Indian's Loyalty; 6.8; (8.16;13); (1); Bitzer; (Indian-American Western Melodrama); Cal.

Two Men of the Desert; 6.8; (8.23;13); (1); Bitzer; (Western Prospector Drama); Cal. (San Fernando).

The Reformers, or *The Lost Art of Minding One's Business;* 7.6; (8.9;13); (2); Bitzer; ("Uplifter" Melodrama Comedy); Cal.

The Battle of Elderberry Gulch; 7; (3.28;14); (2); Bitzer; (Western Action Melodrama); San Fernando, Cal.

In Prehistoric Days; (Original Title: *Wars of the Primal Tribes;* Re-released as *Brute Force*); 7; (13); (2); Bitzer; (Melodrama of Primitive Man); Cal. (Chatsworth Park).

Judith of Bethulia; 7; (3.7;14); (4); Bitzer; (Biblical Melodrama); Chatsworth Park, Los Angeles, Cal. Reissued in 1917 as *Her Condoned Sin* in (6) reels.

LIST OF PLAYERS

The Player List includes the names of the known principal actors and actresses who appeared in the films directed by D. W. Griffith from 1908 to 1913. The name of the actor is followed by the year or years of his appearances and the known list of films for that year in which he appeared in a principal or supporting role. It was the custom for members of the Biograph acting company to double as extras in films in which they did not play major roles. No attempt is made here to list these appearances.

AITKEN, SPOTTISWOODE
1911
The Battle

ARVIDSON, LINDA (née Johnson;
    Mrs. D. W. Griffith)
1908
The Adventures of Dollie
The Greaser's Gauntlet
The Man and the Woman
The Barbarian, Ingomar
The Planter's Wife
The Curtain Pole
1909
The Salvation Army Lass
Tragic Love
Politician's Love Story
Edgar Allen Poe

The Deception
A Drunkard's Reformation
The Cricket on the Hearth
Her First Biscuits
A Convict's Sacrifice
The Mills of the Gods
1776, or The Hessian Renegades
Comata, the Sioux
Pippa Passes
Lines of White on the Sullen Sea
The Death Disc
1910
The Unchanging Sea
Heart Beats of Long Ago
1911
Fisher Folks
Enoch Arden, Part I, Part II

AUGUST, EDWIN (Edwin August
   Philip Von der Butz)
  1910
The Fugitive
Simple Charity
Winning Back His Love
His Daughter
Madame Rex
  1911
A Tale of the Wilderness
A Blot on the 'Scutcheon
  1912
The Girl and Her Trust
The Lesser Evil
The Old Actor
The School Teacher and the Waif
The Sands of Dee

BARKER, FLORENCE
  1909
A Fool's Revenge
Choosing a Husband
The Dancing Girl of Butte
Her Terrible Ordeal
The Call
The Last Deal
  1910
Faithful
The Usurer
His Sister-in-law
A Wreath of Orange Blossoms
The Two Paths
The Diamond Star
  1911
His Daughter

BARRYMORE, LIONEL
  1911
Fighting Blood
The Battle
  1912
Friends

The One She Loved
The Musketeers of Pig Alley
Gold and Glitter
My Baby
The Informer
The New York Hat
My Hero
Oil and Water
The Burglar's Dilemma
A Cry for Help
The God Within
Fate
An Adventure in the Autumn
  Woods
  1913
The Sheriff's Baby
The Perfidy of Mary
A Misunderstood Boy
The Wanderer
The House of Darkness
Just Gold
The Yaqui Cur
The Ranchero's Revenge
A Timely Interception
Death's Marathon
Judith of Bethulia

BARRY, VIOLA
  1913
The Mothering Heart

BERNARD, DOROTHY
  1910
Fate's Turning
  1911
The Failure
Sunshine Through the Dark
A Tale of the Wilderness
A Sister's Love
A Blot on the 'Scutcheon
The Root of Evil

1912
A Siren of Impulse
The Goddess of Sagebrush Gulch
The Girl and Her Trust
The Female of the Species
His Lesson
Heaven Avenges

BOOTH, ELMER
1912
The Narrow Road
An Unseen Enemy
Two Daughters of Eve
So Near, Yet So Far
The Musketeers of Pig Alley
The Unwelcome Guest

BRACY, CLARA T.
1909
Eloping with Auntie
The Awakening
1910
Three Sisters
A Decree of Destiny

BRUCE, KATE
1909
One Touch of Nature
The Better Way
1776, or The Hessian Renegades
In Old Kentucky
A Midnight Adventure
1910
The Two Brothers
Her Father's Pride
The Usurer
Wilful Peggy
The Fugitive
His Trust Fulfilled
1911
Fighting Blood
1912
Home Folks

An Indian Summer
The Old Actor
A Feud in the Kentucky Hills
The Tender Hearted Boy
1913
The Sheriff's Baby
The Little Tease
Just Gold
The Yaqui Cur
Death's Marathon
The Battle of Elderberry Gulch
Judith of Bethulia

BURNS, FRED
1913
During the Round-up
An Indian's Loyalty

BUTLER, WILLIAM J. (Daddy)
1909
1776, or The Hessian Renegades
In Old Kentucky
One Night, and Then—
1910
The Purgation
A Flash of Light
The Usurer
1911
The Two Sides
A Romany Tragedy
The Last Drop of Water
Fighting Blood
The Unveiling
Dan the Dandy
A Blot on the 'Scutcheon
1912
Man's Lust for Gold
1913
The Hero of Little Italy
A Timely Interception

CABANNE, CHRISTY W.
1912
Under Burning Skies

The Punishment
  1913
Judith of Bethulia

CAHILL, LILY
  1910
The Fugitive

CAREY, HARRY
  1912
An Unseen Enemy
Friends
In the Aisles of the Wild
The Musketeers of Pig Alley
Heredity
The Informer
The Unwelcome Guest
An Adventure in the Autumn
    Woods
  1913
Love in an Apartment Hotel
Broken Ways
The Sheriff's Baby
The Hero of Little Italy
The Left Handed Man
Olaf—An Atom
The Ranchero's Revenge
Judith of Bethulia

CARLTON, LLOYD
  1910
The Fugitive

CARROLL, WILLIAM
  1912
Black Sheep

CLARGES, VERNON
  1909
Was Justice Served?
1776, or The Hessian Renegades
In Old Kentucky
  1910
The Face at the Window

A Flash of Light
Little Angels of Luck
The Lesson
His Trust Fulfilled

COOPER, MIRIAM
  1910
The Duke's Plan

COTTON, LUCY
  1910
The Fugitive

CRAIG, CHARLES
  1909
The Rocky Road
The Englishman and the Girl

CRISP, DONALD
  1910
The Two Paths
Fate's Turning
  1911
The Battle

COMPSON, JOHN
  1909
Monday Morning in a Coney
    Island Police Court
A Smoked Husband
Mr. Jones at the Ball
Mrs. Jones Entertains
Mr. Jones Has a Card Party
Jones and the Lady Book Agent
The Jones Have Amateur
    Theatricals
His Wife's Mother
Her First Biscuits
Mr. Jones' Burglar

DARK CLOUD
  1910
The Song of the Wildwood Flute
  1911
The Squaw's Love

1913
An Indian's Loyalty

DAVENPORT, DOROTHY
1910
A Mohawk's Way
The Fugitive

DE GARDE, ADELE
1909
The Roue's Heart
The Medicine Bottle
A Drunkard's Reformation
What Drink Did
The Lonely Villa
Through the Breakers
1911
The Trail of the Books

DEL RIO, DOLORES
1911
The Voice of the Child (? British
Film Institute Catalogue)

DILLON, EDWARD (Eddie)
1908
The Feud and the Turkey
The Reckoning; After Many Years
The Welcome Burglar
The Salvation Army Lass
1909
The Brahma Diamond
The Little Teacher
1910
As the Bells Rang Out
The Sorrows of the Unfaithful
Examination Day at School
Muggsy Becomes a Hero
The Fugitive
His Sister-in-law
1911
The Miser's Heart
Sunshine through the Dark

1912
The Spirit Awakened
1913
Love in an Apartment Hotel
An Indian's Loyalty
Judith of Bethulia

DILLON, JOHN (Jack)
1908
The Greaser's Gauntlet
1910
The Iconoclast
A Decree of Destiny
1913
Love in an Apartment Hotel
The Sheriff's Baby

EGAN, GLADYS
1908
The Stolen Jewels
The Christmas Burglars
1909
The Lonely Villa
In the Watches of the Night
A Trap for Santa Claus
1910
Unexpected Help
The Broken Doll
A Child's Impulse
A Child's Faith
A Salutary Lesson
A Child's Strategem
1911
The Two Sides; A Romany
Tragedy
The Crooked Road
The Ruling Passion
1912
A Child's Remorse

EVANS, FRANK
1908
The Vaquero's Vow

1909
The Death Disc
1911
A Woman Scorned

FINCH, FLORA
1908
Mrs. Jones Entertains
1909
Jones and the Lady Book Agent

FOSTER, EDNA
1911
The Adventures of Billy
The Baby and the Stork

GEBHARDT, FRANK
1908
The Tavern Keeper's Daughter
The Greaser's Gauntlet
The Man and the Woman
The Fatal Hour
Balked at the Altar
The Devil
Romance of a Jewess
Mr. Jones at the Ball
The Song of the Shirt
The Feud and the Turkey
One Touch of Nature
1909
The Cord of Life
At the Altar

GISH, DOROTHY
1912
An Unseen Enemy
The New York Hat
The Burglar's Dilemma
1913
The Perfidy of Mary
Her Mother's Oath
Judith of Bethulia

GISH, LILLIAN
1912
An Unseen Enemy
In the Aisles of the Wild
The One She Loved
The Musketeers of Pig Alley
Gold and Glitter
My Baby
The Informer
The Unwelcome Guest
The New York Hat
Oil and Water
A Cry for Help
1913
A Misunderstood Boy
The Left Handed Man
The House of Darkness
Just Gold
A Timely Interception
The Mothering Heart
During the Round-up
An Indian's Loyalty
The Battle of Elderberry Gulch
Judith of Bethulia

GRANDIN, FRANK
1910
The Duke's Plan
In Old California
1911
The Lonedale Operator
The Chief's Daughter
Enoch Arden, Part I, Part II
The Primal Call
Swords and Hearts

GRAYBILL, JOSEPH
1910
A Victim of Jealousy
The Purgation
The Italian Barber
A Decree of Destiny

1911
A Romany Tragedy
The Last Drop of Water
Bobby, the Coward
Italian Blood
The Making of a Man
Love in the Hills
Through Darkened Vales
Saved from Himself
The Voice of the Child
1912
The Painted Lady

HARRON, ROBERT (Bobby)
1909
Sweet Revenge
1910
Ramona
In the Season of Buds
1911
Enoch Arden, Part I
The White Rose of the Wilds
The Last Drop of Water
Bobby, the Coward
The Unveiling
Billy's Strategem
1912
Fate's Interception
A Pueblo Legend
The Sands of Dee
An Unseen Enemy
Home Folks
Friends
So Near, Yet So Far
The Musketeers of Pig Alley
Brutality
The New York Hat
The Massacre
My Hero
Oil and Water
The Burglar's Dilemma

A Cry for Help
Fate
The Tender Hearted Boy
1913
Love in an Apartment Hotel
Broken Ways
The Sheriff's Baby
A Misunderstood Boy
The Little Tease
His Mother's Son
The Yaqui Cur
A Timely Interception
Death's Marathon
Her Mother's Oath
The Reformers
The Battle of Elderberry Gulch
In Prehistoric Days
Judith of Bethulia

HEDLUND, GUY
1910
The Modern Prodigal
1911
Bobby, the Coward

HENDERSON, DELL
1909
Lines of White on the Sullen Sea
1910
The Purgation
That Chink at Golden Gulch
When a Man Loves
1911
Teaching Dad to Like Her
In the Days of '49
The Crooked Road
The Last Drop of Water
The Making of a Man
A String of Pearls
1913
The Battle of Elderberry Gulch

HENDERSON, GRACE
  1909
Lucky Jim
A Corner in Wheat
  1910
The Marked Time-Table
The Purgation
A Midnight Cupid
The Usurer
His Trust Fulfilled
  1911
Enoch Arden, Part I
Her Sacrifice
The Old Confectioner's Mistake
The Unveiling
Sunshine Through the Dark
A String of Pearls
  1912
An Unseen Enemy

HENDRY, ANITA
  1909
The Road to the Heart
The Peach Basket Hat

HYDE, HARRY
  1911
Her Awakening
A String of Pearls
The Root of Evil
  1912
The Punishment
The Narrow Road

INSLEE, CHARLES
  1908
The Adventures of Dollie
The Redman and the Child
For Love of Gold
For a Wife's Honor
The Girl and the Outlaw
The Red Girl
Where the Breakers Roar

Romance of a Jewess
The Call of the Wild
After Many Years
Mr. Jones at the Ball
Money Mad
One Touch of Nature
  1909
The Girls and Daddy
The Cord of Life
His Wife's Mother
The Lure of the Gown
A Burglar's Mistake
Confidence
Her First Biscuits

JEFFERSON, THOMAS
  1913
Judith of Bethulia

JOHNSON, ARTHUR V.
  1908
The Adventures of Dollie
The Bandit's Waterloo
The Greaser's Gauntlet
The Red Girl
The Vaquero's Vow
The Planter's Wife
After Many Years
Concealing a Burglar
The Ingrate
The Test of Friendship
  1909
Tragic Love
The Drive for Life
The Voice of the Violin
A Drunkard's Reformation
A Rude Hostess
Confidence
Tis an Ill Wind That Blows No Good
Resurrection
Eradicating Auntie

Her First Biscuits
The Necklace
The Way of Man
A Strange Meeting
The Indian Runner's Romance
The Mills of the Gods
The Sealed Room
The Awakening
Pippa Passes
The Gibson Goddess
The Expiation
Nursing a Viper
A Midnight Adventure
The Mountaineer's Honor
The Trick That Failed
A Corner in Wheat
To Save Her Soul
The Cloister's Touch
  1910
The Final Settlement
Taming a Husband
The Newlyweds
The Thread of Destiny
Faithful
The Unchanging Sea
Unexpected Help
The Usurer
Rose O'Salem Town
The Lily of the Tenements
  1912
Iola's Promise

KENT, CHARLES
  1910
Examination Day at School

KIRKWOOD, JAMES
  1909
The Road to the Heart
The Message
Was Justice Served?
The Renunciation

The Seventh Day
A Convict's Sacrifice
The Mended Lute
The Indian Runner's Romance
The Better Way
Comata, the Sioux
Pippa Passes
The Death Disc
1776, or The Hessian Renegades
Through the Breakers
A Corner in Wheat
The Redman's View
The Rocky Road
The Honor of His Family
The Last Deal
  1910
The Final Settlement
A Victim of Jealousy
The Modern Prodigal
Winning Back His Love

KERBY, MARION
  1912
Two Daughters of Eve

LA BADIE, FLORENCE
  1911
The Broken Cross
Enoch Arden, Part I, Part II
The Primal Call
The Thief and the Girl
Fighting Blood

LAWRENCE, FLORENCE
  1908
A Calamitous Elopement
The Girl and the Outlaw
Betrayed by a Hand Print
Behind the Scenes
The Heart of Oyama
Where the Breakers Roar
A Smoked Husband
The Vaquero's Vow

The Barbarian, Ingomar
The Planter's Wife
The Devil
The Zulu's Heart
Romance of a Jewess
The Call of the Wild
Mr. Jones at the Ball
Concealing a Burglar
Taming of the Shrew
The Ingrate
A Woman's Way
The Song of the Shirt
Mr. Jones Entertains
An Awful Moment
The Christmas Burglars
Mr. Jones Has a Card Party
The Salvation Army Lass
  1909
The Brahma Diamond
The Jones Have Amateur
    Theatricals
His Wife's Mother
The Deception
The Lure of the Gown
Lady Helen's Escapade
Jones and His New Neighbor
The Winning Coat
The Road to the Heart
Confidence
The Note in the Shoe
Resurrection
Eloping with Auntie
Her First Biscuits
The Peach Basket Hat
The Necklace
The Way of Man
Mrs. Jones' Lover
The Cardinal's Conspiracy
The Slave
Mr. Jones' Burglar
The Mended Lute

LEE, JENNIE
  1913
His Mother's Son
Her Mother's Oath

LEHRMAN, HENRY (Pathé)
  1910
As the Bells Rang Out
The Iconoclast
Her Sacrifice
  1912
A Beast at Bay

LENOR, JACQUE (Jaque)
  1911
Bobby, the Coward
Italian Blood
The Long Road
  1912
The Spirit Awakened
Lena and the Geese

LEONARD, MARION
  1908
The Fatal Hour
Father Gets in the Game
An Awful Moment
The Maniac Cook
The Christmas Burglars
A Wreath in Time
The Criminal Hypnotist
The Welcome Burglar
  1909
The Roue's Heart
The Voice of the Violin
A Rude Hostess
The Eavesdropper
The Lonely Villa
With Her Card
The Mills of the Gods
The Sealed Room
Pippa Passes
Fools of Fate

His Lost Love
The Gibson Goddess
The Expiation
The Restoration
Nursing a Viper
Through the Breakers
A Trap for Santa Claus
In Little Italy
On the Reef
  1910
In Old California
Gold Is Not All
Love among the Roses
The Two Brothers
Over Silent Paths
A Salutary Lesson
The Sorrows of the Unfaithful
The Two Paths

LESTINA, ADOLPH
  1909
The Cord of Life
  1910
The Two Paths
What Shall We Do With Our Old?
  1911
A Woman Scorned
  1912
The Inner Circle

LEWIS, WALTER
  1912
My Hero

LONGFELLOW, STEPHANIE
  1909
Eradicating Auntie
The Necklace
A Convict's Sacrifice
A Strange Meeting
The Better Way
Two Women and a Man
The Rocky Road

  1910
Thou Shalt Not
Love among the Roses
The Impalement
As the Bells Rang Out
In Life's Cycle
The Message of the Violin
The Lesson
Winning Back His Love
  1911
The Chief's Daughter
Madame Rex
The Crooked Road

LUCAS, WILFRED
  1908
The Barbarian, Ingomar
  1909
1776, or The Hessian Renegades
  1910
Winning Back His Love
His Trust
His Trust Fulfilled
The Diamond Star
Heart Beats of Long Ago
  1911
Fisher Folks
Was He a Coward?
The Spanish Gypsy
His Mother's Scarf
The New Dress
Enoch Arden, Part I, Part II
The White Rose of the Wild
The Primal Call
The Indian Brothers
The Thief and the Girl
The Rose of Kentucky
The Sorrowful Example
Swords and Hearts
The Old Confectioner's Mistake
Dan the Dandy
Italian Blood

A Woman Scorned
The Miser's Heart
The Failure
As in a Looking Glass
A Terrible Discovery
The Transformation of Mike
Billy's Strategem
1912
Under Burning Skies
The Girl and Her Trust
Fate's Interception
Just Like a Woman
When Kings Were the Law
Man's Genesis
A Pueblo Legend
The Massacre

MAC DOWELL, CLAIRE (Mrs. Charles
    Mailes)
1910
His Last Burglary
Wilful Peggy
A Mohawk's Way
The Golden Supper
His Trust Fulfilled
In the Days of '49
A Romany Tragedy
The Primal Call
The Sorrowful Example
1911
Swords and Hearts
A Woman Scorned
As in a Looking Glass
A Blot on the 'Scutcheon
Billy's Strategem
The Sunbeam
1912
The Female of the Species
Lena and the Geese
The Sands of Dee
The Daughters of Eve
In the Aisles of the Wild

The Unwelcome Guest
The Massacre
1913
A Welcome Intruder
The Wanderer
The House of Darkness
Olaf—An Atom
The Ranchero's Revenge

MAC PHERSON, JEANNIE
1908
The Vaquero's Vow
Mr. Jones at the Ball
Mr. Jones Entertains
1909
The Death Disc
A Corner in Wheat
1910
Winning Back His Love
Heart Beats of Long Ago
Enoch Arden, Part I
The Last Drop of Water

MC DERMOTT, JOSEPH
1913
The Sheriff's Baby
A Timely Interception
The Mothering Heart

MAILES, CHARLES HILL
1909
At the Altar
1911
A Woman Scorned
The Miser's Heart
A Terrible Discovery
A Tale of the Wilderness
A Blot on the 'Scutcheon
1912
The Girl and Her Trust
Just Like a Woman
A Beast at Bay

Home Folks
Lena and the Geese
Man's Genesis
The Sands of Dee
The Narrow Road
Iola's Promise
A Change of Spirit
Friends
So Near, Yet So Far
The Painted Lady
The Unwelcome Guest
The New York Hat
An Adventure in the Autumn
    Woods
1913
A Welcome Intruder
The Hero of Little Italy
A Misunderstood Boy
The House of Darkness
Olaf—An Atom
Her Mother's Oath
The Coming of Angelo
The Reformers
The Battle of Elderberry Gulch
Judith of Bethulia

MARSH, MAE
1912
One Is Business, the Other Crime
Lena and the Geese
Man's Genesis
The Sands of Dee
Brutality
The New York Hat
The Telephone Girl and the Lady
An Adventure in the Autumn
    Woods
1913
Love in an Apartment Hotel
The Perfidy of Mary
The Little Tease
The Wanderer

His Mother's Son
The Reformers
The Battle of Elderberry Gulch
In Prehistoric Days
Judith of Bethulia

MARSH, MARGUERITE
1912
The Mender of the Nets

MERSEREAU, VIOLET
1909
The Cricket on the Hearth

MILES, MRS. HERBERT
1909
His Wife's Mother
Her First Biscuits
The Peach Basket Hat

MILES, HERBERT
1908
The Feud and the Turkey
The Test of Friendship
The Helping Hand
1909
Tragic Love
Lady Helen's Escapade
The Eavesdropper
The Violin Maker of Cremona

MILLER, W. CHRISTY (Christie)
1909
The Redman's View
The Rocky Road
1910
The Newlyweds
The Thread of Destiny
In Old California
The Way of the World
The Two Brothers
Her Father's Pride
A Plain Song

Examination Day at School
The Lesson
What Shall We Do with Our Old?
　1911
In the Days of '49
The Last Drop of Water
Swords and Hearts
The Old Bookkeeper
　1912
An Indian Summer
Man's Genesis
The Sands of Dee
The Old Actor
My Baby
The Informer
The Unwelcome Guest
　1913
The Little Tease
His Mother's Son
A Timely Interception
The Reformers
The Battle of Elderberry Gulch

MILLER, WALTER
　1912
Oil and Water
Two Daughters of Eve
So Near, Yet So Far
A Feud in the Kentucky Hills
The Musketeers of Pig Alley
Brutality
*An Adventure in the Autumn
　Woods*
　1913
Love in an Apartment Hotel
The Perfidy of Mary
The Wanderer
His Mother's Son
Death's Marathon
The Mothering Heart
The Coming of Angelo

MOORE, OWEN
　1908
The Honor of Thieves
The Salvation Army Lass
　1909
The Winning Coat
A Baby's Shoe
The Cricket on the Hearth
The Violin Maker of Cremona
The Mended Lute
Pippa Passes
1776, or The Hessian Renegades
Leather Stocking
A Change of Heart
His Lost Love
The Expiation
The Restoration
The Light That Came
The Open Gate
The Dancing Girl of Butte
Her Terrible Ordeal
The Last Deal
The Iconoclast

MORENO, ANTONIO
　1912
Two Daughters of Eve
So Near, Yet So Far
　1913
Judith of Bethulia

MURRAY, WALTER
　1913
The Reformers

MYERS, HARRY
　1908
The Guerrilla
　1909
Her First Biscuits

NEILAN, MARSHAL
　1913
Judith of Bethulia

NICHOLS, GEORGE
1908
Behind the Scenes
1909
The Jilt
Lines of White on the Sullen Sea
The Gibson Goddess
In the Watches of the Night
The Death Disc
In Little Italy
The Rocky Road
Her Terrible Ordeal
The Cloister's Touch
The Woman from Mellon's
1910
His Last Burglary
As It Is in Life
A Child of the Ghetto
A Midnight Cupid
A Child's Faith
A Flash of Light
As the Bells Rang Out
The Usurer
What Shall We Do with Our Old?
The Lily of the Tenements
Fighting Blood
1912
Two Daughters of Eve
Heredity

NORMAND, MABEL
1911
The Unveiling
The Eternal Mother
The Squaw's Love
Her Awakening
Saved from Himself
1912
The Mender of the Nets

OPPERMAN, FRANK
1912
The Old Actor

O'SULLIVAN, ANTHONY (Tony)
1908
The Red Girl
The Pirate's Gold
1909
'Tis an Ill Wind That Blows No Good
What Drink Did
A Convict's Sacrifice
A Strange Meeting
Getting Even
In the Watches of the Night
Her Terrible Ordeal
The Honor of His Family
1910
The Final Settlement
The Newlyweds

PAGET, ALFRED
1910
The Newlyweds
The Call to Arms
A Mohawk's Way
The Oath and the Man
The Spanish Gypsy
The Primal Call
1911
A Terrible Discovery
The Old Bookkeeper
1912
Iola's Promise
The Girl and Her Trust
One Is Business, the Other Crime
When Kings Were the Law
A Beast at Bay
The Spirit Awakened
The Inner Circle
Oil and Water
Heredity
1913
The Sheriff's Baby

A Misunderstood Boy
The Battle of Elderberry Gulch

PICKFORD, JACK (Jack Smith)
   1910
The Modern Prodigal
The Iconoclast
Examination Day at School
A Child's Strategem
   1912
Heredity
The Unwelcome Guest
The New York Hat

PICKFORD, MARY (Gladys Smith)
   1909
Her First Biscuits
The Violin Maker of Cremona
The Lonely Villa
The Son's Return
The Way of Man
The Mexican Sweethearts
The Country Doctor
The Renunciation
A Strange Meeting
Sweet and Twenty
They Would Elope
The Indian Runner's Romance
His Wife's Visitor
Oh, Uncle
The Sealed Room
1776, or *The Hessian Renegades*
In Old Kentucky
Getting Even
The Broken Locket
The Awakening
The Little Teacher
The Gibson Goddess
In the Watches of the Night
The Restoration
The Light That Came
A Midnight Adventure

The Mountaineer's Honor
The Trick That Failed
To Save Her Soul
   1910
The Woman from Mellon's
The Englishman and the Girl
The Thread of Destiny
The Twisted Trail
As It Is in Life
A Rich Revenge
A Romance of the Western Hills
The Unchanging Sea
The Two Brothers
Ramona
In the Season of Buds
Muggsy's First Sweetheart
What the Daisy Said
Muggsy Becomes a Hero
An Arcadian Maid
The Sorrows of the Unfaithful
Wilful Peggy
Simple Charity
The Song of the Wildwood Flute
A Plain Song
When a Man Loves
The Italian Barber
Three Sisters
A Decree of Destiny
   1912
The Mender of the Nets
Iola's Promise
Fate's Interception
The Female of the Species
Just Like a Woman
The Old Actor
A Lodging for the Night
A Beast at Bay
Home Folks
Lena and the Geese
An Indian Summer
The School Teacher and the Waif

A Pueblo Legend
The Narrow Road
Friends
So Near, Yet So Far
A Feud in the Kentucky Hills
The One She Loved
My Baby
The Informer
The Unwelcome Guest
The New York Hat

POWELL, BADEN
1911
The Crooked Road
A Smile of a Child
The Thief and the Girl
The Sorrowful Example
1912
The Inner Circle

POWELL, FRANK
1908
The Honor of Thieves
1909
Politician's Love Story
His Duty
The Necklace
Was Justice Served
The Country Doctor
The Cardinal's Conspiracy
The Seventh Day
With Her Card
His Wife's Visitor
The Broken Locket
Fools of Fate
Two Women and a Man
A Corner in Wheat
The Rocky Road
1910
Faithful
The Impalement
1911
A Knight of the Road

PRESCOTT, VIVIEN
1910
A Flash of Light
A Salutary Lesson
Winning Back His Love
Three Sisters
1911
Teaching Dad How to Like Her
How She Triumphed
The Primal Call
Her Sacrifice
Italian Blood
A Woman Scorned

PRYOR, HERBERT
1909
Tis an Ill Wind That Blows No
    Good
The Cricket on the Hearth

QUIRK, WILLIAM (Billy)
1909
The Son's Return
The Renunciation
Sweet and Twenty
They Would Elope
His Wife's Visitor
Oh, Uncle
1776, or The Hessian Renegades
Getting Even
The Little Teacher
The Gibson Goddess
A Midnight Adventure
A Corner in Wheat
1910
The Woman from Mellon's
A Rich Revenge
The Two Brothers
Muggsy's First Sweetheart

ROBINSON, GERTRUDE
1909
Pippa Passes

The Open Gate
The Death Disc
1910
Gold Is Not All
The Purgation
What the Daisy Said
A Summer Idyll
Examination Day at School
1913
Judith of Bethulia

SALTER, HARRY
1908
The Redman and the Child
A Calamitous Elopement
For Love of Gold
For a Wife's Honor
Balked at the Altar
Sunday Morning in a Coney Island
    Police Court
The Vaquero's Vow
Father Gets in the Game
The Barbarian, Ingomar
The Devil
Mr. Jones at the Ball
Taming of the Shrew
The Guerrilla
The Song of the Shirt
The Test of Friendship
The Reckoning
The Helping Hand
The Criminal Hypnotist
The Welcome Burglar
1909
The Roue's Heart
At the Altar
A Burglar's Mistake
The Winning Coat
The Eavesdropper
What Drink Did
Was Justice Served?
The Renunciation

The Cardinal's Conspiracy
The Slave
1910
The Iconoclast

SENNETT, MACK (Michael Sinnott)
1908
Balked at the Altar
Father Gets in the Game
Mr. Jones at the Ball
The Curtain Pole
An Awful Moment
A Wreath in Time
Mr. Jones Has a Card Party
The Salvation Army Lass
1909
Politician's Love Story
The Lure of the Gown
Lucky Jim
The Jilt
The Seventh Day
A Convict's Sacrifice
The Slave
The Better Way
Getting Even
The Awakening
The Gibson Goddess
In the Watches of the Night
A Midnight Adventure
The Trick That Failed
In a Hempen Bag
A Corner in Wheat
The Dancing Girl of Butte
1910
The Newlyweds
A Midnight Cupid
An Arcadian Maid
A Mohawk's Way
Examination Day at School
1912
Man's Genesis
The New York Hat

SIEGMAN, GEORGE
1909
The Sealed Room
1913
In Prehistoric Days

SUNSHINE, MARION
1908
The Tavern Keeper's Daughter
The Red Girl
1909
Her First Biscuits
1910
In the Season of Buds
Sunshine Sue
Three Sisters
A Decree of Destiny
1911
The Rose of Kentucky
The Stuff Heroes Are Made of
Dan the Dandy
1912
Heredity

SWEET, BLANCHE (Sarah)
1909
The Rocky Road
1911
Was He a Coward?
How She Triumphed
The White Rose of the Wilds
A Smile of a Child
The Last Drop of Water
A Country Cupid
The Stuff Heroes Are Made of
The Eternal Mother
The Making of a Man
The Long Road
The Battle
Love in the Hills
Through Darkened Vales
The Voice of the Child
The Transformation of Mike

1912
Under Burning Skies
The Goddess of Sagebrush Gulch
The Punishment
One Is Business, the Other Crime
The Lesser Evil
Blind Love
The Spirit Awakened
Man's Lust for Gold
The Inner Circle
Oil and Water
A Change of Spirit
The Painted Lady
The Massacre
The God Within
1913
Love in an Apartment Hotel
Broken Ways
The Hero of Little Italy
Death's Marathon
The Coming of Angelo
The Battle of Elderberry Gulch
Judith of Bethulia

TANSEY, JOHNNY
1908
The Redman and the Child

TONCRAY, KATE
1911
The New Dress
The Long Road
1912
A Change of Spirit
1913
The Hero of Little Italy

WALTHALL, HENRY
1909
A Convict's Sacrifice
The Sealed Room
1776, or The Hessian Renegades
In Old Kentucky

Pippa Passes
Leather Stocking
Fools of Fate
A Corner in Wheat
In Little Italy
The Call
The Honor of His Family
On the Reef
The Cloister's Touch
1910
His Last Burglary
The Converts
Gold Is Not All
Thou Shalt Not
The Gold Seekers
The Face at the Window
The Usurer
The Sorrows of the Unfaithful
In Life's Cycle
A Summer Idyll
1912
The Inner Circle
Oil and Water
A Change of Spirit
Friends
A Feud in the Kentucky Hills
In the Aisles of the Wild
The One She Loved
My Baby
The Informer
The Burglar's Dilemma
The God Within
1913
Love in an Apartment Hotel
Broken Ways
The Sheriff's Baby
The Little Tease
The Wanderer
Death's Marathon
His Mother's Oath
During the Round-up

The Battle of Elderberry Gulch
Judith of Bethulia

WEST, CHARLES
1909
Lines of White on the Sullen Sea
1910
In Old California
A Child's Impulse
A Flash of Light
As the Bells Rang Out
In Life's Cycle
The Message of the Violin
Sunshine Sue
The Golden Supper
The Italian Barber
The Two Paths
Fate's Turning
What Shall We Do with Our Old?
1911
The Broken Cross
His Mother's Scarf
In the Days of '49
Her Sacrifice
The Last Drop of Water
Dan the Dandy
The Long Road
The Battle
Love in the Hills
Through Darkened Vales
A Tale of the Wilderness
1912
The Mender of the Nets
A Siren of Impulse
The Goddess of Sagebrush Gulch
Fate's Interception
Blind Love
The Old Actor
The Lesser Evil
A Lodging for the Night
Black Sheep

The Massacre
The Burglar's Dilemma
1913
A Welcome Intruder
The Hero of Little Italy
The Left Handed Man

WEST, DOROTHY
1909
The Girls and Daddy
The Deception
Lines of White on the Sullen Sea
1910
His Last Burglary
A Child of the Ghetto
The House with the Closed
*   Shutters*
A Salutary Lesson

Rose O'Salem Town
The Fugitive
The Golden Supper
The Italian Barber
The Lily of the Tenements
1911
A Knight of the Road
His Mother's Scarf
The New Dress
Swords and Hearts
The Revenue Man and the Girl
The Squaw's Love

YOST, HERBERT (stage name: Barry
    O'Moore)
1909
Edgar Allen Poe
The Deception

Others who appeared as extras during Griffith's Biograph period but who did not play major roles include Florence Auer, William Beaudine, Gene Gauntier, Charles Gorman, Ruth Hart, Eleanor Hicks, Eleanor Kershaw (Mrs. Thomas Ince), Florence Lee, Fred Mace, Marie Newton, Lester Predmore, Paul Scardon, Mabel Stoughton, and the Wolfe children.

LIST OF AUTHORS AND SOURCES

The following list includes the names of the known authors, adaptors, and sources for films directed by D. W. Griffith during the Biograph period, 1908 to 1913. The plays are listed under the author's name, followed by the source, if known; the date of the film's production; the title of the film; and the name of the adaptor, if any.

ACKER, EDWARD; (original)
    1911; *The Old Confectioner's Mistake*
    1911; *A Terrible Discovery*
    1912; *An Unseen Enemy*
    1912; *A Cry for Help*
    1913; *The Telephone Girl and the Lady*

ARVIDSON, LINDA; (original)
    1911; *How She Triumphed*

BARRYMORE, LIONEL; (original)
    1912; *The Burglar's Dilemma*

BAYER, F. P.; (original)
    1911; *The Unveiling*
    1912; *The God Within*
    1913; *Broken Ways*

BELL, EDWARD; (original)
    1913; *The Sheriff's Baby*

BROWNING, ROBERT
    (*Pippa Passes*); 1909; *Pippa Passes;* D. W. Griffith
    (*Blot on the 'Scutcheon*); 1911; *Blot on the 'Scutcheon;* Linda Arvidson

BUTLER, W. J.; (original)
　　1910; *A Salutary Lesson*

CABANNE, WILLIAM CHRISTY; (original)
　　1912; *An Adventure in the Autumn Woods*
　　1912; *A Chance Deception*
　　1913; *The Sorrowful Shore*
　　1913; *The Misunderstood Boy*
　　1913; *His Mother's Son*
　　1913; *A Timely Interception*

CARROLL, JAMES; (original)
　　1910; *A Child's Faith*
　　1911; *The Adventures of Billy*

CERR, JAMES; (original)
　　1913; *Near to Earth*

COOPER, JAMES FENIMORE
　　(*Leather Stocking Tales*); 1909; *Leather Stocking;* Stanner E. V.
　　　　Taylor
　　(unknown); 1910; *A Mohawk's Way;* Stanner E. V. Taylor

DE MAUPASSANT, GUY
　　(unknown); 1909; *The Son's Return;* (unknown)

DICKENS, CHARLES
　　(*The Cricket on the Hearth*); 1909; *The Cricket on the Hearth;*
　　　　(unknown)

DONNELLY, ANTHONY; (original)
　　1910; *Winning Back His Love*

ELIOT, GEORGE
　　(*Silas Marner*); 1909; *A Fair Exchange;* (unknown)

HALL, EMMETT C.; (original)
　　1910; *The House with the Closed Shutters*
　　1910; *That Chink at Golden Gulch*
　　1910; *Rose O'Salem Town*
　　1911; *Swords and Hearts*
　　1911; *His Trust*
　　1911; *His Trust Fulfilled*
　　1911; *Was He a Coward?*
　　1911; *Teaching Dad to Like Her*

1911; *The Primal Call*
1912; *For His Son*

HAVEY, M. B.; (original)
1910; *His Sister-in-law*
1911; *The Diamond Star*
1911; *A Smile of a Child*
1911; *In the Days of '49*
1911; *The Failure*

HENDERSON, DELL; (original)
1910; *The Modern Prodigal*
1910; *The Lesson*
1911; *A Knight of the Road*
1911; *Bobby, the Coward*
1911; *Love in the Hills*

HENDERSON, GRACE; (original)
1911; *The New Dress*

HENKELS, MRS. WILLIAM G.; (original)
1912; *Fate*

HENNESSY, GEORGE; (original)
1911; *Saved from Himself*
1911; *A Woman Scorned*
1911; *The Miser's Heart*
1911; *As in a Looking Glass*
1911; *The Voice of the Child*
1911; *Billy's Strategem*
1911; *The Root of Evil*
1911; *The Sunbeam*
1912; *The Baby and the Stork*
1912; *The Girl and Her Trust*
1912; *The Punishment*
1912; *Fate's Interception*
1912; *The Lesser Evil*
1912; *Just Like a Woman*
1912; *The Old Actor*
1912; *One Is Business, the Other Crime*
1912; *A Lodging for the Night*
1912; *His Lesson*
1912; *A Beast at Bay*
1912; *An Indian Summer*

1912; *A Temporary Truce*
1912; *Heaven Avenges*
1912; *Man's Lust for Gold*
1912; *Black Sheep*
1912; *The Narrow Road*
1912; *A Child's Remorse*
1912; *The Inner Circle*
1912; *Two Daughters of Eve*
1912; *So Near, Yet So Far*
1912; *The One She Loved*
1912; *The Informer*
1912; *Heredity*
1912; *Gold and Glitter*
1913; *The Unwelcome Guest*
1913; *The Perfidy of Mary*

HICKS, ELINORE; (original)
1910; *The Two Brothers*

HODGE, EARL; (original)
1910; *The Banker's Daughters*

HOOD, THOMAS
(*The Song of the Shirt*); 1908; *The Song of the Shirt;* (unknown)

HUGO, VICTOR
(*Rigoletto*); 1909; *A Fool's Revenge;* (unknown)

JACKSON, HELEN HUNT
(*Ramona*); 1910; *Ramona;* (unknown)

LEIST, BERNARDINE R.; (original)
1910; *Waiter No. 5*
1910; *The Iconoclasts*
1911; *Dan the Dandy*
1911; *The Long Road*
1911; *Italian Blood*
1911; *A String of Pearls*

LONDON, JACK
(*Just Meat*); 1908; *For Love of Gold;* (unknown)
(*The Call of the Wild*); 1908; *The Call of the Wild;* (unknown)

LOONEY, J. F.; (original)
1913; *The House of Darkness*

LOOS, ANITA; (original)
1912; *The New York Hat*

LUCAS, WILFRED; (original)
1910; *Sunshine Sue*
1911; *The Ruling Passion*
1911; *The Transformation of Mike*
1912; *When Kings Were the Law*

MARSTON, WILLIAM M.; (original)
1913; *Love in an Apartment Hotel*

MC DONAGH, J.; (original)
1910; *The Fugitive*

MONTAGNE, E. J.; (original)
1912; *Oil and Water*

NOLTE, H. M. L.; (original)
1912; *Brothers*

NORRIS, FRANK
(*The Pit*); 1909; *A Corner in Wheat;* (unknown)

O'HENRY
1909; *Trying to Get Arrested;* Mack Sennett
His Duty; (unknown)

OLSEN, JEROME J.; (original)
1911; *The Trail of Books*

PICKFORD, MARY; (original)
1911; *Madame Rex*
1912; *Lena and the Geese*

PIERCE, GRACE A.
(*The Apocrypha*); 1913; *Judith of Bethulia;* Frank Woods

PIERSON, MRS. E. G.; (original)
1912; *A Sister's Love*

POE, EDGAR ALLAN
(*The Raven*); 1909; *Edgar Allen* [sic] *Poe;* (unknown)
(*The Cask of Amontillado*); 1909; *The Sealed Room;* (unknown)

QUIMBY, HARRIET; (original)
1911; *His Mother's Scarf*
1911; *The Blind Princess and the Poet*

1911; *Fisher Folks*
1911; *Sunshine through the Dark*
1911; *The Broken Cross*

REARDON, M. S.; (original)
1912: *Three Friends*

REYNOLDS, ISOBEL M.; (original)
1911; *The Jealous Husband*

RYAN, MRS. JAMES H.; (original)
1910; *The Song of the Wildwood Flute*
1910; *Two Little Waifs*

SENNETT, MACK; (original)
1911; *The Lonedale Operator*

SHAKESPEARE, WILLIAM
(*The Taming of the Shrew*); 1908; *The Taming of the Shrew;*
Harry Salter

SIMONE, CHARLES; (original)
1910; *In Life's Cycle*

TAYLOR, BELLE; (original)
1910; *The Broken Doll*
1910; *A Child's Strategem*
1910; *A Wreath of Orange Blossoms*
1911; *His Daughter*
1912; *The Old Bookkeeper*
1912; *Iola's Promise*

TAYLOR, STANNER E. V.; (original)
1908; *The Adventures of Dollie*
1910; *His Last Burglary*
1910; *A Rich Revenge*
1910; *The Man*
1910; *A Child of the Ghetto*
1910; *In the Season of Buds*
1910; *The Impalement*
1910; *In the Border States*
1910; *The Face at the Window*
1910; *A Victim of Jealousy*
1910; *As the Bells Rang Out*
1910; *A Child's Impulse*

1910; *Serious Sixteen*
1910; *The Purgation*
1910; *A Midnight Cupid*
1910; *What the Daisy Said*
1910; *The Sorrows of the Unfaithful*
1910; *An Arcadian Maid*
1910; *Her Father's Pride*
1910; *A Flash of Light*
1910; *The Oath and the Man*
1910; *A Plain Song*
1911; *Through Darkened Vales*
1911; *A Romany Tragedy*
1911; *The Squaw's Love*

TENNYSON, ALFRED LORD
(*Enoch Arden*); 1908; *After Many Years;* Frank Woods
(*The Golden Supper*); 1910; *The Golden Supper;* Dorothy West
(*Enoch Arden*); 1911; *Enoch Arden;* Linda Arvidson

TERWILLIGER, GEORGE W.; (original)
1911; *When a Man Loves*

TOLSTOY, LEO
(*Resurrection*); 1909; *Resurrection;* (unknown)

TWAIN, MARK
(*The Death Disc*); 1909; *The Death Disc;* (unknown)

WING, W. C.; (original)
1913; *Death's Marathon*
1913; *Olaf—An Atom*

WOODS, FRANK E.; (original)
1910; *The Marked Time-table*
1910; *Muggsy's First Sweetheart*
1910; *Simple Charity*
1913; *The Reformer*

Frank Woods and Stanner E. V. Taylor have been credited by a number of the Biograph participants, notably Linda Griffith and Billy Bitzer, with having written the synopses for many of the Griffith films in 1908, 1909, and 1910. No direct evidence of individual scripts or films written by them has been found, other than for those scripts listed.

Index

D.W. Griffith: the years
at Biograph.

JUDITH OF BETHULIA

COPYRIGHT, 1913, BY
BIOGRAPH COMPANY
New York, N.Y.

JUDITH OF BETHULIA

COPYRIGHT, 1913, BY
BIOGRAPH COMPANY
New York, N.Y.

JUDITH OF BETHULIA

COPYRIGHT, 1913, BY
BIOGRAPH COMPANY
New York, N.Y.